THE QUEEN'S SPEECH

THE
QUEEN'S
SPEECH

An Intimate Portrait of the Queen
in Her Own Words

INGRID SEWARD

**SIMON &
SCHUSTER**

London · New York · Sydney · Toronto · New Delhi

A CBS COMPANY

First published in Great Britain by Simon & Schuster UK Ltd, 2015
A CBS COMPANY

1 3 5 7 9 10 8 6 4 2

Simon & Schuster UK Ltd
1st Floor
222 Gray's Inn Road
London WC1X 8HB

www.simonandschuster.co.uk

Simon & Schuster Australia, Sydney
Simon & Schuster India, New Delhi

A CIP catalogue record for this book
is available from the British Library.

Hardback: 978-1-47115-097-5
Trade paperback: 978-1-47115-154-5
Ebook ISBN: 978-1-47115-099-9

Typeset in Sabon by M Rules
Printed and bound by CPI Group (UK) Ltd, Croydon, CR0 4YY

MIX
Paper from
responsible sources
FSC® C020471

*For Bella and Nou in memory of their father,
my inspiration.*

Contents

1 History and the Queen   1
2 The Early Years   18
3 The New Queen   44
4 The Age of Change   73
5 Celebrations and Tribulations   97
6 Weddings, Wars and Worries   119
7 The Diana Years   145
8 The New Millennium   172
9 Time for Reflection   197
10 Milestones   220
11 Conclusion   256

Queen's Speech Timeline   263
List of Speeches Quoted   271
Bibliography   277
Acknowledgements   279

Chapter 1

HISTORY AND THE QUEEN

*Each Christmas, at this time, my beloved
father broadcast a message to his people in
all parts of the world. Today I am doing
this to you, who are now my people.*

CHRISTMAS BROADCAST, 1952

Perhaps the most remarkable thing about Her Majesty Queen Elizabeth II is how hard it is to realise she is actually almost ninety. Her brain is still razor sharp, her skin is perfect. Her teeth are white and her smile, when she chooses to use it, is as wide and generous as ever. She moves like someone twenty years younger in that unmistakable Windsor gait that actress Helen Mirren perfected so well in her Oscar-winning role as the Queen in the 2006 film of the same name. Slightly bent forward, head down, with large purposeful strides. Since her birth in April 1926, the year of the General Strike, the world has changed beyond all recognition, but she seems remarkably unchanged and unchanging.

Her dedication and the efficiency with which she carries out her role as head of state are unsurpassed. While she wins no prizes for imagination, charisma or small talk, and was widely regarded as ill-educated as a child – she spent just seven and a half hours a week with her governess – she is the most reliable, unflappable, least complaining monarch in history. She has always enjoyed the regimented side of royal life and is a stickler for order – she will notice the minutest detail. On one occasion during a parade, she spotted a guardsman fiddling and remarked, 'That man in the back rank, third man from the right, kept moving his fingers on his rifle. Why did he do that? Is he mad?'

Her dogs, which she feeds herself, are fed in strict order: the eldest first and the youngest last. They wait for their names to be called out and, because of the strict hierarchy, there is never any fighting when this task is being performed by Her Majesty. Her love of horses and dogs is well documented and, at Windsor weekends, the talk is usually about animals. For a woman who is constantly surrounded by people, the natural world has played a large part in keeping her sane. With animals, she has no role to play and no dangerous words to stifle.

That is not to say that the Queen does not have her unguarded moments, and she has a wonderfully waspish sense of fun if she chooses to use it. Three days after her grandson Prince William's engagement to Catherine Middleton was announced in November 2010, the Queen and Duke of Edinburgh were being entertained to lunch at Sheffield University by Sir Peter Middleton, former chairman of Barclays Bank and chancellor of the university. The Queen, who was seated next to Sir Peter, turned to him and said impishly, 'Any relation?' When he replied in the negative, she then said, 'A little research perhaps?'

Now, it would have been easy for him to let his guard drop, but being socially adept he knew however friendly the Queen might be, you cannot become overfamiliar yourself. Even her children bow to her when they come into a room; and a friend of Princess Anne, witnessing her take a telephone call from her mother, noticed she automatically stood up as she started talking.

In the Queen's unchanging routine, any little mishap becomes an adventure and any situation a potential part in the play of her life. Her own brand of humour is delivered with impeccable timing, which comes from her years of public speaking. Her skill for mimicry is honed from observing and listening to the hundreds of characters she meets. A couple of years ago, an elegant and impeccably mannered American gentleman from Atlanta, Georgia, was introduced to Her Majesty at a reception at St James's Palace. He bowed low and informed the Queen in his deep southern drawl that he came from one of Her Majesty's former colonies. The Queen replied that, indeed, she could tell from the way he was talking that he came from the southern states. Looking at her straight in the eye, he told her he had heard she was an excellent mimic and, before he lost his nerve, challenged her to have his accent perfected by the next day.

Without hesitating the Queen said that if he kept on talking the way he was, she would have his accent perfected before dinner.

Energetic and open-minded though she is, the Queen is still the person she always was. Controlled, unemotional, punctilious and dignified, it is difficult to understand what kind of woman she really is, and none of her biographers has successfully managed to penetrate her private world. Even the experienced BBC documentary-maker, Edward Mirzoeff, who produced *Elizabeth R* to mark the Queen's fortieth anniversary of her accession to the throne, confessed that, after a whole year spent with her and her entourage, he still could not claim to know her. During that time, he lunched privately with the Queen, talked with her in her sitting room and sat with her while she had her portrait painted, as well as travelling with her to Sandringham and Balmoral.

Having spent more time with her in intimate circumstances than any of her biographers, he felt she remained a mystery. He admitted he came to know her mannerisms and style of her daily behaviour well, but never the woman herself. So is it possible to get to know and understand the Queen better than we do? Is there a way we can shed more light on her character, personality and interests?

Arguably the best clues lie in the speeches she actually writes for herself. Her Christmas speech is more or less the only time in the year when she has the chance to express her own opinion, however understated it might be, without having government officials, diplomats or other figures to guide her. As such, the Queen's speeches provide a unique and valuable insight into her personality. Accordingly, in writing this book I have delved into all of her speeches to find the key moments when she opens up, however subtly, to reveal her thoughts on subjects as diverse as modern technology, families and the role of women, immigration and much else besides.

The stories told by those close to the Queen might not reveal a great deal about her, but they do say something about the reality of the relationship between her and her husband. On one occasion, for instance, they were picnicking at Balmoral and for some reason or other Prince Philip was late, and there was a huge row as she let rip at him: 'This is ridiculous ... Where on earth have you been? Why were you doing that?' Of course, they ended up the best of friends, but it was uncomfortable for those around who witnessed the scene.

Her late private secretary, Lord Charteris, recalled once many years ago when President Mobutu of Zaire (now the Democratic Republic of Congo) came on a state visit and his wife smuggled her pet dog through customs in a fur muff and into Buckingham Palace. She then demanded steak for the dog to eat. Naturally, the Queen heard about it through her staff grapevine and said with tremendous force, 'Martin, that dog is to be out of my house by three o'clock this afternoon!' He recalled she was 'really shaking with anger and someone from customs came immediately and picked the dog up'.

Probably those who know the Queen best, apart from her family and very close friends, are her trusted group of personal staff, such as her dresser and her page and, of course, her security protection officers. They are the only ones who see Her Majesty in her unguarded moments and could, if they chose to do so, paint us a true picture of the monarch with all her fears and foibles.

A former chauffeur recalls driving the Queen in a convoy of three cars returning to London from Luton Hoo at two in the morning. A local constable's suspicions were aroused when he saw three Daimlers coming along the narrow road and he put his hand up to stop them. The front car came to a halt and the window went down. The chauffeur enquired, 'Good evening, officer. Can I help you?'

'Well,' said the policeman. 'It is a matter of, can I help you? What are you doing driving round here at this time in the morning?'

The chauffeur leaned forward and said quietly: 'I have the Guv'nor in the back. The Queen. In the next car is the Queen Mother. In the third is Princess Margaret, and this man next to me is Chief Inspector Perkins, who looks after the Queen.'

'Yes,' said the policeman. 'And if that's right I'm Roy Rogers and this bike's Trigger.'

Then a little voice from the back of the car said: 'I'd get on Trigger if I were you because you're ahead at the moment.'

The policeman nearly died of shock, but there was a happy ending. The Queen sent a letter from Buckingham Palace to Hertfordshire's chief constable, complimenting the policeman on his vigilance – and he was promoted.

She looks after her staff – never servants – listens to their problems, helps their families and is prepared to put up with all kinds of small indiscretions, such as same-sex love affairs and drunken behaviour, as long as no one else gets to know about them. As her son Prince Andrew revealed, there is nothing that goes on in her household that the Queen doesn't know about, but she prefers to keep it to herself.

However, she would be inhuman if she didn't occasionally forget things, such as in the case of Paul Burrell. The late Princess of Wales's former butler had a meeting with the Queen in which he told her he had taken some of Diana's possessions into his safekeeping. She only remembered when his trial was at its height and admitted to Prince Charles and Prince Philip that she recalled him saying something to her about keeping Diana's belongings. The result was the trial was halted and Burrell was acquitted.

Like her mother before her, the Queen has the ability to compartmentalise and, if things get too difficult, she will take off for a walk with her dogs and forget about it. Prince Philip calls it her 'dog mechanism'. On the day Prime Minister John Major announced the separation of the Prince and Princess of Wales in the House of Commons, the Queen was staying at Wood Farm on the Sandringham estate. It was a poignant setting, for it was here that, in 1919, in this red-brick house hidden from view at the end of a long tree-lined drive, the Queen's thirteen-year-old uncle, the pathetic Prince John, had died of an epileptic fit all but forgotten.

She did not watch the prime minister on television. Instead, she did what she always does when she is agitated and took her corgis for a walk through the wintry woods and ploughed Norfolk fields. When she got back, she dried off the dogs and then almost immediately took them out again.

When she returned to the back door, a member of staff approached the solitary figure of his sovereign, who was dressed in Wellington boots, a Loden coat and a headscarf. He said how very sorry he was to hear the news. The Queen replied: 'I think you will find it's all for the best.' She then walked out again into the drizzle.

Like many aristocratic parents of her era, the Queen did not see much of her children, who were cared for by nannies, and, in the case of Prince Charles and Princess Anne, also by their grandmother, the Queen Mother. The Queen was not a tactile mother and in later life blamed the disintegration of three out of her four children's marriages on her lack of availability when they were growing up. She was only twenty-five, with two small children, when she was catapulted into a world of formidable older men and women. She was not only head of state but the first sovereign to be made head of the Commonwealth, with over a billion subjects. She had all the responsibilities and support, but none of the understanding from someone her own age while still learning the job.

'In a way I didn't have an apprenticeship,' she says. 'My father died much too young and so it was all a very sudden kind of taking on and making the best job you can.'

It was not surprising she was too busy for her children's difficulties. If they had a problem, they seldom discussed it with her and developed the habit of talking about only the most trivial of things. When Prince Charles had troubles with Diana, it was to the Queen Mother he turned and later to Camilla Parker Bowles, never to his mother. None of the Queen's children was accustomed to speaking out about their real feelings because they had been left to their own emotional devices for too long. The results, particularly in the case of Prince Charles and Diana, were disastrous.

As a grandmother, the Queen has enjoyed more time with her children's offspring than she ever had with her own. Peter and Zara Phillips were, and indeed are, particular favourites, although it took five weeks before she saw her first great-grand-child, Peter and Autumn's daughter, Savannah Phillips. She is very fond of Princesses Beatrice and Eugenie and proud of the way Prince William and Prince Harry have turned out, despite their troubled early life. She thoroughly approves of the Duchess of Cambridge and doesn't give a fig for her being from an ordi-nary background as long as it is a stable one – which it is. They may have little in common, as Kate gives no signs of being a genuine horsey, doggy lady, but she admires how well the Duchess has embraced royal life, combining it so cheerfully with duty and motherhood. She has high hopes the Cambridges' mar-riage will be as successful as her own and therefore guarantee the future of the monarchy she has sacrificed so much to sustain.

Throughout her long reign, the Duke of Edinburgh, now in his nineties, has been her 'strength and stay', but he is not super-human. His own mother died at eighty-four, his father at sixty-two and the youngest of his four sisters, Sophie, seven years his senior, at eighty-seven. Genetically, he has outlived his whole family and, despite having overcome several major health problems, may not survive into his hundreds. That means that if the Queen has the longevity of her mother, she may live for many years as a widow. Even if this happens, she has no intention of abdicating. She will reign as long as she is fit and well enough to do so, and that is the promise she made long before she became Queen and it is a promise she will keep. She never forgets that, among her many other styles and titles, she is Defender of the Faith. When Elizabeth II, by the grace of God, came to the throne, she was crowned and anointed a queen in a solemn religious ceremony. Not only did she make her vows to her people, she made them to God.

'It's a job for life,' she says. 'Most people have a job and then they go home, but in this existence the job and the life go together. You can't really divide it up. The boxes and the communications just keep on coming and of course with modern communications they come even quicker. Luckily, I am a quick reader so I can get through a lot of reading in quite a short time, though I do rather begrudge some of the hours I have to do instead of being outdoors.'

The Queen adheres to a strict, old-fashioned Christian faith. She does not see going to church as a duty but as something she enjoys and always has done. She loves traditional hymns and has always preferred the all-embracing words of the Authorised Version, which shows her to be both pragmatic and conservative. When she is at Windsor Castle at weekends, she likes to go to the private chapel in the park near Royal Lodge, rather than St George's Chapel, which she considers too grand. She is not a fan of sermons, but four different bishops are invited to preach at Sandringham when she is there at the beginning of each year.

The Queen's Christmas broadcasts, which she has been giving since her accession to the throne in 1952, are again highly significant in enabling us to understand her faith. They are the most predictable clue to her religious beliefs, and she often uses the opportunity of the celebration of the birth of Jesus to make a Christian point. However, in the sixties, she began to play down the specifically Christian aspects of the celebration. It was part of her early acknowledgement of the importance of all faiths, which in recent years she has come back to again and again, reflecting the increasing numbers of the population who have different religious beliefs, or none at all. Accordingly, reconciliation has become a recurring theme in her speeches – it is a Christian virtue, but it is one that all can relate to. She will also often praise those who do boring, repetitive, selfless tasks, perhaps suggesting that they are not unlike her own role.

Once a year, the Queen comes into our homes and speaks to us from her home, in her own words, not repeating some political platitudes drafted by a government speechwriter. It is the one time in the year she has licence to express some of her own feelings, as the Queen is probably the only individual in a free country who does not enjoy a constitutional right to freedom of speech. Usually, she is required to speak her lines as if from a continuous play written by an ever-increasing circle of scriptwriters. In the UK, everything she says in public must be in accord with the sentiments of her government of the day, and if she happens to be in one of the sixteen countries where she is head of state, she has to reflect the local prime minister, whose views about freedom or the Commonwealth or religion might be far removed from those of Downing Street or indeed her own.

Her role as head of the Commonwealth has, however, given the Queen the opportunity to say what she wants to the world, not only in her Christmas message but in her Commonwealth Day speech in March. It is her bid for freedom, but the use she makes of it reveals as much about her personality and outlook as do her words. She never directly mentions a crisis, whether it is personal or political. The departure of South Africa from the Commonwealth in 1961 never got a mention; instead, she welcomed Jamaica, Trinidad and Uganda to 'our Commonwealth family' when they joined the following year.

On the domestic front, when unemployment was soaring in 1980 and the government was being blamed, she said we 'faced grave problems in the life of our country', but added little more on a political theme. Instead, she commented on how she was 'glad' the celebrations for her mother's eightieth birthday 'gave so much pleasure'.

While she would prefer to be able to strike a happy note, in tune with the Christmas celebrations, often the tone is sombre, especially when she has to recall sad events that have happened over the previous twelve months. Occasionally, she is called upon to address the nation at times of national mourning. Perhaps the most significant of these occasions was after the tragedy of the death of Diana, Princess of Wales. The outpouring of grief that followed led the Queen to deliver a historic live broadcast to the nation.

Although privately the Queen found it hard to understand the public's reaction to someone they didn't even know personally, in public she maintained her composure and delivered her speech on a sultry Friday afternoon from the Chinese Drawing Room at Buckingham Palace. On Friday 5 September 1997 they did a final run-through fifteen minutes before she went on air. At 5.55 the countdown started, with the two monitors in the corner showing different pictures – the live feed of the BBC programming leading up to the news and the interior palace shot of the Queen staring intently into the lens.

'What I say to you now as your Queen, and as a grandmother, I say from my heart,' she began. 'I for one believe there are lessons to be drawn from her life . . .' The Queen's voice was calm and contrite. It was possibly the most difficult speech she had ever given, because it followed an enormous public uproar after her initial response to the death was deemed to be insufficient. Many in the huge crowd in front of the palace gates were almost mutinous in their reactions towards her. But her speech that day was well received and, by the time of her Christmas message that year, the Queen was able to thank her subjects for the love they had shown for Diana through 'the wonderful flowers and messages left in tribute to her'.

The next time Diana's name was uttered in public by the Queen was seven years later, at the opening of the Diana Memorial Fountain in London's Kensington Gardens in July 2004. The Queen spoke fondly of her late daughter-in-law, in far more intimate and affectionate terms than had been possible in the immediate aftermath of her death.

'I cannot forget – and nor can those of us here today who knew her much more personally, as sister, wife, mother or daughter-in-law – the Diana who made such an impact on our lives,' she said. 'Of course, there were difficult times, but memories mellow with the passing of the years. I remember especially the happiness she gave to my two grandsons.'

Her speech on that occasion reflected many of the themes she has returned to over the years: tolerance and forbearance, children as the future, the vitality of young people, the basic goodness of most people in the community, the necessity of doing one's best in the face of life's inevitable frustrations and tragedies, helping those less fortunate or on the edge of society. The points are familiar because they are of the kind that have been applied by parents (and nannies, in certain echelons of society) to their children all over the globe.

Throughout all her personal speeches and Christmas messages, the Queen's own clear voice comes through. The process of drafting the text, however, is usually a joint effort, involving private secretaries and senior members of staff, and the themes for inclusion will be discussed over many months. Any interesting or unusual events are potential topics and even a chance remark on a walkabout could produce a theme for consideration. During the summer court at Balmoral, written drafts are

passed back and forth between the Queen and her private secretary, Sir Christopher Geidt. The Queen makes comments in
the margin in pencil, and takes the shrewd advice of Prince
Philip, who is not only an experienced speechwriter, but a well-
informed theologian. Naturally, he has his own strong opinions,
but he understands the Queen's insistence on adjusting the
speech until it is as it should be. Out of courtesy, Buckingham
Palace will show a draft of the speech to Number 10 before it is
finalised, but they are not compelled to do so. During the year,
the broadcasters will have been doing their bit, too, searching
for the right moments to capture on camera, so the completed
ten-minute film will take almost the whole year to pull together.

It is not easy to grip an audience with the sort of worthy
material that usually makes its way into the Queen's speech, but
gripped they have to be. The Queen takes it seriously and her
views on the world are largely unchanging and unvaried, though
she is aware and reflects on how the world itself is progressing.
Her Christmas broadcasts represent continuity and the reassurance of the familiar, while the predictability of the similar
themes is as comforting as Christmas itself.

The Queen's Christmas address is not just an annual task for
Her Majesty; it has also been woven into the fabric of the nation,
with many families still sitting down after they have completed
their lunch to watch the speech on television. The broadcast
topped its popularity during the Diana years, reaching an all-
time high in 1987 with an audience of 28 million. That year the
Queen struck a chord when she spoke about how much she
enjoyed receiving letters from members of the public, as they
allowed her to get a sense of what people were thinking, even if
they were critical and 'full of advice for me and my family'.

Even now, in the modern world of technology and social
media, the Christmas Day message is still looked forward to

with anticipation by millions of people who regard it as much a part of their day as Christmas itself. Yet the tradition is comparatively recent. It is eighty-three years since the Queen's grandfather, King George V, consented to face up to a radio microphone carved from Australian walnut and send a message to inaugurate the new BBC Empire Service. His words, written by poet and author Rudyard Kipling, reached 20 million people from two rooms at Sandringham converted into a temporary broadcasting studio. The microphones were connected through Post Office landlines to the control room at London's Broadcasting House and from there were connected to BBC transmitters. The General Post Office was then used for the speech to reach Australia, Canada, India, Kenya, South Africa and other parts of the globe.

After he died, the new King Edward VIII never made a Christmas broadcast, as it was less than a year before he abdicated, on 11 December 1936. The following year, the unwelcome task fell to his younger brother George VI. He suffered from a terrible stammer, and the listeners realised what a tremendous personal struggle it was for him to speak coherently through his stammer. His speech went live from Sandringham in December 1937, and the bond between the King and his people intensified when they realised how difficult it had been for him to do this. During the years of war that followed, his broadcasts were particularly significant as they helped give hope to a disembowelled world. So, by the time of the death of her father, the Queen had little choice but to continue with his tradition of giving a Christmas message, and she explained why it was so important to her to follow him in many things that were particular to him:

Each Christmas at this time, my beloved father broadcast a message to his people in all parts of the world ... As he used to, I am speaking to you from my own home where I am spending Christmas with my family ... My father and my grandfather before him worked hard all their lives to unite our peoples ever more closely and to maintain its [the Commonwealth's] ideals which were so near to their hearts. I shall strive to carry on their work.

Over the years the Queen has become aware that what is expected of her is not a performance, but a welcome. She recognises that not only is she bringing her subjects into her home, but equally she is going into theirs. It is a moment of personal connection that is impossible at any other time. When she meets people at functions or on walkabouts, her encounters are almost always brief, yet during her address she is able to give of herself for much longer, and she tries always to keep the tone personal and informal.

She cannot be asked to act, because acting is not the sentiment she wants to convey. An unpretentious feeling of warmth is essential for her message to get across. She does not have to perform her role, merely live it. When she quotes from the great works of literature or the Bible, she chooses a simple message, by far the most frequent being the familiar line about 'peace on earth, goodwill to men'. After sixty-three years on the throne and having reached the significant milestone of being the world's longest reigning monarch, the Queen has seen enough of politics and of life to know how important it is to reach those men of goodwill.

Over a span of sixty years and more, she has met nearly all the leaders of the age – some good, some bad, a few utterly deranged – and handled them all with grace and finesse. In that time, she has shown herself to be a woman of will, determined to carry out her duties in her own way and according to her own beliefs. She has seen the power of the monarchy eroded, but has steadfastly maintained her authority over what areas she can control. When, in 1961, the British government, concerned for her safety, tried to prevent her visiting Ghana, she exerted her prerogative so forcefully that Prime Minister Harold Macmillan backed down and the Queen went to West Africa.

She was just as quick to put Prime Minister Tony Blair in his place when, on a visit to Balmoral in 1999, he said with only three years to go it was time to start making preparations for the Golden Jubilee. The Queen interpreted this as an attempt to hijack the arrangements and sternly reminded him: '*My* Golden Jubilee, Mr Blair.'

She is also physically brave. When at Trooping the Colour in 1981, someone fired blank shots at her. She calmly continued with the ceremony and appeared unaffected by it. When Prince Edward telephoned her from his school that night, she never mentioned the incident. Sometimes actions can speak louder than words, but as we will see throughout this book, the words she speaks on her own behalf can be just as revealing, even if occasionally they need a little bit of decoding.

The Queen lives in unrivalled splendour, with upwards of 200 members of staff on call, but most of them are there to help her fulfil her role as head of state. Left to her own devices, she would have much preferred the homely comfort of a small household surrounded by dogs and horses. She does not enjoy society but prefers the company of the small group of friends who have not left for what she loves to call 'greener pastures'. Her tastes are simple and those who know her well say she is two different people: Lilibet, her pet name, and Her Majesty the Queen.

Lilibet would much rather wear a headscarf than a tiara, and sit on a rug for a country picnic with her family (even in a

chilling wind) than attend a sumptuous glittering state banquet. Less hardy folk have been known to complain she is
apparently quite impervious to cold. However, the two characters come together in her greatest attribute: she is first and
foremost a diplomat, whether on a personal level or on a political one.

No other British monarch has reigned as long as Queen
Elizabeth; she has been a fixed point in the history of the monarchy and she has kept it going. She decided she was going to
follow the approach taken by her father and her grandfather
before that. She has not been immune to change in the way she
lives her life, but she has sometimes been reluctant to embrace it.
She believes that the continuity she has upheld over the years
has proved to be the royal family's salvation.

In her words to parliament on the occasion of her Diamond
Jubilee, the Queen reflected on a life dedicated to the service of
a nation and her gratitude and thanks for the days that have
gone and for those yet to come:

We are reminded here of our past, of the continuity of our
national story and the virtues of resilience, ingenuity and tolerance which created it. I have been privileged to witness
some of that history and, with the support of my family,
rededicate myself to the service of our great country and its
people now and in the years to come.

It was a speech of emotion, reflection and dignity. It revealed
the principles at the heart of her reign, and her pride in the
nation's history. As so often before, the Queen's speech carried
symbolic power, but was also a very personal statement of her
beliefs.

Chapter 2

THE EARLY YEARS

*I declare before you all that my whole life,
whether it be long or short, shall be
devoted to your service and the service of
our great imperial family to which we all
belong.*

TWENTY-FIRST BIRTHDAY SPEECH,
CAPE TOWN, 21 APRIL 1947

Until the time of the abdication in the winter of 1936, the
Duke and Duchess of York were able to enjoy their relatively simple home life at 145 Piccadilly, living quietly with their
children as much as their position would allow; Princess
Elizabeth was ten at the time and Princess Margaret six. The
future George VI was daunted by the world beyond his familiar
walls and sought emotional refuge in the introspective, self-con-
tained family unit he created for himself – his wife and two
daughters he referred to as 'we four'.

They had, for instance, been accustomed to paying a weekly
visit incognito to the nearby cinema at Marble Arch. They
would telephone the manager and tell him they were coming,

dine early and creep into their seats at the back when the lights were low. They would sit together like any young couple, but as the film was about to end and before the lights went up, they would prepare their escape.

It took time before they could resign themselves to the serious destiny being thrust upon them with such unexpected suddenness. They feared for the life they had planned so carefully, with weeks spent at 145 Piccadilly and weekends at Royal Lodge, in Windsor Great Park. There, they spent their time in the garden, always improving, creating and enjoying a country life with their daughters and their pets. Their big worry was not so much for themselves but for their eldest daughter, for whom they had not visualised such a destiny and would not have chosen it for her.

Even before she became heir to the throne, they had little room for outsiders, and Princess Elizabeth mixed with her own carefully vetted social peers. The Duchess of York had laid down the ground rules for bringing up her children and, in common with the daughters of many aristocratic houses at that time, Elizabeth and Margaret were educated privately at home, chiefly by their governess, Marion Crawford. The Duchess's former nanny, Clara ('Allah') Knight, a no-nonsense Hertfordshire woman, believed that to spoil a child was to ruin the adult. What this meant in practice was that everything was done according to a strict routine and at an appointed hour, from breakfast at 7.30am through to bedtime at 7.15pm.

The rigours of this inflexible routine were alleviated somewhat by the arrival of a nursery maid, 22-year-old Margaret MacDonald, whom Elizabeth nicknamed 'Bobo'. A generation younger than the formidable Allah and a lot more easy-going, she came to share the Princess's bedroom and remained her closest confidante and friend until her death in 1993.

However, there was only so far even Bobo and Allah were allowed to go in their efforts to make young Elizabeth's life as pleasant as they could, for there was another significant figure involved in her upbringing – her grandmother, Queen Mary, who was almost seventy at the time. The nannies took their instructions not from the Duchess but from George V's indomitable wife, who ordered Elizabeth be taught to wave to crowds and smile for photographers. 'Teach that child not to fidget,' Queen Mary would bark. In return for the small reward of a biscuit, Elizabeth would learn how to control her bladder for hours on end. It is unfair to judge one generation by the standards of another, but even by the criteria of her own era, Elizabeth's childhood was regimented. Only the strong will of her mother, who insisted her children should be surrounded by affection and happiness and in return offer it to others, prevented them from being lonely. The Duchess made them realise that they had two separate lives to lead – their lives as Princesses and their lives as little girls.

Even so, when Elizabeth was outside her family circle she was timid and shy to the point of gaucheness. She was dressed in clothes of the same cut and colour as her sister, who was four years her junior, and she had a physically fragile father to deal with. Because of his stammer, he was seen as an embarrassment, and the prospect of being King appalled him. When he was told he was to succeed Edward VIII, he admitted that 'he broke down and sobbed like a child'.

Elizabeth was still young and her parents did what they could to shield her from the enormous change that had befallen them, but she was too old not to be affected by the terrible despondency engulfing her family. Told that her Uncle David was going away for a long time, perhaps forever, and that she was going to live in Buckingham Palace, she blurted out in horror: 'What, *for always?*' She saw her mother crumble under the strain, and witnessed her father reduced to helpless misery, as they began to take on their new role and her happy family life as she knew it was torn apart.

Once the family moved into Buckingham Palace, life took on a more even keel again; the Princess was removed from the all-pervading influence of her widowed grandmother, who had moved to Marlborough House. That period was short-lived, however, as international events moved fast. At the outbreak of war, Elizabeth and Margaret were sent to the comparative safety of Scotland, to stay at Birkhall on the Balmoral estate. It meant being estranged from their parents, however, and eventually Royal Lodge beckoned. In 1940 they were moved to the pink-washed house in Windsor Great Park with its wide terraces, green, weed-filled swimming pool and flat-roofed pagoda. It was relatively tranquil there; the only disturbances were the drones of wartime planes overhead. Things were not so calm in London, as the German blitz meant the city was bombed on a regular basis: Buckingham Palace was damaged on 9 September 1940 and four weeks later their old home, 145 Piccadilly, received a direct hit. In the circumstances, only the ancient battlements of Windsor Castle were thought sturdy enough to protect the two Princesses.

'Suddenly we were asked to pack and move to the castle,' Princess Margaret said. 'We packed for the weekend and stayed for five years.'

They were not the only ones to be evacuated. In an operation codenamed Pied Piper, hundreds of thousands of children were sent from the slums of London to homes in a countryside they had often never seen, and many thousands more from all over the country were evacuated to North America and even Australia.

Because supplies from overseas were restricted, as German U-boats sought to stop vessels reaching the UK, food was rationed and meat was in very short supply. Those fortunate enough to own land, especially extensive land such as the royal estates, fared better. Like other children, the Princesses missed out on the luxuries of childhood, such as sweets, which were in very short supply, and bananas, which were not imported because shipping space was needed for other vital things.

Princess Elizabeth still had responsibilities and she had to work much harder than other girls of her age at her lessons, with a larger variety of essential subjects to study. According to contemporary reports that depicted her sharing in the war effort, she knitted for the troops and spent weekend mornings in the garden digging for victory. Otherwise Elizabeth and Margaret enjoyed life very much as it had been. They were still very privileged girls; they had their own bikes; a menagerie of pets, including an aviary of bright blue budgerigars, two grey ponies called Comet and Greylight and several dogs. One of these, a corgi named Jane, had two puppies, which Elizabeth named Carol and Crackers because they were born on Christmas Eve.

There were no unsightly wartime signs at Royal Lodge, and the only change since the Duke of York had become King was the presence of a policeman to open the gates instead of a kindly old lady. The house had no camouflage, and blackout (which all houses were supposed to have) was achieved with green blinds and curtains that hung behind the original drapes. Nor did the girls have the ominous gas masks that all schoolchildren were obliged to carry. Their mother was adamant that their memories of a happy childhood should be just that.

Despite all that was done to shield her from the effects of the war, Princess Elizabeth was deeply affected by its trail of horror and it made a deep and lasting impression on her. She pored over the news and at night, when she had to take shelter from air raids in the dungeons of Windsor Castle, she worried about her parents in London. She had begged earnestly to be allowed to accompany them there, but had to remain at Windsor Castle with her sister, listening to the distant booming of the anti-aircraft guns and occasional exploding bomb.

When photographer Lisa Sheridan was invited to take photographs of the family group that year, she made some acute observations about the young Princess. 'The development of Princess Elizabeth's character interested me in particular,' she wrote in her autobiography. 'It is surprising that in spite of her position Princess Elizabeth might in some ways be considered young for her age. She has of course, as her constant companion, a sister four years her junior. Inversely that may have resulted in Princess Margaret's being somewhat older than her years, so that their lives and interests may converge more closely. But there is a delightful youthfulness and enthusiasm which one might not expect to find in her position. She shows a very loveable emotional security and lack of sophistication, and all she undertakes appears to be inspired by genuine interest.

'Princess Elizabeth seems to be the more contemplative of the two sisters – the more reserved, the more sensitive. Princess Margaret still shows a spontaneous self-assurance and a delightfully quick response to life. The younger sister's brain and the older sister's lack of selfishness bridge the discrepancy of their ages most successfully.'

However much she might have lacked sophistication, Princess Elizabeth was about to discover that her role as heir to the throne meant that she had to take on certain duties, even at the age of fourteen. She was called upon to give a sterling performance on the 'wireless' when she made her microphone debut in

1940. According to the BBC archives, Derek McCulloch, the head of children's broadcasting, was the man responsible for arranging the broadcast. McCulloch, known as Uncle Mac for his work as the presenter of *Children's Hour*, had the idea to start a new programme for children who had been evacuated to Canada, America and Australia. He decided the Princess was the ideal person to introduce this and besieged the top brass at the BBC to get permission, before turning to the Ministry of Information and pointing out how appropriate it would be. The King agreed to these requests, despite concerns that the Princess was too young.

McCulloch recalled the Princess never made a mistake or wrong inflection, but gave a perfect broadcast. Apparently, the King rushed into the room after the first rehearsal, exclaiming to Uncle Mac, 'She's exactly like her!' – meaning the Princess's voice sounded completely natural and familiar to him.

Her governess, Marion Crawford, recorded in her book, *The Little Princesses*, published in 1950, that 'Lilibet' worked hard preparing for the speech. 'She was so good about the endless rehearsals,' Crawfie recalled. 'We had to get the breathing and phrasing right. It was a long and tedious business for a little girl. She read her speech several times to Mummie and Papa and put in several phrases of her own.'

On Sunday 13 October 1940, in a special edition of *Children's Hour*, the Princess gave her first ever broadcast. Together with her sister Margaret, she sat at a mahogany table at Windsor Castle and, as the radio producer counted her down for her first act of national duty, she talked to the children evacuated to Canada, New Zealand and the United States. Anxious to include her sister at the end of the broadcast, she asked ten-year-old Princess Margaret, who was sitting beside her, to join her in saying goodbye.

Before I finish I can truthfully say to you all that we children at home are full of cheerfulness and courage. We are trying to do all we can to help our gallant sailors, soldiers and airmen and we are trying too to bear our own share of the danger and sadness of war. We know, every one of us, that in the end all will be well; for God will care for us and give us victory and peace. And when peace comes, remember, it will be for us, the children of today, to make the world of tomorrow a better and happier place.

My sister is by my side and we are both going to say goodnight to you. Come on, Margaret, say goodnight.

Thereupon, a small, rather pompous, voice chipped in, 'Goodnight children, and good luck to you all.'

The next day the BBC representative in New York, Gerald Cock, sent a cable home: 'PRINCESSES YESTERDAY HUGE SUCCESS HERE STOP SOME STATIONS REPORT TELEPHONE EXCHANGES JAMMED WITH REQUESTS FOR A REPEAT.' The *Star* newspaper reported that, following the broadcast, children had even adopted the 'Come on, Margaret' part of the broadcast as their catchphrase.

Churchill's private secretary, Jock Colville, might not have liked its soppy sentimentality, but it was a great success, making the front pages of every New York newspaper. It was certainly seen by some as a political ploy to encourage America to relinquish its neutrality, but if that was the aim it had no political repercussions. However, it did mark the beginning of a regular broadcast feature for children evacuees, which had been McCulloch's plan all along, rather than being part of a broader diplomatic initiative.

As war progressed, the peaceful days at Royal Lodge came to an end and the Princesses were moved permanently to the sturdier confines of Windsor Castle, where they lived for the remainder of the war. Their parents continued to visit them at weekends, travelling from Buckingham Palace, and the King would often draw his eldest daughter's attention to a certain document and explain its contents to her very earnestly. There was a particular bond of understanding between the two, deeper perhaps than a normal family, as he knew they had to share the burden of her life to come and that he had to prepare her for her future role. The Queen realised how sensitive her elder daughter was and made sure she was involved as much as she could be with life at the castle and, together with Margaret, shared in the activities of the Royal School in the Great Park.

The Royal School provided education for local children, including those of the castle retainers, and poignantly a number of evacuees from London. The school was run by Hugh Tanner and his wife, and they decided which of the local children would be suitable to visit the castle as companions for the Princesses. It was an invaluable and eye-opening experience. Princess Elizabeth was horrified to discover that one of the girls evacuated from the East End of London had no proper shoes. Although her own pocket money was rationed, she took the evacuee girl into Windsor the next day and together they bought a pair of strong brogues. The Princess paid for them there and then. On another occasion, she discovered that a child destined for the ballet class was unable to attend because her mother had found it impossible to afford ballet shoes for her. To ensure the girl was not embarrassed, the Princess produced a hurriedly scuffed pair of shoes the next day, claiming they were a spare pair of hers.

Tucked away in Windsor Castle for five years, the Princess could absorb some of the symbolism and traditions of the institution of which she would one day be the integral part. She was meticulous in everything she did, including feeding the dogs, and when one of the young corgis was accidentally run over by the gardener's van, she penned a note to him expressing her sympathy for the shock and assuring him it had not been his fault. She became an expert at plane spotting (she is to this day) and could tell when the Hurricanes made a signal to the castle that dive-bomb practice was about to begin, and almost immediately the sky was filled with screeching planes.

The wartime Christmas pantomimes staged at the castle were, according to Princess Margaret, her father's idea. He felt the barbed wire strung 'feebly' around the castle, which kept them indoors in case of air raids, also imprisoned them mentally. He was anxious to find something for them to do that embraced as many of the castle staff and locals as possible. With the Princesses' love of dressing up, singing, dancing and mimicry, staging a pantomime seemed a good idea and made for many hours of entertainment.

The King entered into the spirit of things, making expeditions around the castle with his daughters 'hunting for junk', as he called it. The castle was a veritable storehouse of treasures and, on one occasion, the King even allowed the girls to use the band of the Royal Horse Guards to provide the music for their show. The pantomimes, written by the schoolmaster and performed in the Waterloo Chamber to an audience of several hundred, proved a release from the restrictions of wartime life, and everyone joined in, the King and Queen bursting into song whenever they had the opportunity.

At the age of seventeen, the painfully shy Princess Elizabeth was deemed ready for the next step on her progress, as she was prepared for her future role: she was dispatched to undertake her first solo official duty. She had been made an honorary colonel of the Grenadier Guards and drove to Salisbury Plain to perform her first grown-up inspection of the battalion.

'What shall I do with my handbag during the march past?' she kept asking of her mother's lady-in-waiting, Lady Delia Peel. A stream of other questions followed. As they drew near their destination, Elizabeth's face started to blanch as her nerves got the better of her. She was on the verge of actually being sick when Lady Delia fished into her bag and produced the last of her sweet ration – a barley sugar. The lady-in-waiting commanded her to eat it slowly, adding that she would find it good for the stomach muscles.

It worked, and she managed to walk up and down the lines of soldiers as if she had been inspecting troops all her life. And when the whole battalion marched past twice, she stood stock still, handbag at her side. Queen Mary's instructions never to fidget had paid off. On the way back to Windsor Castle that evening, she saw Stonehenge for the first time and asked if they could stop and have a look.

'No, we can't – it's not on our schedule,' replied Lady Delia, firmly reminding the Princess of the constraints of being royal, even in her teenage years.

At the end of the war, the Princesses moved back to their old rooms at the rear of Buckingham Palace, but still managed the odd moment of freedom. On VE night, now aged nineteen and fourteen, they escaped into the crowds outside the palace with a party of sixteen friends, including their cousin Margaret Elphinstone, their uncle David Bowes-Lyon, the King's equerry, Group Captain Peter Townsend, and the young Lord Porchester, later the Queen's racing manager. In 1985, the Queen gave an interview on Radio 4 to former BBC royal correspondent, the late Godfrey Talbot, recalling the whole episode.

'I think we went on the balcony nearly every hour, six times, and then when the excitement of the floodlights being switched on got through to us my sister and I realised we couldn't see what the crowds were enjoying.'

They asked their father if they could join in, to which he agreed, and the Queen recalled how she and her sister walked for miles and miles.

'We were terrified of being recognised.' But her attempts to pull her cap over her face to try to remain incognito were scuppered by a fellow officer in their party. He told her in no uncertain terms that it must be worn properly. 'He said he refused to be seen in the company of another officer improperly dressed,' she told Talbot.

'We were swept along on a tide of happiness and relief' by the huge crowds, and it was after midnight by the time they returned to the palace. 'It was one of the most memorable nights of my life,' the Queen added.

'It was most exciting – we went everywhere,' Princess Margaret remembered in an interview for *Desert Island Discs* many years later.

'We rushed down the street and when we got back to the palace we had missed the King and Queen on the balcony,' Margaret recalled. Then, because the Princesses were just part of the crowd, they had difficulty getting back inside the palace; and the moment of anonymity was somewhat spoiled when they had to summon a member of the household to let them in.

Even after the war, Elizabeth was not allowed to go out alone with young men. If she did have male company, it was always in a party of four or preferably six or eight. That was a strict protocol never to be broken or disregarded. She could never allow one of her escorts to take her home. She may have had her own car, given to her by her father, with its distinctive number HRH 1, but she could never drive it anywhere without a detective in the back and a bodyguard following in a second car at a discreet distance. No wonder she was naive and no wonder Prince Philip, whom she had met when she was only thirteen, remained the centre of her male universe.

She had formally met the young Philip of Greece at Dartmouth Naval College in 1939 with her parents and her sister. Aged eighteen at the time, he was assigned to look after the Princesses and made an indelible impact on the young Elizabeth. They started corresponding and the homeless Prince (his family had been exiled from his country when he was a child), encouraged by his uncle, Lord Mountbatten, eventually became a regular visitor at the royal palaces. As she grew into a young woman, his interest in Elizabeth changed and, despite her parents' concern that she was too young, she never looked at another man.

Later on, even he couldn't turn up at the palace without a personal invitation from her parents. If she asked him to have a sherry before dinner in her pastel pink apartments, there always had to be a chaperone in the room. Somewhat irritatingly for Philip, it was often Princess Margaret. If Philip and Elizabeth were invited to the same parties, the most they could hope for was a couple of dances together during the evening. She could not discuss her feelings for him with anyone, and perhaps she didn't know herself, but she constantly played the score from *Oklahoma!*, especially the song 'People Will Say We're in Love', which is still a favourite of hers today.

If it hadn't been for the hostilities, Elizabeth's life might have been different, but as it was she went almost straight from the nursery to the office. She had her own small staff and her diary began to be filled up months in advance. At Remembrance Day in 1945, the first to be observed for six years, Princess Elizabeth (dressed in the ATS uniform of a junior commander) was proud to place her own wreath on the Cenotaph. She was also giving the occasional, clearly articulated, professionally delivered, public speech; there was one for the YWCA (the Young Women's Christian Association) in 1945, and another for Empire Day in 1946.

Now twenty, in the latter speech Princess Elizabeth addressed the youth of the Commonwealth and the British Empire. In the aftermath of the war, the speech commended the common ideals of 'freedom, justice and humanity' that can be found in every corner of the empire, about which she said: 'For a year the Empire stood together alone and in so doing saved civilisation.' She also used the occasion to announce her intention to spend some of the next twelve months visiting parts of the Commonwealth that she had not been to before.

Her speech was notable for the way she reflected on the changing nature of Britain's colonial role, commenting: 'Our Commonwealth has grown like a garden – not a formal one with enclosed walks and terraces, but one that makes use of nature for its beauty – what used to be known around the world as an "English Garden".' The point she was making was that the Commonwealth was homely, natural and safe; more importantly, she was suggesting that it was no longer too centralised, as it had once been at the height of imperial power. In truth, in the aftermath of the war, Britain no longer had the energy, finances or appetite to cling on to its empire, and her speech reflected that new reality.

The need to make speeches on numerous occasions became an increasingly regular feature of her life. Accordingly, she gave no sign of the nerves she must have felt when she delivered one on her twenty-first birthday from Cape Town during a four-month royal tour with her parents. Although it was a national holiday in South Africa, it was hardly one for her. The previous day she had reviewed troops, civil defence workers, nursing services, women's corps, and cadet battalions, and finally took the salute at a huge march past in her honour.

On her birthday, she had the most important speech of her life to deliver – which was broadcast live on the radio from Cape Town. It was significant because in it she announced that she was to dedicate her life to her royal duty, and she recognised that meant relinquishing her individuality and, with it, her freedom to do and say what she thought. For a young woman, it was a highly important statement to make, but it was to prove the basis of her view on how she ought to conduct her role throughout the rest of her life.

There is a motto, which has been borne by many of my ancestors – a noble motto, 'I serve.' Those words were an inspiration to many bygone heirs to the throne when they made their knightly dedication as they came to manhood. I cannot do quite as they did, but through the inventions of science . . . I can make my solemn act of dedication with a whole empire listening.

I declare before you all that my whole life, whether it be long or short, shall be devoted to your service and the service of our great imperial family to which we all belong. I shall not have the strength to carry out this resolution alone unless you join in it with me, as I now invite you to do. I know that your support will be unfailingly given. God help me to make good my vow; and God bless all of you who are willing to share in it.

It was her first live address to the nation and the Commonwealth, and she spoke in the certain knowledge that one day she would be Queen. In the speech, she also touched upon Britain's traditional role in the world, quoting William Pitt on how, in an earlier era, 'England had saved herself by her exertions and would save Europe by her example.' She expressed the pride felt by many at how Britain and its empire had 'the high honour of standing alone seven years ago in defence of the liberty of the world'. This balancing act, between looking back at what had previously been achieved, while also studying what could be done now and in the future, was one that was to become a familiar theme throughout her subsequent reign.

The next day the royal family set sail from the warmth and beauty of Cape Town to return to a war-ravaged Europe. But Britain's position in the world was changing, and Princess Elizabeth's speech tried to highlight a possible new role, as being an 'example' to others. Now, in the post-war world, it was clear that the era of empire was drawing to a close – India, the 'jewel', would be declared independent within three months. The United Kingdom was broke and exhausted by the war, as were its subjects. Many looked to the King for an invisible support and saw the monarchy as one of the few stable institutions remaining. The speech also highlighted how much, in a new era of democracy in which a Labour government was transforming the basis on which society was governed, the monarchy recognised it was also dependent on the support of the people.

Just over two months later, Elizabeth finally had someone to provide personal support when, on 10 July 1947, her engagement to Lieutenant Philip Mountbatten was announced. The night before, she had been at a magnificent candlelit coming-out party at Apsley House, Number One London at Hyde Park Corner, where successive Dukes of Wellington had lived since just after the Battle of Waterloo. It was the last time she would have to attend such a function as a single woman.

Their engagement was relatively brief, and on 20 November

they were married, with Philip taking the title of Duke of Edinburgh. Within a year, their first child, Charles, was born, securing the succession for another generation. Princess Anne followed on 15 August 1950, as the young couple grew used to family life and their royal role together.

However, King George's health had been badly affected by the stresses of the war, and his heavy smoking helped cause his lung cancer, which increasingly incapacitated him. By 1951, the King was seriously ill and in September his left lung was removed in an operation, which caused the Princess and her husband to delay a month-long royal visit to Canada, a trip that included a stop-off in the United States.

The Princess was adamant she would not leave before she knew the operation on her father had been successful, so Prince Philip suggested they fly. In 1951, Atlantic crossings were almost always done by sea on one of the great liners, although plenty of businessmen made the journey by plane. The government had reservations about the heir to the throne using air travel as a means of crossing the Atlantic, but after Philip had personally made appointments to see both Prime Minister Clement Attlee and Leader of the Opposition Winston Churchill, they were given approval to go ahead.

The seventeen-hour flight to Montreal on board the BOAC plane 'Atlanta' was the beginning of an exhausting initiation into the responsibilities of their royal role. They covered the vast breadth of the country – Atlantic to Pacific coasts twice – a total of over 10,000 miles, through ten provinces and sixty cities. With the help of her private secretary, Martin Charteris, Princess Elizabeth made some fifty-odd speeches, several of them in French. By now, she had been making them since the age of fourteen, so she felt increasingly capable of doing so, but these, unlike her subsequent Christmas speeches, were all written for her. Delivering them in just the right tone still took a nerve-wracking amount of effort, and once one was finished there was another to be anxious about.

On their return to England, the King looked weak and pale, but the whole family gathered at Sandringham as usual for Christmas. On 29 January 1952, the King returned to London for a consultation with his doctors and the following evening the royal family attended a performance of the musical *South Pacific* at Drury Lane theatre. Both Philip and the Princess feared it might be the last celebration they had together, as they had known for some time that the King was terminally ill with cancer. It was an emotional evening, as the next day Elizabeth and Philip were off on a six-month tour of East Africa, Australia and New Zealand.

Not only did they have to say goodbye to their children, Prince Charles and Princess Anne; worse still, father and daughter were to be parted with the knowledge they might never see each other again. As a precaution, the Princess was given a sealed dossier containing the draft Accession Declaration, to be opened in the event of the King's death. A Royal Standard was also tucked away in the luggage, as were the black mourning clothes always packed among the royal family's personal luggage.

The colonial magnificence of Nairobi's Government House was a shot of adrenaline for the weary travellers. For their few days of official duties, they based themselves amid the splendour and colour of its tropical gardens as guests of the governor, Sir Philip Mitchell. Their wedding present from the Kenyan people was a wooden hunting lodge at Sagana, in the Aberdare Forest game reserve, 20 miles from Nyeri and 100 miles along dirt roads from Nairobi.

It had been agreed that they could visit, despite the tense situation in the country, which was facing the beginning of the so-called Mau Mau uprising. The idea was that the young couple could enjoy relative peace before commencing the next part of the tour. The highlight of their stay was to spend a night at Treetops, a renowned game-viewing lodge built in the branches of an enormous tree, accessible only by ladder. The wooden construction overlooked a lake that was a favourite watering hole for the big game of the area. Although it was February and the height of Kenyan summer, when game movements are unpredictable, they still expected to see plenty of wildlife, as a salt lick was put down to encourage a variety of animals.

Even in those early days, accommodation had to be made for the press. The day before the royal visit, an international party from London's *Evening Standard*, the *Argus* of South Africa, the *Sydney Morning Herald*, and *Time* and *Life* magazines in America spent the night at Treetops before returning to their hotel.

In those days, the lodge was situated in an oval-shaped clearing and had three narrow bedrooms for visitors, and one for the hunter. For the royal visit, renowned British hunter and conservationist Colonel Jim Corbett was seconded. Inside the lodge was a dining room with a wood-burning stove and an elevated viewing platform. Everything was set for the royal party's afternoon arrival when a large herd of forty-seven elephants loomed out of the forest and edged their way towards the salt lick under the tree. When the royal party, which included lady-in-waiting Lady Pamela Mountbatten, Prince Philip's equerry Michael Parker, and Eric Sherbrooke Walker, the founder of Treetops, arrived at the appointed spot they made cautious progress. In single file, they walked along the track, which was only a few feet wide with the bush pressing in on either side.

As they approached the hut, the squealing and trumpeting of restless elephants got louder, and Walker asked Prince Philip if they should abandon the idea or risk the possibility of being charged by an elephant protecting her calf. Unsurprisingly, Prince Philip wanted to continue, so the group moved as silently as they could to where Eric's wife, Lady Bettie, was waiting halfway up the ladder. There was a fifty-yard run of comparative open ground to cross before reaching the narrow wooden struts into the tree. The Princess did not falter and walked straight towards the ladder, ignoring the nearest elephant, which was standing right underneath Treetops flapping her ears menacingly. She then handed Eric's wife her handbag and her camera and climbed the steep ladder.

Meticulously, the Princess filmed the unfolding scene with her cine camera and couldn't be drawn from the array of game that gathered at the water hole. When the sunset had faded and it was no longer possible to use the cameras, the group talked in hushed voices about the game they had seen and what they might expect later. Concern was expressed for the Princess's father, who had stood hatless at London airport on a bitterly cold day in order to wave her goodbye. Walker recalls in his book, *Treetops Hotel*, that the Princess replied warmly: 'He is like that. He never thinks of himself.'

'She then referred to her father's long illness and the family's great pleasure when it was believed he had reached the turning point. She told us that one day he raised his walking stick to his shoulder and declared, "I believe I could shoot now." She was closely informed of her father's plans and was able to say he was planning to shoot on the following day. Clearly from the tone of her conversation when she said good-bye to her father, she was hoping for a complete recovery.'

At sunrise, the Princess – or the Queen as she had unknowingly become during the night – was out on the balcony again with her cine camera, filming a rhino, silhouetted against the

African dawn, at the salt lick. Meanwhile, Prince Philip was keeping an eye on another rhino, which arrived at the scene puffing and blowing as if a bitter battle might ensue. Instead, peace descended and after breakfast they all climbed down from the tree and walked back through the clearing, this time without incident. Mindful of the previous afternoon, Walker turned to the Princess and said rather pompously, 'If you have the same courage, Ma'am, in facing what the future sends you as you have at facing an elephant at eight yards, we are going to be very fortunate indeed.'

Little did he know how prophetic his words would be and, as the Princess drove away, she waved and called, 'I will come again!' It was many years before she was able to do so, but she kept her promise.

The news of her father's death did not reach the Princess until she was back at Sagana Lodge later that morning. The task of conveying the dreadful news was left to Prince Philip, who had been informed by Michael Parker only minutes before. According to Parker, Philip looked as if the whole world had dropped on his shoulders. 'He took the Queen up to the garden and they walked up and down the lawn while he talked and talked to her.'

In the following hours, when preparations were made to return to England as quickly as possible, the Queen wrote letters and telegrams while Philip sat beside her. 'Poor guy,' Parker recalled years later in 1999. 'He needed something to do. But he was there with the Queen; that was the thing; he was like a bloody great pillar.'

Back in London, the news had been relayed to Prime Minister Winston Churchill. Edward Ford, one of the King's private secretaries, had called him, saying, 'I've got bad news, Prime Minister. The King died last night. I know nothing else.'

Churchill's private secretary, Jock Colville, recalled that when he went to Churchill's bedroom he was sitting alone with tears in his eyes staring into space. 'I had not realised how much the King meant to him,' he said. 'I tried to cheer him up by saying how well he would get on with the new Queen, but all he could say was that he did not know her and that she was only a child.'

Child she was not. Two days after her father's death, on 8 February, she was together with Privy Counsellors and representatives from the Commonwealth and the City of London at St James's Palace. 'There must have been two hundred Privy Counsellors present in the large room next to the picture gallery,' Lord Chandos, the Colonial Secretary, recalled. 'The door opened and the Queen in black came in. Suddenly the members of the Privy Council looked immeasurably old, gnarled and grey. The Queen made one of the most touching speeches to which I have ever listened and I, like many others, could hardly control my emotions.'

The 26-year-old Queen, a slight figure in deep mourning, entered the room alone and went through the exacting tasks of the constitution. Her speeches were delivered perfectly and steadily in her strong, clear and somewhat high-pitched voice.

By the sudden death of my dear father I am called to assume the duties and responsibilities of sovereignty. I know that in my resolve to follow his shining example of service and devotion, I shall be inspired by the loyalty and affection of those whose Queen I have been called to be, and by the counsel of their elected Parliaments. I pray that God will help me to discharge worthily this heavy task that has been laid upon me so early in my life.

My heart is too full for me to say more to you today than I shall always work as my father did throughout his reign, to advance the happiness and prosperity of my peoples, spread as they are all the world over.

Prince Philip, who was in the room as a Privy Counsellor, then stepped forward, his head slightly bowed, and went out of the door two steps behind the Queen. His symbolic role as her consort was further reinforced when it was decided that the family should continue to be known as the House of Windsor, rather than the House of Mountbatten after his family name.

As 1952 drew to a close, and she prepared to make her first Christmas speech, the Queen had to contend with the worst 'pea-souper' fog in London's history, between 4 and 9 December, as well as making a significant speech in the City. The smog clung to the windows, leaving sooty deposits behind, and visibility was reduced to a few yards, making driving difficult or impossible. Buses couldn't run and the ambulance service stopped functioning, so those who were ill had to make their own way to hospital. Londoners, wearing handkerchiefs tied around their faces, were obliged to walk along pavements armed with umbrellas to feel where the pavement ended and the road began. Government medical reports in the following weeks estimated that, up until 8 December, 4,000 people had died prematurely and 100,000 more were made ill because of the smog's effects.

Despite the terrible conditions, the Queen and Prince Philip's car managed to crawl its way from Buckingham Palace to the Bank of England in Threadneedle Street on 4 December at the invitation of the Court of Governors of the Bank. In her message of thanks, the Queen said: 'We were all brought up to be familiar with the phrase: "As safe as the Bank of England". We know that the truth of this saying rests on the loyalty and efficiency of all those who have served and still serve the "Old Lady of Threadneedle Street". This is not my first visit, for I remember coming here as a child with my grandmother and being fascinated, as all children are, by the sight of so much gold.'

Three weeks later, when the Queen gave the first Christmas message of her reign, she was already familiar with speaking on the radio. However, in those days, the broadcast went out live at 3.07pm. This meant that it was difficult for her to enjoy the traditional festivities, as she had to be ready and waiting for the moment it was time for her to address the nation. Despite her experience as a public speaker, and the frequent rehearsals to ensure she was completely familiar with the words, Prince Philip stayed nearby to give her confidence.

Clinging to the vestiges of the familiar, she used the same desk and chair in the study at Sandringham as her father and grandfather had done before her to make their broadcast. In fact, it was exactly twenty years since George V had instituted the royal custom, which (with only two exceptions at the beginning of her father's reign) had by now become an annual event. Her maiden address set the tone for her reign, as she referred to some of the events of the year she considered important, seldom mentioned her personal life, and never forgot the true meaning of Christmas and its religious implications. She began speaking in a clear, high voice:

Each Christmas, at this time, my beloved father broadcast a message to his people in all parts of the world. Today I am doing this to you, who are now my people. As he used to do, I am speaking to you from my own home, where I am spending Christmas with my family; and let me say at once how I hope that your children are enjoying themselves as much as mine are on a day which is especially the children's festival, kept in honour of the Child born at Bethlehem nearly two thousand years ago.

Later in her speech, she began to talk about 'the British Commonwealth and Empire', the 'far larger family' to which everyone belonged:

My father, and my grandfather before him, worked all their lives to unite our peoples ever more closely, and to maintain its ideals which were so near to their hearts. I shall strive to carry on their work.

She made her commitment clear in her closing words:

At my Coronation next June, I shall dedicate myself anew to your service. I shall do so in the presence of a great congregation, drawn from every part of the Commonwealth and Empire, while millions outside Westminster Abbey will hear the promises and the prayers being offered up within its walls, and see much of the ancient ceremony in which Kings and Queens before me have taken part through century upon century.

You will be keeping it as a holiday; but I want to ask you all, whatever your religion may be, to pray for me on that day – to pray that God may give me wisdom and strength to carry out the solemn promises I shall be making, and that I may faithfully serve Him and you, all the days of my life.

It was a straightforward message emphasising the importance of duty – something that people felt passionately about in those post-war years. For the Queen, it was to be the defining commitment of her reign. And it was clear where she had found her inspiration for this approach. When Princess Elizabeth became Queen, she had little choice but to follow the example set by her father and do everything as he had done before her. Fortunately, they were both alike and had the same orderly mind and insistence on attention to detail. In her teenage years at Royal Lodge, her father had tried to explain to her just how things were done. Although Princess Elizabeth felt unprepared when the job was unexpectedly thrust upon her, everything she knew had come from him and his example of how one carried out the role of being the monarch.

So when the Queen was faced with the daunting prospect of taking control of the reins of the monarchy, she did it his way. 'It was all very sudden,' she said, and made what she described as the 'best job' she could. In the winter following her coronation, she circumnavigated the globe and visited ten Commonwealth countries, opened seven parliaments, made 157 speeches and four broadcasts. She was only twenty-seven years old. She may not have been like her mother, but she was now the Head of the Commonwealth. Today, the success of the Commonwealth is credited to the Queen and her vast personal knowledge of its members. She is like a mother confessor and knows and understands the political situation in every country. Prince Philip accurately describes her role as the 'Commonwealth physiotherapist'. And, as she said forty years later, 'It's a job for life.' She was about to find out just how demanding the role would be.

Chapter 3

THE NEW QUEEN

*We would like our son and daughter to
grow up as normally as possible so that
they will be able to serve you and the
Commonwealth faithfully and well when
they are old enough to do so. We believe
that public life is not a fair burden to place
on growing children.*

CHRISTMAS BROADCAST, 1958

Five days before her twenty-seventh birthday, on 16 April
1953, the Queen travelled to the shipbuilding yards at
Clydebank in Scotland to name the new 4,000-ton royal yacht
Britannia. Her late father had been delighted when the
Admiralty decided to commission the ship, and he even discussed the plans for it with his eldest daughter. It was also
hoped an inaugural convalescence cruise would help the ailing
King's health. Sadly, the John Brown shipyard in Clydebank
received the order from the Admiralty on 4 February 1952, just
two days before he died, so he never got to see it built.

John Brown & Co was one of the most famous shipyards in

the world, having built the great liners *Queen Elizabeth* and *Queen Mary*. It was the Queen's third visit, but the first since her accession. *Britannia* was one of the last fully riveted ships to be built and she had a remarkably smooth painted hull. The ship's name had been kept a closely guarded secret, being revealed only when the Queen smashed a bottle of Empire Wine across her bows (champagne was considered too extravagant in post-war Britain) and announced to the expectant crowds of dock-workers and guests, 'I name this ship *Britannia* …' Her words were almost drowned out by the cheers, as she continued: 'I wish success to her and all who sail in her.' She then pressed the launch button and *Britannia* was released into the muddied waters of the Clyde. Later, in an emotional speech to Lord Aberconway, the chairman of John Brown, the Queen explained what it meant to her:

It has been a great pleasure to come to Clydebank today and once again to launch a ship in John Brown's yard. This time it means more to me than ever before because the *Britannia*, which is now floating in the waters of the Clyde, is not only the most modern addition to a long line of Royal Yachts which goes back to the reign of King Charles II, but it is to be at times the home of my husband and myself and of our family.

I am sure all of you who are present here realise how much the building of this ship meant to the late King, my father. For he felt most strongly, as I do, that a yacht was a necessity not a luxury for the head of our great British Commonwealth, between whose countries the sea is no barrier but the natural and indestructible highway. With the wise advice of the Admiralty and of your firm, he laid the plans of a vessel which should wear the Royal Standard in times of peace and which, in the event of war, should serve the cause of humanity as a hospital ship. Had he been in Clydebank today, he would have been as delighted as I am to see what a fine ship our yacht promises to be.

As we have already seen, at this period air travel was relatively rare, and considered risky, so *Britannia* was a physical symbol of the Queen's desire to be linked with the whole of the Commonwealth. Her speech, though formal in tone, also highlighted in a very personal way why all the royal family had such an emotional attachment to *Britannia*, because of its connection with her father. So, when it was decommissioned in 1997, the Queen was photographed wiping a tear from her eye. One of Prince Charles's enduring memories is of being on board for the first time as he sailed to meet his parents at the end of their Commonwealth coronation tour: 'There was the thrill – as a small boy – of witnessing the entire Mediterranean Fleet of the Royal Navy steam past the Royal Yacht at high speed, with my mother and father waving to all the ships' companies from the afterdeck.'

A few weeks later, there was an even more significant event for the Queen. Prince Charles, who was just four and a half at the time, has a clear memory of the night before the coronation, when his mother arrived in the Buckingham Palace nursery to say goodnight to him and his sister Anne wearing the bejewelled St Edward's Crown, which weighed almost five pounds, 'so that she could get used to its weight on her head before the Coronation ceremony'. He also remembers the voices 'of thousands of people gathered outside Buckingham Palace chanting "we want the Queen" and keeping me awake'.

On the morning of the coronation, 2 June 1953, the Queen woke to discover rain lashing against her bedroom windows.

The date had been picked so as not to clash with the Epsom Derby, which was scheduled to run the following Saturday, 6 June, and because it had the best chance of fine weather. Naturally, it turned out to be as cold, wet and windy as only England in June could be. The downpour that started the night before was unremitting, and guests on their way to Westminster Abbey, who had to be in their places before eight in the morning, knew they were in for a long, chilly wait.

Everybody had been talking about the coronation for weeks and months, and the ballroom at Buckingham Palace had been marked out with tape to indicate the approximate shape of the abbey. Members of the household were pressed into assuming various roles for the endless rehearsals considered necessary to get everything coordinated with royal precision. Wearing a long sheet pinned to her slight shoulders, the Queen went through the repetitive and tiring rehearsals time and time again without complaining. Everything was planned down to the minutest detail, even the second the crown would be placed on the Queen's head. Characteristically, she took all her responsibilities very seriously, but above all with great patience.

The coronation invasion of London had begun on 23 May, when on that day alone a million people arrived in the capital to see the decorations along the processional route. Post-war Britain was austere, many types of food were still rationed, but the British people knew exactly how to enjoy themselves, and they desperately wanted to welcome their young Queen. The lavish pageant was a break from a grim period that seemed to date back for a generation, taking in the Great Depression, the war and its aftermath. The coronation was a symbol of better times ahead, and the public wanted to make the most of the event.

Those who had not secured seats in the stands began to camp

out on the streets in order to get a standing place and, with typical British spirit, the crowd sang and shared cups of tea laced with the occasional nip of brandy. Bakers ran out of sliced bread for sandwiches, and up and down the country people prepared to celebrate the day with street parties, with bunting and trestle tables piled high with such simple culinary delights as paste sandwiches, jam rolls and jelly.

There were even two coronation state banquets on 3 and 4 June, and two evening receptions on 4 and 9 June to accommodate the large number of guests, including visiting heads of state and over twenty crowned sovereigns. Each banquet was held in the ballroom, with the guests seated at individual round tables with the Queen's rectangular table in the centre of the room. They dined on lamb, green beans and new potatoes from the crown estates served on Sevres porcelain, with the finest silver gilt cutlery and crystal glass. The magnificent flower displays were arranged by Moyses Stevens and Edward Goodyear and arranged so that the Queen and the Duke of Edinburgh would be visible to their guests.

Just before dawn on Coronation Day, the news reached the palace that Mount Everest had been conquered by a British expedition of which the Duke of Edinburgh was patron. Four days earlier, climbers Sherpa Tenzing and Sir Edmund Hillary had set foot on the summit and toasted Prince Philip with rum. They were amazed that news of their success had not only been in that morning's *Times*, but also relayed to the coronation crowds through loudspeakers along the route. It all added to the sense that a glorious, new Elizabethan era was dawning.

In the 1950s, television was still in an embryonic stage and mistrusted by many of the Queen's advisors, so when the idea of televising the coronation was first mooted it met with a firm refusal. 'Whereas film of the ceremony can be cut appropriately,' the Queen's private secretary wrote to Prime Minister Churchill, 'live television would not only add considerably to the strain on the Queen (who does not herself want TV), but would mean that any mistakes, unintentional incidents or undignified behaviour by spectators would be seen by millions of people.'

Eventually, the Queen changed her mind and decided that it would make sense if everyone could see her coronation live, and after it was announced that the event would be televised, there was a huge rush of people looking to buy their first television set. It was also a breakthrough in broadcasting and became the first major international television event, as much of Europe was able to link up to watch it, though it was not yet possible to send the pictures live to the Commonwealth or North America.

There were eight television commentators in various spots around London, including outside Buckingham Palace, outside the abbey on Victoria Embankment and at Grosvenor Gate, while Richard Dimbleby broadcast from a position inside the abbey high up on the triforium. Fifteen radio broadcasters produced a continuous flow of information from along the route, inside the palace quadrangle and in the abbey itself. To put it all together, hundreds of technicians and tons of equipment were required.

Although there was no live television to America, still pictures were transmitted with a seven-minute delay, so the Queen had actually been crowned some time before the images were shown. They were also treated to images of her alighting from the coach, assisted by the Duke of Edinburgh; they saw Prime Minister Winston Churchill bow to the crowd before entering the abbey; while Prince Charles was seen with his grandmother in the abbey and there was also the moment that the crown was placed upon the Queen's head.

For those who wanted to see television images, the logistics of getting the pictures across the Atlantic in 1953 was a massive technical performance in itself. For the shipping of the film a pooling system between NBC and CBS – the two giants of American broadcasting – had been arranged, but NBC plotted to be first. They arranged for a British Canberra bomber to take off two hours before the others and fly direct from London to Boston. The plot failed when the plane had to turn back two hours over the Atlantic because of a damaged fuel tank. NBC had to rely on the original Canberras, which took off for Goose Bay in Labrador with films for both networks. The resulting footage was shown in cinemas throughout the United States and the rest of the world, narrated by Sir Laurence Olivier.

On coronation night, London was packed with revellers and there were dozens of parties in the clubs and hotels of the West End. The Savoy hotel hosted one of the grandest of all, the Coronation Ball, attended by heads of state, ambassadors and much of London society. Beneath hundreds of yards of dove-grey silk made from parachutes, the ballroom was transformed into a vast tented Elizabethan garden laid out with camellia plants and box hedges. For that night at least, austerity was forgotten, and 5,000 bottles of champagne were produced together with fine wines to accompany a dinner of foie gras and lamb. After dinner, guests had a magnificent view of the firework display across the river on the South Bank, which featured a tableau of the Queen, Prince Philip and their two children. When Sir Winston Churchill made his entrance in his white tie and tails on the arm of his old friend, the Pasha of Marrakesh, the other guests burst into spontaneous applause.

Back at the palace, the Queen and Prince Philip had been called out on to the balcony at least half a dozen times. After their final appearance around midnight, the crowd, which was by then a solid mass all the way to Trafalgar Square, sang 'Auld Lang Syne'. The BBC Home Service, Light Programme and Third Programme all had celebratory shows and music; and the BBC produced a commemorative issue of the *Radio Times*, which sold 9 million copies.

Earlier that evening, the Queen had given her historic coronation radio broadcast to the world, thanking the public for their support. Introduced at five minutes to nine by Sir Winston Churchill from Downing Street, the Queen spoke at exactly nine o'clock from the Royal Closet next to the White Drawing Room in Buckingham Palace. It was broadcast on both the Home Service and Light Programme, as well as on the single television channel, though they had sound only. Television came into its element later that evening when cameras joined the crowds thronging the Thames at Westminster to watch the fireworks display until 11.30pm.

In her speech, the Queen set the tone for her reign, and what she hoped to achieve, as well as thanking the public for their enthusiastic support:

> Throughout all my life and with all my heart I shall strive to be worthy of your trust. As this day draws to its close, I know my abiding memory of it will be not only the solemnity and beauty of the ceremony, but the inspiration of your loyalty and affection ... In this resolve I have my husband to support me. He shares all my ideals and all my affection for you. Then, although my experience is so short and my task so new, I have in my parents and grandparents an example which I can follow with certainty and with confidence.

The daunting burden of the young Queen's responsibilities, especially around the time of the coronation, meant that she saw far less of her children than she would have liked. On the day of her crowning, she had organised for Prince Charles to give a party for fourteen children and had a television set specially installed in her private sitting room so that they could all watch the ceremony. Prince Charles had to leave for the abbey, where he stood next to his grandmother, but his young guests were well looked after. They were assigned a footman to serve them cakes and jellies and ice cream from a buffet, and when the Queen returned from the abbey she popped in to see how things were going. The children were overawed by the glittering lady in her coronation robes, and instead of hugging her they bowed and curtsied formally.

On 13 June, the Queen made a state entry into Windsor, a town tradition shared only with Edinburgh and Belfast where, amid great celebration, the new monarch processes into the town centre. The Queen received a short address of welcome before joining the River Carnival to Eton College. In the National Maritime Museum at Greenwich is a wooden step, specially made for Queen Elizabeth II's visit to Eton College on board the *Windrush*. After the loyal address given by the provost of Eton College on behalf of the fellows and masters, the Queen replied: 'I have spent much of my life in sight of Eton, and enjoyed the memorable experience of learning history from your predecessor, Sir Henry Marten. I feel therefore that I have a special attachment to this college founded by my ances- tor King Henry VI.'

The Queen then thanked the captain of the school for his welcome and loyal assurances expressed on behalf of the King's Scholars and Oppidans, and asked the headmaster to give the boys an extra three days' holiday to mark the happy occasion. After the reception, the Queen changed from her royal car into a carriage drawn by Windsor Greys. A Captain's

Escort of the Household Cavalry accompanied the carriages into Windsor over Windsor Bridge, followed by a tricky climb up Thames Street hill where the horses can lose their footing. The procession then halted by Queen Victoria's statue and was greeted by the mayor and Corporation in their ceremonial robes. After presentations, the Queen stepped back into her carriage to continue along the High Street to Park Street and the Long Walk, where Guides, Scouts and children from all over Berkshire, Buckinghamshire, Surrey and Middlesex were waiting. The Windsor schoolchildren were gathered by the Cambridge Gate, all waving their flags enthusiastically. Flag-waving children are central to the Queen's processions all over the world. To her, they represent the future and stability of the monarchy, and she seldom fails to mention them in her Christmas messages.

With such massive interest in the Queen around this time, it was difficult for her and Prince Philip to shield their own growing children from the insatiable public appetite for information about their lives. They organised occasional photo sessions with a favourite photographer, but otherwise kept the children's lives private. The Queen eventually received so many letters from members of the public begging her to allow her children to be more visible that she even mentioned it in her Christmas speech of 1958. The Queen was being protective and wanted her offspring to have a more normal upbringing than she had herself. She and Philip both felt this would enable their children to relate to the increasingly less deferential world they would inherit.

Some of you have written to say that you would like to see our children on television this afternoon. We value your interest in them and I can assure you that we have thought about this a great deal before deciding against it.

We would like our son and daughter to grow up as normally as possible so that they will be able to serve you and the Commonwealth faithfully and well when they are old enough to do so. We believe that public life is not a fair burden to place on growing children. I'm sure that all of you who are parents will understand.

This desire to maintain a sense of privacy around the royal children would be an ongoing theme throughout the Queen's reign, and the royal family have never tried to make a spectacle of their children. When Princess Charlotte was born in May 2015, it was a rare moment that her brother, Prince George, made a public appearance. More than the adult members of the royal family, it was the children, in all their burnished innocence, in all their ordinariness, who provided the symbolic hope for the future of the royal family and of the nation it reigned over.

From the moment of their birth, every detail of their development – no matter how mundane or insignificant – was recorded in gushing terms. When a royal baby cut its first tooth, took its first step or uttered its first word, the news was broadcast in terms of reverential excitement. The colour of its hair and eyes was discussed, the clothes it wore studied and copied. Even the names of the nannies, handmaidens to this live offering on the secular altar of Britain's national life, made front-page news. The Queen's greatest wish was, she said, for her children to be brought up as normal people. As she often told her friend Eileen Parker, wife of Prince Philip's equerry, who later became his private secretary: 'I would so like them to live ordinary lives.'

However much the royal couple might have wanted normality for their children, being surrounded by servants and having a nursery footman, who polished the baby's pram every day, even whitening the tyres, was not ordinary. Their parents saw them between 9.15am and 10am every day, and they kept the time between after tea and bedtime free for them whenever possible. During these times, they played games with them, they read to them, taught them nursery rhymes, and Prince Charles would amuse his parents by reading from a book he already knew by heart. They were not encouraged to use baby talk, although Charles insisted on calling all birds 'billies', a name he had found for himself, probably from the pelicans he had seen in St James's Park. Neither he nor his sister had any conception at that time of their position and, like other children, were in awe of stories of kings, queens and princesses in nursery rhymes and fairy tales, not relating them to their own family.

It was not without difficulty that the new Queen tried to blend the two roles of sovereign and mother. She had been trained since childhood by her father that duty came before everything, and when duty called she reluctantly had to relinquish her family into the hands of the nursery staff. They taught the children manners – particular emphasis was placed on politeness – and dished out discipline when it was necessary, which was rare with Charles. They made the nursery a home and filled it with a menagerie of animals; as well as the corgis, there were a pair of lovebirds, a hamster and Charles's white rabbit called Harvey.

Like many families, it was her own mother that the Queen came to rely upon as the constant affectionate force, and being a grandmother suited Queen Elizabeth. She brought more affection to the role than Queen Mary had ever been capable of. In her dying days, the old Queen had unbent a little, allowing her great-grandson to play with her collection of jade objects, a pleasure she had sternly denied her granddaughters Elizabeth and Margaret. By contrast, the Queen Mother was gentle and welcoming, and looking after her grandchildren gave her a purpose in life after she had been left bereft by the premature death of the King. According to her page, the late William Tallon, who was always on hand to do her bidding, the Queen Mother practically brought the children up. It was a slight exaggeration, because they had nanny Helen Lightbody and, when she left, her assistant Mable Anderson. They also had governess Miss Catherine Peebles, who set up a schoolroom in Buckingham Palace. In the Fifties, there was no such thing as a royal child without a retinue of nannies and housemaids to look after them.

Before the coronation year was over, the Queen had to put duty over family, when on Monday 23 November she and the Duke of Edinburgh embarked on their long-delayed tour of the Commonwealth. They flew to Bermuda then Jamaica, processing via the Panama Canal to the South Seas on board HMS *Gothic*. The tour focused on New Zealand and Australia and was a marathon of five-and-a-half months' travel. There were continual wardrobe changes, speeches, handshakes, openings, inspections and galas. It was probably the most daunting trip ever undertaken by a British head of state. The night before the Queen and Prince Philip left London, the Queen Mother threw a grand party at Clarence House, where the guests were entertained by actor and raconteur Peter Ustinov. Her favourite, Noel Coward, was among the guests, and Prince Philip and the Queen stayed dancing until 3am.

When the royal couple arrived in Auckland, the Queen was welcomed like a sovereign deliverer. It was the first time she had spent a Christmas away from home, let alone that far away. As she prepared to give her Christmas broadcast from Government House, the Queen was summoned to the front door to listen to children singing carols and watch Father Christmas appear in a coach drawn by four tiny ponies. He bowed to the Queen and then produced all kinds of gifts, including a walkie-talkie doll for Princess Anne and a train for Prince Charles, which were spectacular children's presents at the time.

The Christmas broadcast proved a rare technical challenge to the radio technicians of the day. It was sent from Auckland to Wellington via landline, then by radio telephone directly via Sydney and via Barbados. It was also transmitted from a Royal New Zealand Navy transmitter, from the short-wave transmitters of the New Zealand Broadcasting Service in Malaya as a back-up in case of poor reception. The message went from Auckland at 9pm local time to London, where it was 9am on Christmas Day, and was then rebroadcast from London at 3pm.

Auckland, which I reached only two days ago, is, I suppose, as far as any city in the world from London and I have travelled some thousands of miles through many changing scenes and climates on my voyage here ...

Some people have expressed the hope that my reign may mark a new Elizabethan age. Frankly, I do not myself feel at all like my great Tudor forbear, who was blessed with neither husband nor children, who ruled as a despot and was never able to leave her native shores.

Here the Queen was creating an interesting definition of herself as a wife and mother of her rainbow Commonwealth family and United Kingdom subjects. She successfully made the monarchy sound warm and homely, the exact opposite of her ancestor. She was acknowledging not only the change in her own role, but also that of her country, which was no longer to be seen as a conquering imperial power, but as a much more benevolent force in the world.

At the end of the scripted version of her speech, the Queen

added a personal note about a rail disaster at Tangiwai, where late on Christmas Eve a railway bridge collapsed underneath an express train, killing 151 people:

> I know there is no one in New Zealand, and indeed throughout the Commonwealth, who will not join with my husband and me in sending to those who mourn a message of sympathy in their loss. I pray that they and all who have been injured may be comforted and strengthened.

If the six weeks in New Zealand was a cocktail of excitement for the royal caravan, Australia was a true exotic tipple. Tens of thousands lined the streets in crowds twenty deep to catch a glimpse of the Queen as she drove by in an open-topped car or stood on the steps of a town hall, resplendent in her Norman Hartnell couture outfits. Her husband, 'handsome and cheerful', was at her side and they appeared the picture of a truly romantic young couple. Together, the historian Philip Ziegler declared, they heralded 'a brighter and more successful future'.

In the cities, onlookers fainted in the crush, while out in the bush families waited for hours in the searing heat, on roads usually empty, just to see her pass by in a whirl of dust. Earl Mountbatten's daughter Lady Pamela, who was in the royal party, noted: 'She was very meticulous in the motorcades that the car should go slowly enough for people to get a proper view. She used to say: "What's the point in coming unless they can see me?"'

Sometimes she was forced to stop and make as many as six impromptu little speeches a day, but her public demeanour never faltered, despite one unavoidable challenge. 'It's awful – I've got the kind of face that if I'm not smiling I look cross,' she said. 'But I'm not cross. If you try to smile for two hours continuously it gives you a nervous tick. But the moment I stop smiling somebody will say, "Doesn't she look cross?"' So she smiled until her face hurt. Her reward was adulation, and by the time she ended her tour it was estimated that three-quarters of Australia's entire population of 12 million had turned out to see her in person.

There were times when it was more than the Queen was able to handle. She came from a background as sheltered as they come and she remained shy. She was still only twenty-seven, in a distant land, and her children and the familiar things of home were half a world away. After one particularly gruelling twelve-hour day, when she had been greeted by more dignitaries than she could count in more towns than she could name, her composure nearly deserted her. She had been gaped at, waved at, cheered at, blinded by old-fashioned camera bulbs and had her hand shaken until it ached. She was tired and overwrought and her crowded schedule allowed her no privacy; when she went to what was euphemistically referred to as 'repair her make-up', she had to do so in a public lavatory in front of an audience of the attendant and her friends. In a snatched moment alone with Prince Philip and on the verge of tears, she turned to him and in a trembling, high-pitched voice demanded: 'Why is everyone so boring, boring, boring ...'

It was hard right from the outset, and there would be occasions on that Australian tour when she would wonder if it was worth the strain – and whether she was truly worthy of the homage bestowed on her. She had been Queen for only two years and the responsibility still frightened and sometimes confused her. But she kept her misgivings to herself. She was the head of a great and venerable institution, and by her way of thinking it would have been an egotistical abjuration of the sacred obligation to surrender to self-doubt. After the tensions had been released by that uncharacteristic outburst, she again took steel-willed control of herself and set off on her next round of engagements, her smile firmly in place.

At the state opening of parliament in Canberra, the Queen spoke to the Australian people with unusually emotional words: 'It is a joy for me today to address you not as Queen from far away, but as your Queen and part of your Parliament.' Although the Queen never writes her own addresses to parliaments, she likes them to emphasise the fact that even though she may be based in the United Kingdom, she also feels herself to be a local monarch wherever she visits. She understands the importance of stressing that direct link.

The state banquet in Parliament House that evening was the brilliant climax of a day of ceremony. Sitting next to Prime Minister Robert Menzies, who had presented her with a diamond brooch made up of a number of sprays of wattle, the national flower, the Queen spoke over the radio to the people of Australia, which had been relatively untouched by the Second World War and had a booming industry supplying Europe with all the things they needed. Noting the confidence of the nation and its positive attitude, she said: 'This is a spacious country with a healthy and vigorous people and vast natural resources. Only a pessimist would set bonds to its future.'

The impact of the young couple's May 1954 homecoming was maximised when the new Royal Yacht *Britannia* set sail on her maiden voyage from Portsmouth to Grand Harbour, Malta. On board were a very excited Prince Charles and Princess Anne, who continued on and greeted their parents in Tobruk on 1 May. It was the first time the Queen and Prince Philip had been on board for a sea voyage and, after stopping in Malta and Gibraltar en route home to Portsmouth, the *Britannia* sailed up the Thames into the Port of London.

It was a special moment for the Queen, for, as we have seen, she had been closely involved in the design of the royal yacht, even picking furnishings and materials for the royal apartments on board with the help of architect Sir Hugh Casson. The single gold line painted around the yacht's navy blue hull was also the Queen's idea, and she wanted the yacht to be admired as a symbol of Great Britain. Having spent thousands of pounds on the interior, the Queen intriguingly decreed that the old sheets and blankets from the previous royal yacht could be reused, and she supplemented them with a dozen new linen mono-grammed sheets and pillowcases.

The coronation and the Commonwealth tour had unleashed a different type of interest in the royal family; with the spread of television and radio broadcasting, people no longer had to rely on going to the cinema to catch the Pathé newsreels for their information. As the royal yacht *Britannia* approached Portsmouth, hundreds of small ships put out to escort her home, while the guns of the fleet thundered a salute. It was less than ten years after the war had ended and just over two years since the death of the King, but even to the sternest of critics, the Queen's arrival on board *Britannia* at Tower Bridge was a symbol of all that was great with Great Britain.

That Christmas the Queen talked of the tumultuous welcome she had received when she had arrived in New Zealand. Surrounded by stiff, formal courtiers all her life, the 28-year-old Queen had found the informality and friendliness of the Antipodeans as refreshing as the sunshine and rugged beauty of their country. When she emphasised how touched she had been by the 'affectionate greeting' she had received 'among people who are my own people', she obviously meant it. She was no longer the Queen from far away, but a tangible person who was enveloped by their enthusiasm, which she would remember 'all my life long'. She mentioned almost as an afterthought, although it certainly was not, that it was two years since she had spent Christmas with her children and what it meant for families to be together.

Part of the Queen's enormous impact abroad was due to the way she dressed and presented herself. The maestro of fashion, Sir Norman Hartnell, knew this and created a wardrobe that was not only appropriate for the different climates and events she would experience, but for the huge assortment of people who might have waited hours to see her for the first and last time.

Months before her departure, Hartnell had been having weekly audiences with the Queen to submit designs and discuss fabrics. The Queen's meticulous eye could spot an uneven hemline or a crooked press stud at a glance, and although she was said not to care much about clothes, she cared about the impact they made. Her dresser and confidante, Bobo MacDonald, and her two assistants spent hours packing and unpacking and sending things ahead. Hartnell gave Bobo small notebooks with sketches of all the clothes, with details of the matching shoes, gloves and handbags to go with the 150 day dresses. For the many evening gowns appropriate for state opening banquets and even normal dinners (as evening dress was still worn in the Fifties), there was another set of books, so nothing was left to chance.

It couldn't be. There was no possibility of an article of forgotten clothing being sent on a commercial flight, as it was to the Princess of Wales during her Australian trip thirty years later. It would have been a logistical nightmare. When the Queen's father died and hurried arrangements were made to get her back to London as quickly as possible, it was discovered that the black mourning outfit she always carried had already gone ahead and she had only a floral dress to wear. When the aircraft landed in North Africa, a message was sent ahead and a second black outfit was taken to London airport. Upon the flight's arrival, it stopped in a remote area of the airport, and the dress was taken aboard. The Queen quickly changed before emerging from the plane to meet the official line-up, including her uncle the Duke of Gloucester and Prime Minister Winston Churchill.

The next major national occasion came on 21 October 1955, the 150th anniversary of the Battle of Trafalgar. On that day, a memorial to the late King George VI was unveiled by the Queen in Carlton Gardens, just off the Mall near Admiralty Arch. It features a relatively simple statue by the Chelsea-based sculptor William McMillan of the King dressed in naval uniform, standing on a plinth of Portland stone. In paying tribute to her father, the Queen said: 'Today is Trafalgar Day and it is fitting that this ceremony should take place on the anniversary of one of the great events in our history as a sea-faring nation. Throughout his life, my father had a deep concern for the welfare of the services ... he saw active service in the Royal Navy.'

The Queen rarely forgets the role of the services, and her family's close links with the armed forces, but this was a more personal message. That same evening, the Queen was entertained to dinner by the Royal Navy in the Painters Hall at the Royal Naval College at Greenwich. Two spectacular dishes are always served at the Trafalgar Day dinner – the Baron of Beef and the chocolate Ships of the Line. The Baron of Beef is said to have originated when Henry VIII, whose favourite palace was in Greenwich, was so taken by a spit-roasted double sirloin of beef that he dubbed it 'Sir Loin, the Baron of Beef'. The Baron of Beef is always paraded around the dining hall at shoulder height, accompanied by music from the naval cadets.

Adding to the spectacle, dessert takes the form of a flotilla of flaming chocolate ships. In her speech thanking the Board of Admiralty for drinking a toast to her health, proposed by Lord Mountbatten, the Queen said: 'I have been wondering this evening what the collective noun should be for admirals. On the whole I think I like "a foam of Flag Officers", although perhaps for this unique occasion when nearly a hundred have sat down together for a meal, we should speak of "an ocean of Admirals".'

For her first visit to the United States as monarch, in October 1957, the Queen wanted to ensure that she made the right impression. At the banquet hosted by the garrulous old President Dwight D. Eisenhower, she chose her long beaded dress and jewellery with extra care, instructing Bobo her dresser it had to be perfect. She did not want to impress anyone by looking pretty; she wanted to ensure that her hosts saw her as the Queen she was. That meant jewellery, which was carried in a large leather case that never left her side in transit, long gloves over the elbow, and the beaded gowns the House of Hartnell made so beautifully.

Prince Philip knew he needed to charm the Americans, as his extended world trip the previous year on board the royal yacht *Britannia* had sparked rumours of a marriage rift. The Queen and the children had spent Christmas 1956 without him, and the American press had been particularly rough on him. When Buckingham Palace took the unwise decision of denying any problems within the marriage, the Americans had leapt on the story. 'London Hushes Royal Rift', they printed on their front pages.

To make matters worse, 1956 had also been the year of the Suez crisis, when Britain and France had sought to take control of the canal that runs through Egypt. In America, this action had been seen as a return to colonialism, and they had not supported their wartime allies, resulting in a humiliating failure. Unsurprisingly, media interest in the royal couple was huge and the Queen was nervous the bad publicity – both personal and national – might have a negative impact. Fortunately, when she arrived there was another prominent story: everyone was talking about how the Russian satellite had beaten the Americans in the space race.

She couldn't believe how awful American television was and how they chose to present the news. Writing to Prime Minister Sir Anthony Eden, who had succeeded Churchill in 1955, she confided: 'I suppose when one gets used to it, it's not so terrible!'

By the time she left, the Queen was feted somewhat incongruously as a 'living doll', but said she had gained a real understanding of how stressful the responsibilities of the American president's job really were. She was determined to do all she could to cement the relations between the two countries after the difficulties of the previous year, and at Williamsburg courtiers inserted a passage into her speech expressing her delight that the state of Virginia had counties named after every British monarch from Elizabeth I to George III.

In 1957, the Queen agreed to allow her Christmas message to be televised for the first time. That year marked the twenty-fifth anniversary of the first Christmas broadcast, and it was suggested this was the perfect occasion to take things forward. Preparations began eight months earlier, in the spring, when the BBC had tickled Prince Philip's enthusiasm for new technology. The final sell had been made by BBC executive Anthony Craxton, who had been a school contemporary of Philip's at Gordonstoun.

By Christmas 1957, the Queen had made only one television broadcast, during her visit to Canada earlier in the year, so the whole experience was a novel one, and it caused her a great deal of concern. Initially, her private secretary had agreed to the broadcast only on the condition that the Queen would be in front of a microphone reading a script with no teleprompter, although that was later changed by the Queen, who insisted she didn't want the broadcast to look unnatural. She was also worried that, as much of the Commonwealth had no television sets in their homes, they would feel unhappy if they were unable to see her.

During her Canadian broadcast, the Queen had found it virtually impossible to feel at ease in the unnatural environment of a television set-up. There were so many technicians and production staff to one solo performer, who seemed to exist in a vacuum, while a producer and a floor manager and several cameramen were in constant communication with each other through earpieces and microphones. She had to develop an almost inhuman degree of concentration amid the distractions, but because of her royal training she proved to be very capable of doing this. Luckily, Prince Philip had a little experience of the tension in the minutes before the transmission and stood off camera, where the Queen could see him, and made her laugh. The result was that she relaxed enough to smile just as she went on air and the broadcast was enthusiastically received.

When it came to the Christmas broadcast, Prince Philip's verbal expertise was an enormous help, especially with the rewriting of the script in the Queen's own words. According to a BBC official, the final draft was in fact Prince Philip's, and that made it all the more difficult. 'The fact the Queen had nothing to do with the script made our job a tough one,' he recalled. 'It is the most difficult thing in the world to give a personal message that is in fact not personal.'

The criticism was a little unfair as Philip had been central to all the Queen's television and radio broadcasts. Helping with the script was something he enjoyed doing with his wife. His ability to make her laugh before she went on air was again invaluable, as it certainly improved her performance and made her more relaxed with all the technicians and production staff involved. The level of concentration required to get everything right was enormous, and with all the distractions, she knew it required a performance from her to appear her normal self.

When the television circus arrived at Sandringham at Christmas 1957, the whole local area was overtaken by the vast numbers of people deemed necessary in those days to make a live television broadcast, and great attention was paid to technicalities. Although it was still a black-and-white transmission, details of colour and texture – of both the Queen's clothing and the furniture visible on screen – were important to know beforehand. Weeks in advance, the Queen and her dresser Bobo MacDonald had selected three frocks to show the producer and they all finally agreed the Queen's favourite by Norman Hartnell would be best. Make-up artist Tommie Manderson was brought in, as she had been on every previous occasion, to prepare the Queen's face with the heavier make-up needed for the cameras.

The rehearsals for the broadcast began in early October. Craxton and his team, weighed down with equipment, arrived at the State Dining Room at Buckingham Palace to begin work. The Queen walked in at three o'clock as planned and promptly froze. Peter Dimmock, the producer, recalled how the Queen kept on telling him: 'I am not an actress.' He added: 'She was not, and the first two takes were less than encouraging. She found the teleprompter unnerving and kept staring straight at the camera. I told her to look down occasionally. Prince Philip came in and suggested a few alterations to the script. It helped –

but not much – and every time the Queen started to speak, nerves pushed her voice up two octaves.'

Four times the camera team went back to Buckingham Palace, even bringing the desk and curtains from Sandringham to simulate exactly the same conditions as she would face when she made the broadcast itself. On the afternoon of 23 December, the Queen held her final rehearsal. She was still unsure in her performance and she wanted more time. But Craxton was adamant: too many rehearsals, he insisted, would only add to her nerves. So the finishing touches were put to her speech. Finally, the Queen wanted to check a passage from Bunyan's *Pilgrim's Progress* she intended to quote.

'I know we have a copy of the book here,' she said, and staff were dispatched to find it. Dimmock was left alone in the royal presence, desperately trying to make small talk. 'It was awkward to say the least,' he remembers. 'Things were very different then, and the royal family did not have the same ease with the media they have now. It was one of the longest half-hours I have ever spent.'

In the end, it was Prince Philip who saved the day. When the Queen entered the library at Sandringham where the broadcast was to take place, he remained in the room throughout, watching on a spare camera on the reserve circuit. He told a silly joke and the Queen at last relaxed and managed to do what Dimmock had been trying to get her to do all those months – smile for the cameras.

The broadcast made history because independent television, then just two years old, was taking the BBC sound and pictures and transmitting them live on its own channels. The Commonwealth received the usual sound-only broadcast because the technical limitations of 1957 restricted live television coverage to an international audience. The message was a resounding success when it was broadcast at 3pm, before *Billy Smart's Family Party* on BBC and the film *The Lady from Boston* on ITV. Viewers in Britain were able to see the royal Christmas cards and the photographs of both Charles and Anne on the Queen's desk in her study, and were intrigued to be told that the bowl of holly was a hiding place for the microphone.

And so began the slow progress of allowing the Christmas message to evolve into the slick performance it is today. Press reaction to the Queen in vision was apparently as lyrical as that which greeted her grandfather's first Christmas message in 1932. The *New York Times* and the *New York Herald* published the text of the broadcast in full, and London's *Daily Mirror* reported the Queen spoke with 'easy friendliness'. In a year when the royal family had received much criticism, instead of the usual sycophancy, it was positive news.

Twenty-five years ago my grandfather broadcast the first of these Christmas messages. Today is another landmark because television has made it possible for many of you to see me in your homes on Christmas Day. My own family often gather round to watch television, as they are at this moment, and that is how I imagine you now.

It was a typically domestic note for the Queen to strike, highlighting how – like many other families across the nation – hers was also to be found sitting around the television. But she was also keen to stress how the royal family had moved with the times, reflecting the era they were all living in. For this was a time when rationing had at long last been ended, more people owned cars, fridges and other modern conveniences (as well as their TV sets), and the dawning of the rock'n'roll era gave a new

emphasis to youth. The Queen's 1957 speech was in part, therefore, designed to welcome in this new age and to show that the
monarchy still had an important part to play in a fast-changing
world.

The Queen continued to look forward when she broadcast
another message, this time from the Commonwealth Games in
Cardiff on 25 July 1958. She would have delivered the speech in
person but for a bout of sinus trouble, and it was her pre-
recorded voice that Prince Charles and some of the other boys
who were invited into their headmaster's study at Cheam heard.
She declared: 'The British Empire and Commonwealth Games in
the capital, together with all the other activities of the Festival of
Wales, have made this a memorable year for the Principality. I
have therefore decided to mark it further by an act, which will,
I hope, give as much pleasure to all Welshmen as it does to me.
I intend to create my son, Charles, Prince of Wales today. When
he is grown up, I will present him to you at Caernarfon.'

In the year Harry Webb renamed himself Cliff Richard and
My Fair Lady opened in the West End, with Rex Harrison and
Julie Andrews, Charles had just become His Royal Highness
Prince Charles Philip Arthur George, Prince of Wales. (He also
had a host of other titles: Earl of Chester, Duke of Cornwall,
Duke of Rothesay, Earl of Carrick, Lord of the Isles and Baron
Renfrew, Prince and Great Steward of Scotland and Knight
Companion of the Most Noble Order of the Garter.) He was
nine years and eight months old. His housemaster remembered
the outward look of trepidation on his face and Charles
recalled the inner turmoil and acute embarrassment he felt
when it was announced. When he heard the enormous cheer
coming from the stadium in Cardiff, he remembers it was all
very bewildering when everyone turned and looked at him in
amazement.

In retrospect, the Queen was said to regard the pronounce-ment, dropped on to an unsuspecting child, as one of the few mistakes she made in Charles's upbringing and she never men-tioned it in her Christmas message that year. Instead, her words touched on some of her pet subjects – standards of living, which she applied to her Commonwealth countries – and spoke of those who 'worked in our cities' and might be missing their homeland.

It was an important note for the Queen to strike, for by then the British were trying to get used to the first major wave of immigration to the country from the Commonwealth nations, in particular from the Caribbean. West Indian families had been encouraged to leave their homes behind and come to the UK, often to take up jobs such as working on the buses. Their arrival hadn't been welcomed by everyone, but this was the Queen insisting that they were very welcome as far as she was concerned.

Elsewhere in her speech, her theme was one of travel and she spoke of the journeys her extended royal family would be undertaking the following year. Once again, the Queen embraced these developments: 'So, between us we are going to many parts of the world. We have no plans for space travel – at the moment.' The new space age had excited many of her gen-eration, and the Queen was certainly no exception, and she would refer to it many times over the years.

In 1959, the Queen was pregnant with Prince Andrew, so she decided that, as the baby was due only two months after Christmas, she would record a one-minute sound-only message for transmission on Christmas Day. It was her first break from the 'live' broadcast which her father had deemed so important, and on 17 December it was recorded from Buckingham Palace.

It is testimony to how stressful the Queen found the whole

process that she decided to continue the practice of pre-recording her Christmas message for both radio and television after that year. There was a distinct advantage to doing it that way, as it meant each country in the Commonwealth could transmit it at a time that suited them. Although it was not publicised how it was done, on a personal level it freed her from the anxieties that had marred her enjoyment of Christmas Day over the first eight years since her accession.

The pre-recording of the Christmas message was just one of the myriad of technological advances the next decade would bring as the pace of change gathered momentum, and the royal family had to adapt to a rapidly moving world.

Chapter 4

THE AGE OF CHANGE

The wise men of old followed a star:
modern man has built one. But unless the
message of this new star is the same as
theirs our wisdom will count for nought.

CHRISTMAS BROADCAST, 1962

The 1960s were a decade of great technological development, as space travel became a reality and global communications changed beyond all recognition. Like many of her subjects, the Queen was fascinated by space travel, and in her Christmas address of 1962 she referred to the recent achievements in space. With the launch of *Telstar 1* in July 1962, followed by other satellites, live television pictures could be beamed around the world. The Queen's coronation had started a boom in television ownership in the UK, which continued into the 1960s. Whereas in 1950 only 4 per cent of households had a television set, by 1960 this had risen to 80 per cent.

The 1960s also saw a revolution in society, with the newly affluent young embracing London's music, art and fashion. Established norms were being challenged at every level, as old class barriers were torn down. The royal family were not immune to this social revolution. Both in print in the satirical magazine *Private Eye* and on television's *That Was the Week That Was*, they were being made fun of for the first time in almost a century.

For the first time, in 1963, the Queen's government was tainted by scandal when John Profumo, a cabinet minister and a friend of Prince Philip, lied to parliament about his brief affair with Christine Keeler, a showgirl who was also believed to be having an affair with a Russian diplomat. Profumo soon resigned, and Prime Minister Harold Macmillan asked Lord Denning to lead a commission of inquiry. When his report was published later that year, the general public was amazed by scandalous stories of the political elite prancing around naked at dinner parties when they were meant to be governing the country. The publication of the report did a great deal of damage to the reputation of the Conservative Party and the Establishment, and the Profumo affair was seen by many as marking the end of the post-war era of deference and the beginning of a more modern, permissive society.

Even though Profumo had lied to parliament, in 1975 he received a CBE for services to charity. Twenty years later, Margaret Thatcher, who called him 'one of our national heroes', invited him to her seventieth birthday dinner, and seated him next to the Queen. This was a prime example of the Queen practising reconciliation as well as preaching it, as she did frequently in her Christmas broadcasts.

The political scene was changing, too. Macmillan resigned in the autumn of 1963, due to ill health, and was replaced by Alec Douglas-Home, who disclaimed his earldom in order to do so. In the general election that followed a year later, the contrast between the aristocratic Douglas-Home and the grammar school-educated Yorkshireman Harold Wilson personified the difference between the old era and the new. After thirteen years of Tory rule, Labour came to power by the narrowest of margins and Wilson became prime minister. By all accounts, he would become one of the Queen's favourite premiers. Years later, she did him the honour of attending his retirement dinner at 10 Downing Street – something she had done previously only for Churchill.

When the MP Anthony Wedgwood Benn was obliged to leave the House of Commons after his father, Viscount Stansgate, died in 1960, he began a campaign against hereditary titles. Eventually, in 1963, he was successful in being able to renounce his peerage, and was able to resume his career as an MP. As Postmaster General in 1964, he continued to campaign against hereditary privilege when he tried to get the Queen's head removed from postage stamps. He had an audience with the Queen, when he showed her a number of designs for new stamps omitting the royal portrait. Although the Queen displayed a polite interest, she made certain that the monarch's head would remain on all postage stamps while she was Queen.

On a personal level, the decade started well enough for the Queen with the arrival of her second son, Prince Andrew, on 19 February 1960, the first child to be born to a reigning British monarch in 103 years. By that stage, the Queen and Prince Philip had been married for twelve and a half years.

Just eight days prior to the birth, an order in council was issued applying the surname Mountbatten-Windsor to those descendants of the Queen not holding royal styles such as HRH. Prince Philip wanted the royal family to be known as the House of Mountbatten when the Queen came to the throne in 1952. He is famously said to have told friends: 'I am the only man in the country not allowed to give his name to his children. I'm nothing but a bloody amoeba.' Winston Churchill had blocked previous moves to incorporate the Mountbatten name into the royal family, but Harold Macmillan was more sympathetic to Prince Philip's case and advised the Queen to accept the compromise, at the same time retaining as the family name the 'House of Windsor'.

The birth of a new baby is a cause for some celebration among the palace staff; by tradition a bottle of fine vintage port is sent to each department of the household, 'to drink a toast to Her Majesty'. In some departments the port is raffled, and one lucky footman won a special bottle after the births of both Prince Andrew and later Prince Edward. The port had been a gift to the Queen from the president of Portugal.

The Queen was determined to enjoy motherhood to what she considered its fullest extent, which was not very much by ordinary standards, but more than she had been able to give to either Charles or Anne. This did not run to changing nappies or nightly bathing of the baby, but it did mean she allotted as much time to her baby as her role as monarch allowed.

In her typically orderly way, she pencilled into her leather-bound appointment book the times she would be with Andrew. And during that time, nothing short of a crisis would prevent her from being with the baby. It was a lesson she had learnt when, as a young monarch with two small children, the affairs of state had had to take precedence.

Both Prince Philip and the Queen were of the opinion that Charles and Anne had suffered unnecessarily from overzealous media attention during their formative years – especially Charles, who was extremely shy. They decided the best way of avoiding a repetition of the situation was to keep the baby, who was second in line to the throne, away from public places. Instead of going to the park, nanny Mabel Anderson would restrict walks to the garden of Buckingham Palace or Windsor Castle, a discreet distance from any public highway. That way the palace could control the amount of coverage he received.

Later that month, the Queen announced her consent to Princess Margaret's engagement to photographer Tony Armstrong-Jones. (She had to do this because of the Royal Marriages Act of 1772, and in 1953 had been advised by the cabinet to reject Margaret's previous suitor, Peter Townsend, a divorcee.) The news took most of the press by surprise, as the relationship had developed largely out of the public eye. On 4 May, two nights before the wedding, the Queen gave a reception for 2,000 guests at Buckingham Palace in honour of her sister and her fiancé. It was not exactly what the avant-garde photographer would have chosen, and he had to stand in line with the Princess to greet all the important guests, with a footman whispering in his ear their names and titles. His bohemian friends mixed with the Establishment figures as they quaffed champagne and danced to the Joe Loss Orchestra playing songs from the popular musical, *Fings Ain't Wot They Used T'Be*.

However, the main drama came at the end of the evening when there was a rumpus after it was discovered that the Duchess of Buccleuch's brooch, worth thousands of pounds, had fallen off her dress. In the search to find it the following day, footmen moved every bit of furniture, dismantled heating units and even some of the floorboards were taken up. Eventually the brooch was found.

On 6 May, the wedding took place in Westminster Abbey with guests including a frail Sir Winston Churchill, Noel Coward, poet John Betjeman and many of the bridegroom's artistic friends. It was the first royal wedding to be televised and, with its eclectic group of guests, it made fascinating viewing.

The bride was dressed by Norman Hartnell, the Queen's favourite couturier, and her hairdresser Rene rather indiscreetly admitted he had to use a hairpiece to hold the tiara in place. If the Queen was happy to see her 29-year-old sister marrying at last, she did not show it, and the television audience of an estimated 300 million thought that she plainly wished she was elsewhere. Even when the couple bowed and curtsied to her after the marriage vows, she gave them only the briefest of nods. The Queen has often been accused of looking glum when in fact she is simply controlling her emotions, as she was in this instance.

In July, the Queen celebrated the tercentenary of the Royal Society, of which she is patron, at the Royal Albert Hall. The Royal Society, founded in 1660, is a fellowship of the world's most eminent scientists and is the oldest scientific society in continuous existence. Its fundamental purpose is to recognise, promote and support excellence in science for the benefit of humanity. The Queen again showed her evident interest in the boundaries of scientific exploration when she said: 'The Royal Society has a tradition of tireless curiosity. It urges you on in the ever-widening fields of research and investigations of outer space, of the depths of the ocean, of the mysteries of particles and of the origins of life.'

The Christmas address of 1960 was recorded in the White Drawing Room at Buckingham Palace. Because it had been pre-recorded, it was also able to be seen on Christmas Day in many Commonwealth countries. Among them was Nigeria, which had gained its independence that year, as part of the 'wind of change' that Prime Minister Macmillan had alluded to in a famous speech a few months before. The Queen saw this as one of the 'encouraging signs' coming out of Africa in what was a period of 'tension and uncertainty all over the world'. At a time when some were concerned about the loss of the empire, the

Queen was looking forward to the fact that new countries were being admitted to the Commonwealth, an organisation that has remained central to her thinking. The Queen also focused on personal matters: 'This year I was delighted to get so many kind messages when my second son was born. The telegrams and letters which came flooding in at that time made me feel very close to all the family groups throughout the Commonwealth.'

Despite her new family commitments, the Queen continued to travel widely, visiting numerous countries in 1961, including India, Pakistan, Nepal and Iran. In India, she laid a wreath on Mahatma Gandhi's tomb, and she also visited Pope John XXIII in the Vatican, so unsurprisingly she ended up mentioning 'the varied peoples who profess different faiths' during her 1961 Christmas speech. And she spoke up for the 'quiet people who fight prejudice by example'. She was determined to give new countries her support, even when there were concerns for her own safety, during a visit to Ghana.

But her main theme was addressed to the younger generation:

Angry words and accusations certainly don't do any good, however justified they may be. It is natural that the younger generation should lose patience with their elders, for their seeming failure to bring some order and security to the world. But things will not get any better if young people merely express themselves by indifference or by revulsion against what they regard as an out-of-date order of things. The world desperately needs their vigour, their determination and their service to their fellow men. The opportunities are there and the reward is the satisfaction of truly unselfish work.

As we have seen, 1962 saw the beginnings of the communications revolution, with the launch of *Telstar 1*, but for the

Queen – who remained excited by such developments – this also raised another important question for her address that year: 'What is it all for, they ask, if you can bounce a telephone conversation or a television picture through the skies and across the world, yet still find lonely people living in the same street?' It was a typically Christian message at a time when scientific innovation was gaining all the attention.

During the following year, she became pregnant again, so her Christmas address was broadcast on radio only. And while it was traditional for pregnant women to keep a lower profile in those days, the Queen was about to take a modern approach to childbirth. When Prince Edward was born on the evening of Tuesday 10 March 1964, it was a most unusual confinement, for there at the bedside was the Duke of Edinburgh. It was the first time he had seen one of his children born.

As a keen reader of women's magazines, which had been devoting an increasing number of pages to articles expounding the part fathers can play in childrearing, the Queen had become interested in the new hands-on approach. Her life had always been subject to the advice of others. Even in matters as intimate as how they were delivered of their own children, the royal family had to submit to checks and scrutiny. Since the reign of the Stuarts it had been customary for a selection of Privy Counsellors and ladies-in-waiting to be in attendance at royal births to ensure that the baby was not switched. In 1894, Queen Victoria ruled that henceforth only the home secretary need be summoned. In 1948, shortly before the birth of his grandson, Prince Charles, George VI did away with the archaic law.

Now, for the first time in 300 years, royal women in labour were mistresses of their own confinement room. The Queen was determined to enjoy the experience and she wanted her husband to be there with her. How quickly social mores had changed. Prince Philip had been barred from the birth of Charles, Anne and Andrew. The idea of having him there would have been incomprehensible, if not distasteful, in an age so decorous that it forbade publication of any photographs of the Queen in her pregnancy and never officially acknowledged that she had delivered her first born by Caesarean section. But now the Queen had caught the change in mood, and decreed that Philip would be in attendance at the birth – the first time, certainly in modern history, that any royal father had been allowed to see his progeny born. Her decision wasn't publicised at the time, but her example showed her taking a more modern approach, as it would be a few years before it would become commonplace for fathers to be present at their children's birth.

The baby was delivered in the bathroom of the Belgian Suite of Buckingham Palace converted into a delivery suite. Attending the Queen were five doctors plus two midwives. The delivery was slower than they might have hoped and it was at this point that Philip's good humour proved so valuable.

'It's a solemn thought that only a week ago General de Gaulle was having a bath in this room,' he remarked when he saw all the glum faces. It was said in a jocular way, which helped ease the tension that had been building up between the doctors and nurses attending the sovereign.

In her 1964 Christmas broadcast the Queen's purple prose was obviously influenced by Prince Philip when she said:

All of us who have been blessed with young families know from long experience that when one's house is at its noisiest, there is often less cause for anxiety. The creaking of a ship in a heavy sea is music in the ears of the captain on the bridge. In fact little is static and without movement there can be no progress.

She also spoke, as so often, about the Commonwealth and the concept of 'freedom' and how it related to the form of government adopted by the new countries. It was a lesson she hoped that the new ministers from overseas would learn from the UK's experience:

> Freedom, to be effective, must be disciplined ... If it is not to degenerate, freedom must be maintained by a thousand invisible forces, self-discipline, the Common Law, the right of citizens to assemble, and to speak and argue. We do not wish to impose a particular form of government on any peoples in the world; we merely say, 'This is what we do; we know it's not perfect, but it is the best system that we have been able to create after many centuries of trial and error.'

What the Queen called 'my second family' was now complete. Sixteen years separated her eldest and youngest children, but whereas Andrew, born half a generation after his sister, Anne, had been an unexpected and (initially at least) inconvenient arrival – he was conceived shortly before his mother embarked on a 16,000-mile tour of Canada – Edward had been very much on the Queen's maternal agenda.

The Queen was so intent on spending more time with her younger children that she brought her weekly meetings with her prime minister forward by half an hour, so that she would be free to bath Edward and put him to bed herself. There was a limit, however, to how far the Queen and her consort were prepared to go down this path. Change is rarely in the monarchy's best interests. There is security in sameness. It is a bulwark against the agitations of social upheaval and the 1960s were a very perturbing time indeed for the ancient regime.

Outside the palace walls, a veritable social revolution was

taking place, and by 1964 it was well underway. In Britain, as we have seen, Sir Alec Douglas-Home was swept from power by Harold Wilson and a Labour Party committed to tearing down the old class barriers and building a modern, technological state instead – some saw it as a socialist vision, while others claimed it was meritocratic. Either way, the deferential ways of the past were disappearing fast, and this meant that the monarchy would surely have to adapt to the new era.

Globally, much was changing, too – though not always in a positive way. In the United States, still traumatised by the assassination of President John F. Kennedy, his successor Lyndon Johnson was signing the Civil Rights Act, the most sweeping civil rights law in American history, which he said would close the springs of 'racial hatred'. However, in South Africa, a young lawyer named Nelson Mandela was sentenced to life for treason for plotting to overthrow the all-white government. Jawaharlal Nehru, India's prime minister since the country became independent from Britain (thereby stripping George VI of his title of Emperor) died. In the Soviet Union, Nikita Khrushchev was ousted in a coup by hardliner Leonid Brezhnev.

The Western world was gripped by the mass hysteria of the most light-hearted phenomenon: Beatlemania. Even Prince Philip was touched by it. The Beatles, he said, are 'entirely helpful': 'I really could not care less how much noise people make singing and dancing. I would much rather they make any noise they like singing and dancing. What I object to is people fighting and stealing. It seems to me that these blokes are helping people enjoy themselves and that is far better than other things.'

At a luncheon at the Foreign Press Association, Prince Philip was asked if the monarchy had a place in the Swinging Sixties. Philip answered:

What you are implying is that we are rather old-fashioned. Well, it might easily be true; I don't know. One of the things about the monarchy and its place – and one of the great weaknesses in a sense – is that it has to be all things to all people. Of course, it cannot do this when it comes to being all things to all people who are traditionalists and all things to all people who are iconoclasts. We therefore find ourselves in a position of compromise and we might be kicked by both sides. The only thing is that if you are very cunning, you get as far away from the extremists as you possibly can because they kick harder.

Philip had warmed to his theme. 'I entirely agree that we are old-fashioned: the monarchy is an old-fashioned institution,' he concluded. It was a most comprehensive and thoughtful answer to the debate about the role of the monarchy in a modern society.

And that was the way it was going to stay. The Queen's decision to have her husband by her side during Edward's birth notwithstanding, the great ship of royalty continued on its majestic course with the foam of change churning up around it.

After using her 1965 speech to commend the importance of voluntary work, the following year the Queen spoke at Christmas about the important role of women in society:

This year I should like to speak especially to women. In many countries custom has decreed that women should play a minor part in public affairs. It is difficult to realise that it was less than fifty years ago that women in Britain were first given the vote ... In the modern world, the opportunities for women to give something of value to the human family are greater than ever, because, through their own efforts, they are now beginning to play their full part in public life.

The Queen was reacting to other changes in society, at a time when feminism was first gaining widespread attention. Only a year previously, Dame Elizabeth Lane became the first woman judge to sit in the High Court. Also in this decade, Countess Inchcape became the first woman to be allowed to become a Lloyd's underwriter in an event considered so momentous it was captured by Pathé News. Even then, unlike her male counterparts, she was not allowed to conduct business personally and could only communicate with clients through an agent.

Women were positioned at the vanguard of social and cultural change, and one of the central images of the 1960s was the figure of the single, mobile young woman; an icon of the cultural revolution and emblem of female power and sexual liberation. The biggest single element in the 'permissive society', as it was known, was the introduction of the contraceptive pill in 1961. More than half a million women were on the pill by 1964. Ideas of duty, restraint and responsibility, as epitomised by the way in which the Queen conducted herself, were replaced with the politics of self-interest and a commitment to pleasure. But, despite this contrast, she welcomed the fact that women's horizons were broadening.

Princess Margaret and her husband Lord Snowdon, as he had become when he married her, found themselves at the centre of the new culture. They mixed with pop stars, fashion icons, actors and musicians. She was seen in miniskirts and costume jewellery; while he preferred a bohemian casual look to the formal attire of royalty. Although they partied hard, the Princess still found time for her official engagements, which mainly involved the dozens of organisations of which she was president or patron. Snowdon found these engagements boring. Cracks soon began to appear in the marriage, though at this stage they were visible only to those closest to them. The trouble was that both were stars, accustomed to being the focus of attention. Jealous arguments began to break out and by the end of the decade the marriage was as good as over, although they did not divorce until 1978.

But the Queen did not take the same route. The closest involvement with the Swinging Sixties for her came when the Beatles were each appointed Member of the Order of the British Empire in the Queen's 1965 birthday honours. The group received their awards from the Queen at the palace on 26 October. John Lennon famously returned his MBE to the Queen in 1969 as an act of protest against the Vietnam War.

Sir Winston Churchill died in January 1965, marking the end of a public life that dated back to the Victorian era. The Queen instructed the Duke of Norfolk, who was responsible for organising the funeral, that the occasion should be 'on a scale befitting his position in history', thus guaranteeing that it would be the grandest state funeral for a commoner since that of the Duke of Wellington in 1852.

It was at Churchill's own request that no grand memorial was erected in his honour, unlike Britain's memorial to former President John F. Kennedy. JFK, who had been assassinated in 1963, had a memorial at Runnymede, on the site of the signing of the Magna Carta some 750 years earlier. An acre of ground was given to the American people in his memory. The Queen made a deeply emotional speech at the inauguration of the Kennedy Memorial on 14 May 1965:

The unprecedented intensity of that wave of grief, mixed with something akin to despair, which swept over our people at the news of President Kennedy's assassination, was a measure of the extent to which we recognised what he had already accomplished, and of the high hopes that rode with him in a future that was not to be ... This acre of English soil is now bequeathed in perpetuity to the American people in memory of President John Fitzgerald Kennedy, who in death my people still mourn and whom in life they loved and admired.

For most people the highlight of the decade was England winning the World Cup in 1966, beating West Germany 4–2 at Wembley Stadium. The Queen was there to present the Jules Rimet trophy to Bobby Moore, the England captain, but she did not mention the event in her Christmas address that year. However, according to a survey commissioned in celebration of the Diamond Jubilee in 2012, when asked to name the most iconic moment during the Queen's long reign, the resounding answer given by most people was the 1966 World Cup – the coronation and the wedding of Prince William and Kate Middleton came a distant second and third.

In 1967, ten years on from the first televised address, the Christmas message was broadcast in colour for the first time. Pre-broadcast preparations were extremely elaborate. The BBC made a replica set in one of the studios at Television Centre, and former BBC secretary Mrs Binnie Marcus sat in for the Queen. She was chosen because her features and colouring resembled the Queen's, and various different lights and make-up could be tried to get the best result.

While the Queen has frequently talked about the difference an individual can make by his or her actions, she has only rarely mentioned a particular individual by name, as she did in 1967. The individual in question was Francis Chichester, who had made the first single-handed circumnavigation of the globe in his yacht *Gipsy Moth*. He was knighted by the Queen at Greenwich using the same sword as Queen Elizabeth I had used to knight Sir Francis Drake. In her Christmas address from Buckingham Palace, she said: 'Great national events can stir the imagination, but so can individual actions. Few people can have attracted so much universal attention as Sir Francis Chichester during his epic journey in *Gipsy Moth*.'

The Queen's Christmas address of 1968 was arguably one of her most political to date, touching on two issues that would continue to resonate for many years. While discussing the 'brotherhood of man' and urging people to 'support those international organisations which foster understanding between people and between nations', she added: 'The British people together have achieved great things in the past and have overcome many dangers, but we cannot make further progress if we resurrect ancient squabbles.'

Her comments came at a time when there were the first signs of conflict in Northern Ireland, with a civil rights march in Derry in October that year hinting at the troubles to come. Sadly, her advice was not heeded, and the situation would become far worse – eventually costing the life of one of her relatives, as well as many others – before it finally got better.

The second topic she addressed was the subject of industrial relations, then going through a challenging period, with increasing unrest as the trade unions sought greater influence. Without taking sides, the Queen commented:

Rich or poor, we all depend upon the work and skill of individual men and women, particularly those in industry and production who are the creators of wealth and prosperity. We depend on new knowledge, invention and innovation, practical improvements and developments, all of which offer us a better life.

Princess Elizabeth, watched by her younger sister Princess Margaret, prepares to make her first broadcast, on *Children's Hour*, in October 1940.

At the age of twenty-one, Princess Elizabeth made one of her most significant speeches while visiting Cape Town, in which she pledged to devote her life to the service of 'our great imperial family'.

She learned her dedication to her role from her father, whose influence inspired her actions throughout her reign.

The Queen, with Prince Philip in the foreground, on her return to England after the death of her father.

In July 1952, the new Queen visited Hemel Hempstead, one of the post-war new towns built to house the displaced population of London.

The Queen was also quickly introduced to the more formal aspect of her role, as when she hosted the king and prince regent of Iraq at Balmoral. Prince Charles and Princess Anne look on with their father.

The Queen's Coronation Day was the first ever to be televised. Prince Charles has a vivid memory of his mother saying goodnight to him the night before wearing the crown so she could get used to its weight.

The Queen prepares to give her 1953 Christmas address from Auckland, New Zealand, during which she contrasted her own life with that of Elizabeth I.

The Queen and Prince Philip continued on to Australia, during which time the strain of being on constant view finally began to tell.

The Queen and Prince Philip host Ronald and Nancy Reagan on the royal yacht *Britannia* during a visit to California, where the weather was more suited to a wet English April.

The Queen has always been fascinated by the latest scientific developments, and here she makes the first long-distance call without an operator, from Bristol to Edinburgh, in 1958. Afterwards, Prince Philip joked: You can relax now, chaps, it all works!'

The Queen often has to mix a formal occasion with a more personal one. (From top to bottom) At the inauguration of the Kennedy Memorial at Runnymede in 1965, when she made an emotional speech about the loss suffered by the world when JFK was assassinated; the investiture of Prince Charles at Caernarfon Castle in 1969; the wedding of Princess Anne to Captain Mark Phillips in November 1973.

The Queen on a walkabout
in Cheapside during her
Silver Jubilee celebrations,
June 1977.

The Queen and the
Queen Mother shelter
from the rain as they
arrive at Ascot in 1997.

The Queen's speech through the years: (Top left) her first in 1952; (top right) 1957 – the first to be televised; (below left) 1972, when she spoke of her concerns over the situation in Northern Ireland; (below right) 1978, a year after she became a grandmother.

She balanced this message by reminding people of the importance of doing our 'utmost to show our concern for others' and urging us not to be 'obsessed by material problems'.

The sixties revealed the Queen's keen interest in space travel, and references have appeared several times in her Christmas broadcasts. The Queen has met at Buckingham Palace the first man in space, Russian major Yuri Gagarin; the first woman in space, Russian cosmonaut Valentina Tereshkova; and the first men on the moon, American astronauts Neil Armstrong and Edwin 'Buzz' Aldrin, as well as their *Apollo 11* colleague Michael Collins. A microfilmed message from the Queen on a silicon disc was deposited by the *Apollo 11* astronauts during the first landing on the moon. The message read: 'On behalf of the British people I salute the skill and courage which have brought man to the moon. May this endeavour increase the knowledge and well-being of mankind.' When the crew of *Apollo 11* visited London a few weeks later, they were received at Buckingham Palace and presented the Queen with a replica of the disc they'd left on the moon. In another technological success, Concorde, the world's first supersonic passenger aircraft and a joint Anglo-French project, made its maiden UK flight in April 1969.

While the Queen was fascinated by such technological developments, she was also aware of the importance of maintaining tradition. The long-awaited investiture of the Prince of Wales, during which the 20-year-old Prince received the insignia as the twenty-first Prince of Wales, took place as planned on 1 July 1969, at Caernarfon Castle, in front of 4,000 guests inside the medieval walls. Thousands more were in the dry moat and outside the castle, and millions around the world watched on television.

The Queen had created her eldest son Prince of Wales when he was nine years old. She later let it be known that the

investiture would be held when he was old enough to understand fully its significance. In a ceremony with many historic
echoes, directed largely by the Constable of the Castle, Lord
Snowdon, the Queen invested Prince Charles with the insignia
of his principality and the earldom of Chester: a sword, coronet,
mantle, gold ring and gold rod. The Prince's formal response
was: 'I, Charles, Prince of Wales, do become your liege man of
life and limb and of earthly worship and faith and truth I will
bear unto you to live and die against all manner of folks.'

A loyal address from the people of Wales was read in Welsh
and English by Sir Ben Bowen Thomas, president of the
University College of Wales, Aberystwyth, where the Prince had
studied Welsh language and history in the months before the
ceremony. The Prince of Wales replied in Welsh and English. In
the Welsh part of his speech, he commented it was his firm
intention to associate himself with as much of the life of the
principality as possible. He said:

It is with a certain sense of pride and emotion that I have
received these symbols of office, here in this magnificent
fortress, where no one could fail to be stirred by its atmosphere of time-worn grandeur, nor where I myself could be
unaware of the long history of Wales and its determination
to remain individual and to guard its own particular heritage – a heritage that dates back into the mists of ancient
British history, that has produced many brave men, princes,
poets, bards, scholars and, more recently, great singers, a
very memorable 'Goon', and eminent film stars. All these
people have been inspired in some way by this heritage.

After a short religious service in both languages, the Queen,
accompanied by the Duke of Edinburgh, led Prince Charles to

Queen Eleanor's Gate, looking out over Caernarfon's Castle Square, and presented him to the crowds below. However, when Prince Charles had arrived in Wales some weeks before the investiture, his reception was far from friendly. He was faced with jeering demonstrators and obscene graffiti. He won the people of Wales round by speaking to them in their native language. As Prince Philip proudly declared: 'He came, saw and conquered the Welsh.'

He had learnt his lesson from his mother, for addressing the local populace in their native tongue is something the Queen has done with great success on other occasions – in Canada, she has spoken in French for the Quebecois and Inuit for the people of Nunavik, while she also spoke in Irish during her 2011 visit to Ireland.

Towards the end of the decade, the Queen took the momentous decision to allow television cameras into her life. When Prince Philip had previously referred to having the family 'in the public eye', he meant that this had happened at times and in circumstances of its choosing. The television film was to be a quite different matter.

The idea was the brainchild of the Queen's press secretary, William Heseltine, an Australian who had joined the palace staff in 1960 on the recommendation of his prime minister, Sir Robert Menzies. Before his appointment to this role in 1968, the palace had maintained a less-is-better approach to public relations. When, for instance, George V's private secretary, Lord Stanfordham, suggested that he should try to look a little more cheerful on public occasions, the King replied: 'We sailors never smile on duty.'

Heseltine argued forcefully that smiles, along with walkabouts and photo opportunities, had become essential tools of the royal trade in the modern, media-dominated age, when the very notion of monarchy was under increasingly critical examination. A sympathetic, carefully made documentary, he insisted, could only work in the family's favour.

The 105-minute film was called *Royal Family* and, according to Heseltine, 'it enlarged and subtly changed the public's idea of what the Queen and her family are really like'. It certainly did that, though not in the way Heseltine might have hoped. The idea came in part from the television programme about the White House arranged when John F. Kennedy and his wife Jackie were in residence. The American presidency, however, is by constitutional definition a self-renewing institution, which every four, or at the most every eight, years offers up a new first family to be dissected and fawned over in equal measure.

The royal family, on the other hand, is based on continuity. There is no finality to what it does; it must bear the consequences of its mistakes for years and sometimes decades afterwards, and the decision to go ahead with *Royal Family* was bound to have a far-reaching effect. Initially, it had an immediate impact on the popularity of the Queen and the family after the programme had a positive response.

But, by going for the PR option, the royal family was surrendering itself to the vagaries of public taste. If they really thought that the programme would contain public interest, they miscalculated badly. It did precisely the opposite. It has been called 'the most fantastic piece of eavesdropping of all time', and it spawned a multimillion-pound business, employing thousands of people – some honest and well-informed, many no more than journalistic medicine men trading a charlatan's potion of innuendo and lies. And no amount of stonewalling, official denials and charm offensives could get the business back on a sensible course.

The resulting film, *Royal Family*, was a sensation. First

broadcast by the BBC on 21 June 1969, and a week later by ITV, it offered the public an unprecedented glimpse into the private world of the royals, as well as showing highlights of the investiture. Three-quarters of the British population watched it, and it was replayed endlessly on television that same year. It went on to earn several million pounds in today's money in worldwide sales.

Yet the bold attempt to usher the monarchy into the modern age proved highly controversial. Critics claimed that the film destroyed the mystique of the royals by showing them to be ordinary people, including scenes of the Duke of Edinburgh frying sausages at a Balmoral barbecue. It also showed the Queen making small talk with guests, telling US president Richard Nixon: 'World problems are so complex, aren't they now?' They saw Prince Edward throwing snowballs, going on picnics and playing with puppies, helping to decorate the Christmas tree and buying sweets at the Christmas shop out of his pocket money. They saw the Queen point at an old photograph and enquire, 'Who's that?' 'Is it Queen Victoria?' Edward replied. 'No,' the Queen answered, 'Queen Mary. That's Gan-Gan.'

The film certainly had a profound effect on the young Prince. Filming on the joint BBC–ITN project began in July 1968 and carried through to 1969. For weeks on end, an eight-man camera crew provided an animated background to his childhood. The crew were suitably well-bred – the assistant soundman was Philip Bonham-Carter. It was, nonetheless, an adventurous change for a boy who, up until then, had been cosseted in royalty's ivory tower, allowed to mix only with obsequious employees or carefully vetted contemporaries, all of whom belonged to the 'right' background of court and family.

It was living history of the most syrupy yet endearing kind. Jack Gould, writing in the *New York Times*, noted: 'In scenes of Queen Elizabeth at the dinner table with Prince Philip, Prince Charles and Princess Anne, or on a family picnic with Prince Edward or Prince Andrew, one sees an identifiable family unit reflecting a diversity of personalities and interest. The human equation comes through.'

David Attenborough, then the BBC's director of programmes, allegedly told the producer-director Richard Cawston that his film was 'killing the monarchy'. Buckingham Palace, perhaps belatedly realising that it had opened them up to unwanted scrutiny, withdrew it from public view at the end of 1969 and it has not been seen again in public.

Some commentators took the cynical view that there was a financial motive in raising the public profile of the monarchy. On 5 November 1969, *The Times* reported that the Queen was overspending her allowance from the government, in spite of having cut her staff by 15 per cent since her accession. For several years, the article said, the Queen had had to dip into her own personal fortune to keep things running.

Some five days later, Prince Philip, who was on a tour of Canada and the USA, when asked in an NBC 'Meet the Press' interview about *The Times* article, admitted that the royal family 'would probably go into the red next year' and that he would have to give up playing polo to make ends meet. He said he had already been forced to sell a small yacht and that 'we may have to move into smaller premises quite soon'. While it was true that the Queen's allowance had fallen well behind inflation, Prince Philip's remarks that he might have to give up such luxuries as polo and sailing did not go down well and were heavily criticised in the British press. Republicans had a field day and the Queen had to wait until Edward Heath's new

Conservative government put the royal finances on a sound footing.

The 1960s had been a period of severe inflation, but the Queen's allowance from the government had not been raised to keep pace with the increase in running costs of the monarchy. Creative accounting had been applied to relieve the Queen of some expenses: the royal train was paid for by British Rail; the Queen's flight was financed by the RAF; and the running costs of *Britannia*, the royal yacht, were borne by the Royal Navy, as its crew of 250 were naval officers and ratings. In later years, this had an unfortunate result when eleven members of its crew were charged with homosexual activity, which was illegal in the armed forces, although the Sexual Offences Act of 1967 had decriminalised such behaviour between consenting adults. Had they been seamen in the employ of the monarchy, no offence would have been committed.

For the only time in the Queen's reign to date, there was no Christmas broadcast in 1969 because of the televised investiture and the *Royal Family* film. Instead, the Queen issued a short message in which she acknowledged that many people had voiced their concern about the break in the usual Christmas broadcast. As a result, there has been a Christmas broadcast every year since. In her statement, the Queen summed up the decade with these words:

In a short time the 1960s will be over but not out of our memories. Historians will record them as the decade in which men first reached out beyond our own planet and set foot on the moon, but each one of us will have our own special triumphs or tragedies to look back on.

It was time to look forward to a new decade.

Chapter 5

CELEBRATIONS AND TRIBULATIONS

I leave you with the old message, 'On earth peace; goodwill toward men.' No one has ever offered a better formula and I hope that its simple truth may yet take hold of the imagination of all mankind.

CHRISTMAS BROADCAST, 1972

These words, taken from the Bible, appear time and again in the Queen's Christmas broadcasts. They were often quoted to support a plea for reconciliation, one of the Queen's favourite causes, particularly during the 1970s when sectarian violence was raging in Northern Ireland. Although during this decade the Queen suffered a number of personal tragedies, including the deaths of four close members of her family and the break-up of her sister Princess Margaret's marriage, she did not refer to them in her Christmas broadcasts. Her messages were always positive and she preferred to focus on happier matters, such as her own silver wedding and Silver Jubilee and her daughter Princess Anne's wedding in 1973.

As well as seeing herself as the bringer of good tidings, the Queen frequently expressed hope for better times in the future, particularly for the next generation. Like her son Prince Charles, she cares about future generations and what kind of world they will inherit. Her Christmas broadcasts often focused on the themes of the Commonwealth or families.

Her 1970 speech was almost entirely devoted to the Commonwealth, after she had engaged in some far-ranging tours, meeting Eskimos in the north of Canada and Aborigines in Australia. The diversity of the Commonwealth was brought home to her when she hosted a party for the athletes taking part in the Edinburgh Commonwealth Games that year. She also saw strength in the level of support that was given to East Pakistan, now Bangladesh, when a cyclone hit the region in November, killing about 500,000 people.

In the 1971 broadcast, Prince Andrew and Prince Edward were seen on television looking at a family photograph album as the Queen stressed how important it was for parents to set an example for their children. 'We do know we are passing onto our children the power to change their whole environment,' she said. 'But we also leave them with a set of values, which they take from our lives and our example.'

The first close family member to die during the decade was the Duke of Windsor, whose abdication in 1936 had put the then Princess Elizabeth in line for the throne. His decision to put personal happiness before royal duty rocked the monarchy and the stress certainly contributed to George VI's early death, but when it became known that he was dying of throat cancer, the Queen agreed to see him during an official state visit to Paris.

On 18 May 1972, after a day at the Longchamp races in

Paris, the Queen and Prince Philip, together with Prince Charles, stopped off at the Duke's home in the Bois de Boulogne. Although the Duke had been more or less in exile since the abdication, according to his doctor the Queen was moved to tears on seeing her uncle's frail, fragile figure as he bowed deeply to her. He had insisted on getting up from his sickbed and dressing formally for the visit.

Touchingly, the Queen spent fifteen minutes alone with her uncle on the first floor, while his wife Wallis served tea in the downstairs drawing room. He died ten days later, on 28 May, and after a funeral service in St George's Chapel, Windsor, the Duke was buried in the royal burial ground at Frogmore. Fourteen years later, after a long illness which rendered her incapable, his widow, the Duchess of Windsor, was buried beside him. Only the Queen, Prince Philip, the Prince and Princess of Wales and eight old retainers attended the burial, and Diana said afterwards it was the only time she had seen the Queen cry.

In July 1972, there was cause for celebration when the Queen's cousin Prince Richard of Gloucester married a Danish bride, Birgitte van Deurs, his former secretary. The joy was short-lived, however, as Prince Richard's elder brother and best man at his wedding, the dashing Prince William, was killed on 28 August when his aircraft crashed and burst into flames while he was taking part in an air race near Wolverhampton. His plane, a Piper Cherokee Arrow, banked sharply soon after take-off, hit a tree and plunged to the ground. It was said that the Prince piloted the plane so as to avoid crashing on a nearby village, thereby saving many lives.

Prince William, just thirty years old at the time of his death, was a favourite cousin of the Queen. He was intelligent and debonair, with startling blue eyes. He was also something of a rebel. At Eton College, he ran the school's film society and, much to the delight of the other boys, managed to arrange a showing of the film that was banned in England at the time, *The Wild Ones*, starring Marlon Brando as the leader of a biker gang. After Eton and Cambridge, he didn't follow the usual royal route into the armed forces, but became a diplomat in the Foreign Office. When the Queen was informed of the news of his tragic death, she immediately ordered family mourning and cancelled her plans to go to the Munich Olympics. The Queen broke her summer holiday at Balmoral to attend his funeral at St George's Chapel, Windsor, on 2 September. He, too, was buried at Frogmore, just four months after the Duke of Windsor.

Two months later, the Queen and Duke of Edinburgh celebrated their silver wedding. At a speech at Guildhall in London, the Queen uttered the words that have made it into the *Oxford Dictionary of Quotations*: 'I think everybody really will concede that on this, of all days, I should begin my speech with the words, "My husband and I."' She went on to say:

A marriage begins by joining man and wife together, but this relationship between two people, however deep at the time, needs to develop and mature with the passing years ... When the Bishop was asked what he thought about sin, he replied with simple conviction that he was against it. If I am asked today what I think about family life after twenty-five years, I can answer with equal simplicity and conviction. I am for it.

The silver wedding was again the subject of the Christmas broadcast in 1972. The Queen's fervent belief in reconciliation and tolerance was in evidence when she said: 'One of the great Christian ideals is a happy and lasting marriage between man and wife, but no marriage can hope to succeed without a deliberate effort to be tolerant and understanding.'

The Queen had learnt tolerance from childhood. She was gentle with her little sister Margaret, who insisted on being included in everything, although she was four years younger. She was tolerant of her handsome husband, whose sarcastic turn of phrase could verge on the cruel. He used to frighten her by driving too fast and, when she nervously held her breath, told her to shut up or get out. She usually shut up. When he disappeared with his friend and secretary Michael Parker on his voyage on board *Britannia*, she was loyal to him despite the rumours of a marriage rift. Years later, she was tolerant of Diana, allowing the distraught Princess of Wales to pour out her troubles, and tried to give her advice. She is equally tolerant of her staff, listening to their problems and turning a blind eye to any little misdemeanours.

As so often in her speeches, she sought to move beyond the personal and suggest lessons that could be learnt on a broader level, with the deteriorating situation in Northern Ireland specifically in mind:

We all ought to know by now that a civilised and peaceful existence is only possible when people make the effort to understand each other. Looking at the world, one might be forgiven for believing that many people have never heard of this simple idea. Every day there are reports of violence, lawlessness, and the disregard for human life . . .

In the United Kingdom we have our own particular sorrows in Northern Ireland and I want to send a special message of sympathy to all those men, women and children who have suffered and endured so much. But there is a light in this tragic situation. The people are steadfastly carrying on their ordinary business in their factories and places of work.

Voluntary workers, both in and out of uniform, have struggled to keep humanity and common sense alive. The social services have done their job magnificently. The forces of law and order continue their thankless task with the utmost fortitude in the face of appalling provocation. We must admire them greatly for their patience and restraint.

And, for one who found the Commonwealth so central to her view on the world, there was a new body that the UK was about to join. After protracted negotiations, Prime Minister Edward Heath had finally secured the rights for the country to join the Common Market, as the EU was then known, from the start of 1973. The Queen welcomed the move, but also issued a message to the Commonwealth nations, reassuring them that Britain would not forget them, now they had a new group of partners:

The new links with Europe will not replace those with the Commonwealth. They cannot alter our historical and personal attachments with kinsmen and friends overseas. Old friends will not be lost; Britain will take her Commonwealth links into Europe with her.

Britain and these other European countries see in the Community a new opportunity for the future. They believe that the things they have in common are more important than the things which divide them, and that if they work together not only they, but the whole world will benefit.

On the home front, 1973 was a dismal year. England failed to qualify for the soccer World Cup finals, the Icelandic cod wars were at their height, with the Royal Navy having to protect English trawlers, and the country was beset with industrial unrest and constant strikes, culminating in the three-day week to conserve fuel as the electricity workers and coal miners went on a 'go-slow'.

A beacon of light among the gloom was provided by the engagement and then wedding of Princess Anne and Olympic equestrian Captain Mark Phillips, whom she had first met in 1968 at a reception in honour of the medal-winning equestrian team. The dashing captain was considered a perfect match for the horse-mad Princess. Back in 1973, they appeared to be a golden couple, and the Queen's cousin, Lady Elizabeth Anson, organised a lively pre-wedding party at the Berkeley hotel in London. Many of the guests wore their hunting pink and the riotous celebrations lasted well into the night.

In keeping with royal tradition, the Queen offered commoner Mark Phillips an earldom on his wedding day, but he declined, which meant that if the couple had any children, they would become the first grandchildren of a sovereign to have no title.

The British public took the couple to their hearts. They were cheered wherever they went. Thousands of wedding presents arrived from up and down the country, including, from Nottinghamshire county council, the number plate '1 ANN'. Princess Anne said she would prefer a quiet wedding, but in deference to her mother she agreed to Westminster Abbey, the traditional venue for royal weddings. The ceremony, a showcase event for the royal family, was watched by an estimated 500 million television viewers around the world; and, in London, crowds of people lined the streets to share in the big day, which was declared a national holiday.

On the morning of the wedding, according to his valet Stephen Barry, Prince Charles popped into his sister's rooms to wish her good luck and upset her by remarking on her unusually heavy make-up, forgetting the whole event was being televised. The couple spent their honeymoon on board the royal yacht *Britannia*, courtesy of the Queen, and over £2 million worth of wedding presents was waiting for the couple when they returned home.

Unsurprisingly, the wedding was a major theme of that year's Christmas broadcast, when the Queen remarked:

I am glad that my daughter's wedding gave such pleasure to so many people just at a time when the world was facing very serious problems. People all over the world watched the wedding on television, but there were still many in London on the day, and their warmth and enthusiasm ensured it was an occasion my family will never forget.

The euphoria generated by the wedding did not last for long. Some eighteen weeks later, the royal couple were returning to Buckingham Palace along the Mall when their chauffeur-driven Austin Princess was forced to halt by a car, which blocked their route. A man appeared and fired his gun and tried to pull the Princess out of the car. The gunman, Ian Ball, almost killed her protection officer, Jim Beaton, who was shot several times as he tried to protect the couple. As others rushed to help, they too were shot, but in the confusion the Princess was able to escape, while Ball was chased away and eventually arrested by Detective Constable Peter Edmonds.

It subsequently emerged that the shooting was an attempt to kidnap Princess Anne and hold her to ransom when a letter penned by the assailant addressed to 'Queen Elizabeth' was found, demanding 'a ransom of £3 million to be paid in £5 notes' for her release. The lengthy letter went on to list all kinds of bizarre demands, and 26-year-old Ball was prosecuted for the attempted murder of the Princess's detective. He was sentenced to life imprisonment and put in a mental hospital.

Things did not improve much the following year. At home, there was a drought in parts of the south of England, resulting in a shortage of animal food and failure of crops; violence in

Northern Ireland showed no signs of abating; the economy continued to struggle, leading to inflation, high unemployment and more industrial unrest. Matters weren't helped by political uncertainty, as 1974 saw two general elections. The first, in February, resulted in a hung parliament, with Harold Wilson's Labour forming a minority government – hardly ideal in such conditions. In October, a second election resulted in Labour gaining a majority of just three.

Elsewhere in the Commonwealth, there was famine in Bangladesh and floods in Brisbane, Australia. In such circumstances, even the Queen was less than her usual upbeat self in her Christmas broadcast when she said:

We have never been short of problems, but in the last year everything seems to have happened at once. There have been floods and drought and famine: there have been outbreaks of senseless violence. And on top of it all the cost of living continues to rise – everywhere.

Despite all this, she also tried to find ways to rally people's morale, suggesting some important ways in which people could improve their lot. It was the voice of experience, from one who had lived through the dark times of the war, and who had seen how a nation had won through when its very survival was at stake. Already, she was using her knowledge of life to inspire others, something she sees as an important part of her role:

Perhaps we make too much of what is wrong and too little of what is right. The trouble with gloom is that it feeds upon itself and depression causes more depression. There are indeed real dangers and there are real fears, and we will never overcome them if we turn against each other with angry accusations ... We have the lessons of history to show that the British people have survived many a desperate situation when they acted together ...

You may be asking what can we do personally to make things better? I believe the Christmas message provides the best clue. Goodwill is better than resentment, tolerance is better than revenge, compassion is better than anger, above all a lively concern for the interests of others as well as our own. In times of doubt and anxiety, the attitudes people show in their daily lives, in their homes, and in their work, are of supreme importance. It is by acting in this spirit that every man, woman and child can help and 'make a difference'.

Although the Queen lost several family members during the 1970s, there was one other death that devastated her more than the others. Lord Patrick Plunket was one of the Queen's closest friends and confidants, so much so that when he died in 1975 he was buried in the royal family's private burial ground at Frogmore. The Queen erected a memorial to him – a small pavilion – in Valley Gardens, Windsor Great Park, at the top of the valley. His mother, the illegitimate daughter of an actress and the Marquess of Londonderry, married Baron Plunket and their son Patrick succeeded to the title when both his parents were killed in an air crash in 1938.

Patrick Plunket joined the royal household as equerry to George VI and later became one of the Queen's closest advisors for nearly a quarter of a century. Three years older than the woman he called 'my boss', he was a lifelong bachelor, often said to be the brother she never had. He arranged the Queen's private social life, including trips to cinemas and discreet lunches with friends in smart restaurants. He danced with the Queen at parties, occasionally dropping her off with a new partner who wouldn't have dared to ask the monarch for a dance.

'He had a wonderful memory for names and faces, plus the knack of good judgement and an amazing instinct for the right and wrong thing to do, and she relied on that,' said his brother Shaun. He also had an irreverent sense of humour perfectly pitched to hers. An art collector and a trustee of the National Art Collection Fund, he encouraged her love of art and advised her on purchases for the Royal Collection. When he died of cancer at the age of fifty-one, the Queen unusually attended both his funeral at the Chapel Royal and his memorial service at the Guards' Chapel. She even had a hand in writing his *Times* obituary.

The Christmas broadcast of 1975 focused on the difference that each individual, by his or her actions, can make. It was another of her favourite themes, and the descriptive prose she sometimes used reflected her feelings when she said:

> If you throw a stone into a pool, the ripples go on spreading outwards. A big stone can cause waves, but even the smallest pebble changes the whole pattern of the water. Our daily actions are like those ripples, each one makes a difference, even the smallest ... And the combined effect can be enormous. If enough grains of sand are dropped into one side of a pair of scales they will, in the end, tip it against a lump of lead.

On the evening of 20 April 1976, the Queen celebrated her fiftieth birthday in style with a grand ball for almost 600 guests at Windsor Castle. The party began with a dinner for sixty followed by a ball, which started with the guests arriving at 10.30pm. Among them were two previous prime ministers, Harold Wilson and Edward Heath, but James Callaghan (who had taken over from Wilson earlier in the month) stayed away for fear that attending this glittering occasion would make it difficult to sell the austerity package he was promoting to the trades unions.

The dancers paused at midnight to toast the Queen and sing 'Happy Birthday', and there was another pause at 2.40am, the exact moment when Princess Elizabeth was born on 21 April 1926. It was a memorable evening, and the Queen danced to the strains of the Joe Loss Orchestra until 3.15am. *The Times*, in a birthday tribute, said: 'At a time when the country needs all the encouragement it can get, it is a strength and reassurance that the central institution of the monarch is so sound.'

For the Queen, the joy of the occasion must to some extent have been tempered by the announcement from Buckingham Palace the previous month: 'HRH The Princess Margaret, Countess of Snowdon, and the Earl of Snowdon have mutually agreed to live apart. The Princess will carry out her public duties and functions unaccompanied by Lord Snowdon. There are no plans for divorce proceedings.'

The breakdown of her sister's marriage was a sad matter for the Queen. The two women had always been very close, and she felt her sister's unhappiness keenly. Having been thwarted in the course of true love, it was perhaps not surprising that Princess Margaret had grown up to be self-indulgent and insecure. She drank and smoked heavily, and embarked on a series of affairs. The Queen never criticised her; their bond was too strong. They had lived through so much together, including the premature death of their father, and Margaret was one of a small group of people with whom the Queen could be herself.

It was in 1953, the year of the Coronation, that Princess Margaret had been disappointed in love. She told her sister that she wanted to marry divorcee Group Captain Peter Townsend, but was persuaded by the Queen to wait a year before making any final decision. By 1955, in spite of Princess Margaret's insistence that she and Townsend were still in love and wanted to marry, she was forced to end her relationship with him. The Queen was able to remove herself from any personal involvement in the situation by saying that she had abided by the decision of the government (according to the Royal Marriages Act, they had the right to approve the match) and the opposition of the Church of England to the marriage.

The Queen could have intervened on behalf of Townsend, but she refused to do so, failing to give her sister any support in the matter, preferring to allow the government and her own advisors to shoulder the blame. It was not that she didn't care. It was because, like her mother, she disliked any personal confrontation and it set the pattern for her reign. It was the portent of how she would behave when called upon to become involved in the marital troubles of Prince Charles.

Although divorce had become much more common by this time, it was anathema to the Queen, who hated the idea, while the British people considered the royal family as an example of marital stability. When Princess Margaret's divorce from the Earl of Snowdon finally happened two years later, it came when society's norms had moved even further down the road of acceptance. At the beginning of the 1970s, 5.6 per cent of marriages ended in divorce, but by the end of the decade this had risen to 12 per cent. The Queen's family would reflect this trend: within a period of twenty years, she had to deal with the divorce of her sister and three out of her four children.

In July 1976, the welcome that greeted the Queen when she sailed up the Hudson river to New York on board the royal yacht *Britannia* was heartening. Two centuries before, New York had been a focal point of resistance to royal authority, as the American colonies issued the Declaration of Independence, but that July the Queen received an enthusiastic welcome from the crowds, which exceeded all expectations. The royal yacht was always an impressive sight and, as she sailed past the Statue of Liberty – who holds the torch in one hand and the Declaration of Independence in the other – the sight gladdened even the most jaded New Yorkers.

Few who have been on board could fail to be impressed by her elegance and grandeur. It was Prince Edward who later pointed out what an asset the yacht was to Great Britain. 'She is a symbol of the greatness of Great Britain, and one of our best public relations tools of the time,' he said. 'The problem is, ninety-nine per cent of people have never seen *Britannia* out of this country. They have never seen the effect she has when she goes to America. They have never seen the impact she has for this country.'

The real friendship between the United States and the United Kingdom, which she had reinforced on her first visit twenty years earlier, enabled the Queen to return to one of her favourite subjects in her Christmas broadcast of 1976 – that of reconciliation. She said of herself:

Who would have thought two hundred years ago that a descendant of King George III could have taken part in these [bicentennial] celebrations? ... The United States was born in bitter conflict with Britain, but we didn't remain enemies for long. From our reconciliation came incalculable benefits to mankind and a partnership which, together with many countries of the Commonwealth, was proved in two world wars and ensured that the light of liberty was not extinguished.

The Queen went on to talk about Northern Ireland in these words:

Another shining example is the peace movement in Northern Ireland. Here Roman Catholics and Protestants have joined together in a crusade of reconciliation to bring peace to the Province ... The gift I would most value next year is that reconciliation should be found wherever it is needed.

The peace movement the Queen was referring to had been set up that year by Mairead Corrigan and Betty Williams, who would be awarded the Nobel peace prize for their work in trying to draw together the two communities. Sadly, she was wrong to have such high hopes for peace in Northern Ireland. Many years would pass and much sorrow would be endured before her hopes were realised.

For many, the summer of 1976 in the UK was memorable for the extraordinary heatwave that parched the grass, and the Queen found in that experience a suitable metaphor for her hopes for the future:

Those who know the desert know also how quickly it can flower when the rains come. But who in Britain who saw the parched earth and empty reservoirs last summer would have believed that the grass would grow so strong, so green and so soon when the drought ended? When the conflict stops, peace can blossom just as quickly.

In the same way that Princess Anne's wedding had given the nation a much-needed boost in 1973, so the Queen's Silver Jubilee supplied a feel-good atmosphere across the nation in 1977. Towards the end of the previous year, the government had been forced to go to the IMF for a loan, and was required to make hefty cuts to public expenditure as a condition of receiving the money. So these continued to be bleak times indeed, with one union after another calling for strikes. The televising of the state opening of parliament was by blacked out by striking technicians and even the country's undertakers went on strike. The IRA had stepped up its bombing campaign both in Belfast and in London's West End. Inflation was running at a record 16 per cent and unemployment was on the rise.

The Silver Jubilee gave the populace a reason to celebrate on a scale not seen since the Coronation. On 6 June, the Queen lit a bonfire in Windsor Great Park, which started a chain of beacons across the country. The following day more than a million people waving Union flags lined the streets of London to watch the royal family on their way to St Paul's. The Queen, dressed in pink on her jubilee day and accompanied by Prince Philip, led the procession in the Gold State Coach. Despite the rain, thousands camped out overnight to try to get a better view of the procession down the Mall.

At St Paul's, 2,700 specially selected guests, including politicians and other heads of state, joined in the ceremony. It began with Ralph Vaughan Williams' arrangement of the hymn 'All People That on Earth Do Dwell', which was played at the Queen's Coronation in 1953. Millions of people tuned in to watch events on the television. Towns and villages threw elaborate street parties for all their residents to honour the Queen, with bunting strung from rooftop to rooftop. In London alone, there were over 4,000 organised parties for individual streets. In addition to parties, drivers decorated motor vehicles as historical events from Britain's past and drove them about town, organising their own parades, while business was given a boost with the production of a vast array of commemorative memorabilia of all kinds, from coins and postage stamps to china mugs and plates.

In contrast to the celebrations, the punk band the Sex Pistols chartered a boat and sailed down the Thames on jubilee day playing their controversial and offensive track 'God Save the Queen'. Their record company, A&M, was so disgusted by their conduct that it dropped the band from its label, but the Pistols were quickly signed up by Richard Branson's Virgin Records.

In her Silver Jubilee address to parliament, the Queen highlighted the benefits of constitutional monarchy. She also took the opportunity of indirectly criticising the rise of Scottish and Welsh nationalism when she talked about:

> ... the continuing and keen discussion of proposals for devolution to Scotland and Wales within the United Kingdom. I number Kings and Queens of England and of Scotland, and Princes of Wales among my ancestors and so I can readily understand these aspirations. But I cannot forget that I was crowned Queen of the United Kingdom of Great Britain and Northern Ireland. Perhaps this Jubilee is a time to remind ourselves of the benefits which union has conferred, at home and in our international dealings, on the inhabitants of all parts of this United Kingdom.

It was an extremely rare political intervention from the Queen, who normally avoided commenting on such topics, but it revealed her passionately held and very personal support for the United Kingdom. It was an issue that would continue to grow in significance throughout the rest of her reign, and she would rarely speak so frankly again about the subject.

During the summer months, the Queen embarked on a large-scale tour of the country, having decided that she wished to mark her jubilee by meeting as many of her people as possible. No other sovereign had visited so much of the UK in the course of just three months – the six jubilee tours in Britain and

Northern Ireland covered thirty-six counties. The home tours began in Scotland, with greater crowds in Glasgow than the city had ever seen before. The tours continued throughout England and Wales – in Lancashire over a million people turned out on one day – before culminating in a visit to Northern Ireland.

Official overseas visits were also made to Western Samoa, Australia, New Zealand, Tonga, Fiji, Tasmania, Papua New Guinea, Canada and the West Indies, ending with a flight back to London on Concorde, which is still the only supersonic passenger aircraft to have flown commercially. During the year it was estimated that the Queen and the Duke of Edinburgh travelled 56,000 miles. They were elated with how successful it had been, but exhausted by it all and they longed for the tranquillity of the Scottish Highlands and Balmoral.

The Christmas broadcast of 1977 was another mix of joy and sadness, with the jubilee an inevitable focus of her thoughts:

> I shall never forget the scene outside Buckingham Palace on Jubilee Day. The cheerful crowd was symbolic of the hundreds of thousands of people who greeted us wherever we went in this Jubilee Year ... I believe it also revealed to the world that we can be a united people. It showed that all the artificial barriers which divide man from man and family from family can be broken down.

But there was sadness, too, over the desperate need for reconciliation in Northern Ireland, where hundreds of people on both sides had been killed during the year: 'Nowhere is reconciliation more desperately needed than in Northern Ireland. That is why I was particularly pleased to go there.'

The Queen had visited Northern Ireland in August for the first time in eleven years as part of her Silver Jubilee tour. Ever since the Battle of the Boyne in 1690, when William of Orange's Protestant army routed James VII of Scotland's Catholics, there had been sectarian violence between the two factions, particularly in Belfast. The Queen's visit cannot have been described as an unqualified success, because the tour was confined to those areas where the royalist Protestants were ready with their Union flags. However, in the run-up to the Queen's visit, the Provisional Irish Republican Army mounted a campaign of violence, hoping to force its cancellation. They had threatened to give the Queen 'a visit to remember', and organised a spate of arson attacks on Protestant-owned shops in Belfast, doing a huge amount of damage. But, as when her safety had been threatened in Ghana in 1961, the Queen did not turn away.

A twenty-one-gun salute marked the Queen's arrival at Belfast Lough aboard the royal yacht *Britannia*. However, the Queen was advised not to come ashore in Belfast for fear of demonstrations from the staunchly Republican area of west Belfast, even though 32,000 troops and police were on duty in the biggest royal security operation ever to have been mounted. Security considerations meant the Queen made the short trip to the first stop on her tour, Hillsborough Castle, by helicopter – her first ever flight in one.

At Hillsborough, she was greeted by schoolchildren and inspected a guard of honour formed by members of the Ulster Defence Regiment. After the inspection the Queen, dressed in a Kerry green coat and hat, hosted an investiture and a garden party for several thousand guests, who were all rigorously screened. The Queen dislikes the presence of security and always has done, but will do as she is advised by the royal protection squad, no matter how restricting she may find it.

In her address to the people of Northern Ireland, the Queen said:

There are hopeful signs of reconciliation and understanding. Policemen and soldiers have told me of the real cooperation they are receiving. I have sensed a common bond and a shared hope for the future. I look forward to the day when we may return and enjoy with the people of Northern Ireland some of the better and happier times so long awaited and so richly deserved.

Those hopeful signs, alas, didn't immediately develop into peace and so there followed another long break – this time of fourteen years – before the Queen returned to Northern Ireland. Even then it was a fleeting one-day visit on 29 June 1991.

During 1977, the Queen celebrated the birth of her first grandchild, Peter Phillips, on 15 November; he was born in the Lindo Wing of St Mary's hospital at 10.46am. When she heard the news, she was about to conduct an investiture in the Throne Room in Buckingham Palace, starting at eleven. The Queen was so overjoyed she delayed the ceremony for an unprecedented ten minutes while she recovered her composure. Prince Philip, who was away in Germany at the time, was equally pleased. He admired his forthright daughter and had always been very close to her. He was convinced motherhood would soften her edges and give a new dimension to her life.

Peter Mark Andrew Phillips, as the baby was to be known, was fifth in line to the throne and the first royal baby to be born to a commoner for 500 years. Three days before Christmas, he was christened in the Music Room at Buckingham Palace. The Queen agreed to allow film of little Peter to be shown within the Christmas broadcast of 1978, which had the future as its theme, while also highlighting how this was a traditional theme that had been developed by her father and grandfather in their Christmas messages. Her final accolade to her grandchild was to send former royal nanny Mabel Anderson to Gatcombe Park, where his parents lived, to help look after the newborn baby.

As the decade drew to its end, another death brought great sadness to the royal family. On 27 August 1979, Lord Louis Mountbatten was killed when IRA terrorists detonated a fifty pound bomb hidden on his fishing vessel *Shadow V.* Mountbatten, a war hero, elder statesman and second cousin of the Queen, was spending the day fishing with his family in Donegal Bay off Ireland's northwest coast when the bomb exploded. Three others were killed in the attack, including Mountbatten's fourteen-year-old grandson, Nicholas. Later that day, an IRA bombing attack on land killed eighteen British paratroopers in County Down, Northern Ireland.

The assassination of Mountbatten was the first blow struck against the British royal family by the IRA during its long terrorist campaign to drive the British out of Northern Ireland and unite it with the Republic of Ireland to the south. The attack convinced the newly elected Thatcher government to take a hardline stance against the terrorist organisation, as Mrs Thatcher had also lost a close ally in Airey Neave in a car bomb earlier in the year.

The Queen led the nation in mourning as the body of her husband's uncle, Lord Mountbatten, was buried after a day of pageantry in London. The earl had planned much of the funeral himself. Members of Britain's armed forces were joined by representatives of Burma, India, the United States, France and Canada in escorting the naval gun carriage carrying his body. The procession from Wellington Barracks, near Buckingham Palace, to Westminster Abbey was accompanied by the sound of bells and the solemn brass of Royal Marine bands. The cocked hat of an admiral of the fleet, his sword of honour and his gold stick were laid on top of his coffin. Lord Mountbatten's horse,

Dolly, was led near the head of the parade with the admiral's boots reversed in the stirrups.

Thousands lined the route of the procession and the funeral service at Westminster Abbey was attended by royalty, leaders and politicians from all over the world. The Archbishop of Canterbury praised the earl for his 'lifelong devotion to the Royal Navy' and for being 'so rare a person'. After the public ceremony, the coffin was taken to Romsey Abbey, near the Mountbattens' family home in Hampshire, and buried at a private service.

The Queen received messages of condolence from leaders all around the globe, including President Jimmy Carter and Pope John Paul II. But, as was her custom, she made no public statement, nor did she refer to the tragedy in her Christmas message. Instead, she chose to devote her speech to children, 1979 being the International Year of the Child, and with Princess Anne being president of the Save the Children Fund since 1970.

In the end each one of us has a primary and personal responsibility for our own children, for children entrusted to our care and for all the children in our own communities. At Christmas we give presents to each other. Let us also stop to think whether we are making enough effort to pass on our experience of life to our children.

With the 1970s drawing to a close, it was an appropriate note for the Queen to strike – once more looking to the future, and to the children who play such an important part in it.

Chapter 6

WEDDINGS, WARS
AND WORRIES

*Growing older is one of the facts of life,
and has its own compensations ...
experience should help us to take a more
balanced view of events and be more
understanding of the foibles of human
nature.*

CHRISTMAS BROADCAST, 1987

A s the new decade dawned, it was the Queen's own family
that was at the centre of her attention. She felt moved to
include a mention of her mother in her Christmas broadcast,
when she said: 'I was glad that the celebrations of my mother's
eightieth birthday last summer gave so much pleasure.'

The broadcast received a record 28 million viewers in the
United Kingdom alone, but the happy events of the first two years
of the decade were not a sign of what was to come, as the period
was not the best time for the Queen. The monarchy was finding
itself increasingly out of step with the hopes and aspirations of a

growing number of its subjects. There was a sense that Prince Philip's description of the royal family having to look back on tradition while also moving with the times had become unbalanced, and the focus was too much in the past. Furthermore, the question of the royal finances, and how much the nation's subjects should be expected to pay towards the upkeep of the family, had been a rumbling complaint since the early seventies. This issue was only going to intensify as the country fell into a deep recession, which made money all the tighter.

On the political front, the Queen found herself uncomfortable with her government over the question of the Commonwealth. As Princess Elizabeth, she had dedicated her life to the organisation which had replaced the old British Empire – and to a large extent had been invented to disguise its passing. Throughout her reign, as we have seen, she remained deeply committed to its welfare and concerned by the poverty of many of its members. Her governments tended to take a more pragmatic view. Prime Minister Edward Heath regarded most of its leaders with barely disguised contempt, as did Margaret Thatcher. At one juncture, the issue of South African sanctions, and the refusal of successive British governments to impose them, threatened to break up the organisation.

Such controversies were temporarily put aside to celebrate Queen Elizabeth the Queen Mother's eightieth birthday on 4 August 1980. The nation had been merrymaking throughout the year, culminating in a service of thanksgiving in July at St Paul's Cathedral attended by the entire royal family. Wearing her trademark feathered hat and wrapover dress, the Queen Mother was driven in an open carriage, with her grandson Prince Charles at her side, while huge crowds cheered her along the route. The Archbishop of Canterbury, Robert Runcie, spoke of her as being 'the human face' of royalty. Prince Charles spoke

of the 'extraordinary happiness, pleasure and sheer joy' she gave
to so many. In her Christmas message that year, the Queen
thanked the nation:

> The loyalty and affection, which so many people showed my
> mother, reflected a feeling, expressed in many different ways,
> that she is a person who has given selfless service to the people
> of this country and of the Commonwealth.

Endless garden parties, carnivals and celebrations had been
organised specially for the octogenarian Queen Elizabeth, but on
the day of her birthday she was with members of her family outside the gates of Clarence House to wave to the crowds as usual.
After a special luncheon with her two daughters and four of her
grandchildren, the Queen Mother watched a fly-past of ten
jets in 'E' formation roar over Buckingham Palace. In July, the
Queen had given her mother a formal party at Windsor Castle as
a joint celebration with Princess Alice, Duchess of Gloucester,
and the Duke of Beaufort. The guests were a mixture of friends,
royalty and the younger generation, prompting the Queen
Mother to remark the evening was 'a perfect cocktail of people'.

Given what was to happen the following year, it was perhaps
surprising that Lady Diana Spencer was not on the guest list, for
at that stage the fiery Anna Wallace was generally thought to be
the most likely contender to be Prince Charles's bride. But, seven
months later, on 24 February 1981, he announced his engagement to the nineteen-year-old Lady Diana. She was the youngest
daughter of Viscount Althorp and his former wife, Frances
Shand Kydd, and the maternal granddaughter of Ruth, Lady
Fermoy, who was a friend and lady-in-waiting to the Queen
Mother. Diana's father, later the eighth Earl Spencer, had served
as an equerry to the Queen between 1952 and 1954, and to

George VI for the two years before that. The family lived at Park House on the Sandringham estate, and the Queen had known Diana fleetingly most of her life. Diana's elder sister Sarah had been a girlfriend of Prince Charles's, and her other sister, Jane, was married to Robert Fellowes, the Queen's assistant and later her private secretary.

'She is one of us,' the Queen wrote to a friend. 'I am very fond of all three of the Spencer girls.'

If the Queen realised the troubles brewing with Diana during the months leading up to the wedding, she chose to ignore them. The relationship had started so well in Scotland the previous summer, when Diana had joined in with the after-dinner games, laughed at Prince Philip's jokes, got wet, fallen into bogs, said all the right things. The 19-year-old passed into their august royal circle with flying colours. Now the fiancée to the heir to the throne, she received a magnificent oval sapphire and diamond engagement ring. She was dazzled by the romantic story she was involved in after she had caught what she called 'the big fish'.

Unfortunately, it soon became clear that, somewhat naively, Diana had rarely looked into the future and fully considered what being a member of the royal family actually entailed. The life of a princess wasn't a fairy tale, and soon she had to live with the realities of it all. She was given a police escort, moved into Buckingham Palace's old nursery suite on the second floor, and her old freedom was gone.

She was a young girl with time on her hands. The Queen made a big fuss of her and tried to show her that she was interested in her for herself, and not just as an attachment to Prince Charles, but Diana ran out of things to say to her. Understandably nervous, she didn't want to have lunch with 'Brenda' – her nickname for the Queen, taken from the satirical magazine *Private Eye* – on her own and refused the Queen's entreaties by making excuses and inventing non-existent friends.

In hindsight, the Queen clearly failed to understand Diana's predicament as she became a part of the royal family. Furthermore, as we have subsequently learnt, Diana had some emotional difficulties, but in the early 1980s few of the Queen's generation understood such issues, or knew how to deal with her chameleon-like character. The Queen was sympathetic to Diana's anxieties, but had no inkling that she was already suffering from the bulimia that was to plague her for years to come. As much as she wanted to help, the Queen had the affairs of state to deal with and many of her own problems.

On 14 June, just a few weeks before the wedding, she had been riding on her faithful horse Burmese to Trooping the Colour when six pistol cracks rang out. Sudden fear gripped onlookers – had the Queen been shot? Fortunately, they were blanks. The Queen was unharmed and, thanks to her excellent horsemanship, not unseated. A seventeen-year-old unemployed youth was charged the following day. It was a serious threat to her personal security and, in the light of the forthcoming royal wedding, security in general, and surveillance was stepped up.

Just over six weeks later, the Queen threw a pre-wedding party at Buckingham Palace for Prince Charles and Lady Diana. It was the most lavish royal ball in over half a century. The guest list included just about every European royal, both major and minor, as well as America's First Lady, Nancy Reagan, a raft of prime ministers and leaders of the Commonwealth. There were footmen and maids in attendance on each floor, and every room in the palace was full, such was the pressure for accommodation. From the Queen's point of view, the party was a showcase to entertain princes, kings and politicians. The wedding two days later was a state occasion and a showcase for the nation.

On the Prince of Wales's insistence, the wedding ceremony took place in St Paul's, not Westminster Abbey, because the cathedral could accommodate the three orchestras he wanted and the vast number of guests deemed necessary to be invited for such an event. Weddings are a declaration of hope for the future, and this one was seen and shared in by more people than any in history. Before the wedding breakfast, Charles and Diana appeared on the balcony of Buckingham Palace. The crowd roared its instruction and the new Princess of Wales said to her husband: 'They want us to kiss.' They did and the moment was shared by a worldwide television audience of 700 million. No kiss had ever been witnessed by more people.

'I will try my hardest to make your grandson happy and give him all the love and support he needs and deserves,' Diana wrote to the Queen Mother afterwards. It was the Queen's fervent wish, too. Her own marriage had survived because Prince Philip was her supporter. She hoped her son's would be the same.

That night the Queen and many of the important guests from the wedding attended a party at Claridge's hotel in London's Brook Street given by party supremo, Lady Elizabeth Anson. 'I arranged for video screens to be erected so the guests could see the ceremony replayed,' she recalled. 'The Queen sat next to Nancy Reagan and Princess Grace on a circular sofa, all glued to the screens. There was a wonderful atmosphere as people were elated by the day and we all fell about laughing when someone thought the man in Lester Lanin's band was the King of Tonga.'

The wedding came about ten weeks after Princess Anne had had a second baby on 15 May, and she had been baptised Zara Anne Elizabeth two days before the wedding. The Queen was delighted to have become a grandmother again.

When the Queen recorded her Christmas message from the terrace of Buckingham Palace that December, she spoke again of her happiness: 'Last July we had the joy of seeing our eldest son married amid scenes of great happiness, which made 1981 a very special year for us. The wonderful response the wedding evoked was very moving.' However, she did not dwell on the topic, but instead turned to the problems faced by disabled people and gave over much of her speech to this matter:

There had been a very different scene here in the garden at Buckingham Palace when three and a half thousand disabled people, with their families, came to tea with us ... The International Year of Disabled People has performed a very real service by focusing our attention on their problems. We have all become more aware of them and I'm sure that many of you, like myself, have been impressed by the courage they show.

The Queen went on to praise their courage and their perseverance, saying how their situation could inspire those facing the challenges of violence in Northern Ireland, unemployment or racism, before adding:

Perhaps the greatest contribution of the disabled is to give the inspiration and incentive to do more to help others. From this we can gain the strength to try to do that little bit extra, as individuals, as members of our families and as nations. We have seen in 1981 how many individuals have devoted themselves to trying to make life more tolerable for handicapped people, by giving loving care and by providing money and effort to improve facilities and to hasten research.

The Queen decided to put the garden party and disabled people at the centre of her speech, because at the time the event was hardly noticed by the media, as all they cared about that year was Charles and Diana. She believed that the important work done by the Royal Commonwealth Society for the Blind, which had helped restore sight to a million people, needed her public support, and the Christmas address was one time when she could be sure of the uninterrupted attention of her nation.

She had a difficult battle, as by November Diana was expecting a baby and the press frenzy peaked. The Queen was genuinely worried about Diana's ability to cope. She instructed her press secretary to invite all the Fleet Street editors to Buckingham Palace for a meeting and ask them to rein back. In an unprecedented move, she appealed to them personally, hid any animosity she might have felt towards the more intrusive papers, and addressed them in small groups. It worked, but not for long.

Soon there were more important issues at stake. In April 1982, Prime Minister Margaret Thatcher had announced Britain was at war with Argentina after they invaded the remote Falkland Islands in the South Atlantic in a dispute over sovereignty. A task force was sent to engage with the Argentine navy and air force to take back control of the islands by amphibious assault. Among the serving helicopter pilots on board HMS *Invincible* was the 22-year-old Prince Andrew.

The Queen was concerned, not only as head of state but as a mother. However, Buckingham Palace issued a statement confirming she had no doubts that her son should take part. Six days after the British forces had landed in the Falklands, she used the opportunity to express her feelings when she opened the Kielder Dam in Northumberland: 'Before I begin, I would like to say one thing, our thoughts today are with those who are in the South Atlantic and our prayers are for their success and safe return to their homes and loved ones.'

A few days later, President Ronald Reagan paid an official visit to Britain and confirmed America's backing for the United Kingdom over the Falklands. He was met at the airport by a reception committee, including the Duke of Edinburgh, Mrs Thatcher and foreign secretary Francis Pym, all of whom waited in a small white prefab, which was all Heathrow had as a VIP suite. The president and his wife were accompanied by Prince Philip from the steps of Air Force One to Marine One, a helicopter freighted in from the US especially for the visit, and flew off to Windsor, followed by two bigger military helicopters. It was an impressive show of American power, but considered by the Queen to be quite unnecessary. In similar circumstances she would have been far happier with a modest car and a couple of police outriders.

When they arrived, the president was invited to inspect a guard of honour – the First Battalion Grenadier Guards. It was not a state visit and therefore comparatively low-key; and, according to a rather amusing account of the day, one of the most enthusiastic people in the crowd outside the castle was a vagrant who sat on a bench roaring with laughter, singing 'I Feel Like a Million Dollars Today' and asking every sober passer-by if they were members of the CIA.

Before the president left he went riding with the Queen, who was irritated by the press presence and unfamiliar with the American way of treating the media as friends, and going over to talk to them. She eventually rode off and left him to it, but there was no bad feeling and that night a banquet was held in his honour in the magnificent beamed St George's Hall. The Queen spoke of drawing comfort 'from the understanding of our position shown by the American people'. It was the first time an American presidential couple had stayed at Windsor, and Ronald and Nancy Reagan let it be known how impressed they were and how 'charming' they found the British head of state. By 14 June, the Falklands were back under British control.

Just a week later, at 5am on Monday 21 June 1982, the Prince of Wales arrived at the side door of the Lindo Wing of St Mary's Hospital in Paddington with his wife, who was having contractions. Sixteen hours later, at 9.03pm, Diana gave birth to a son, who was second in line to the throne. 'I am very pleased that we have another heir,' the Queen told injured Falklands servicemen, with characteristic understatement. She was of course delighted and saw the birth as one of the few positive things in an otherwise difficult year. It was about to get much worse.

On 20 July, the IRA detonated twenty-five pounds of high explosive from a blue Austin car parked in the South Carriage Drive of Hyde Park just as the Household Cavalry Blues and Royals, the Queen's official bodyguard regiment, rode past. The soldiers were on their way from their Knightsbridge barracks to take part in the Changing of the Guard. The blast killed three soldiers and injured a further twenty-three, of whom one died three days later. But the horses took the worst of it, and seven were killed or so badly injured they had to be destroyed. One of the horses, Sefton, had an eight-hour operation and survived his thirty-four injuries to become a national icon and a symbol of the appalling tragedy. That night the watchman outside the Queen's door said he heard Her Majesty saying over and over again: 'The horses, the poor horses ...'

Two hours later, there was a second blast in Regent's Park underneath the bandstand where the regiment of the Royal Green Jackets were playing music from Lionel Bart's *Oliver!* to a crowd of over a hundred onlookers. Six more soldiers died there, with a seventh eventually succumbing to his injuries, while several of the spectators were also casualties.

Only two weeks before those double atrocities, there had been a much more personal threat to the Queen's security, one that raised even more questions than the incident the year before at Trooping the Colour. On 9 July, an intruder, Michael Fagan, overcame the supposedly foolproof security system of Buckingham Palace and broke into the Queen's bedroom. By unfortunate coincidence, the Queen's family were all out of London, the nightwatchman Sergeant Wren had just left his post and her page, Paul Whybrew, was taking the corgis for their morning walk. The Queen's first reaction on waking and seeing a man at the foot of her bed was that it must be a member of staff and she told him to get out.

Fagan has told many versions of the story, but suffice to say the Queen bravely kept him talking while she tried to summon security with the panic button, but there was no response. Eventually, her housemaid appeared and screamed with shock when she saw the intruder. The Queen, still in her nightdress, ran out of the bedroom while Fagan was lured into the page's pantry opposite, where her maid gave him a cigarette.

When Paul Whybrew returned with the dogs, the Queen signalled to him to go into the pantry, which he duly did, and plied Fagan with whisky until security arrived. The Queen claims she was not unnerved, as it was so surreal she didn't have time to be frightened. But she was very angry that such a thing could happen, although she has dined out on the story and imitated her maid's horrified reaction ever since. It was alarming that someone could scale a wall of the palace, get through an open window, walk along a couple of corridors and enter the Queen's bedroom undetected. Fagan's antics remain one of the most embarrassing breaches of royal security ever, and the atmosphere in the palace was one of complete shock and dread as to when the press would find out. Embarrassed by the lapse, home secretary Willie Whitelaw offered his resignation, but the Queen refused to accept it.

Throughout it all, the Queen was the one person to remain calm. Prince Philip, who had been sleeping next door, was more concerned that the world would know their sleeping arrangements, while the members of the royalty protection squad thought they would all be out of a job. Her summing up of it all showed that the Queen had clearly spent some time watching television with her younger children. 'It is just like *Camberwick Green*!' she said, referring to the popular programme where there were always disasters in the imaginary village.

In between those events, there was another story that had the potential to cause embarrassment. When the Queen went to hospital, ostensibly to have a wisdom tooth removed, it was conveniently at the same time as her long-serving police officer, Commander Michael Trestrail, of whom she had been very fond, had to resign. It was revealed that he had been conducting an affair with a male prostitute.

Where royalty is concerned, the show must go on and after the dramas and tragedies of July there was a happier event on 4 August. With her smile fixed firmly in place, the Queen attended the christening of the heir presumptive in the Music Room of Buckingham Palace. Because the Queen Mother was celebrating her eighty-second birthday that day, she too was the centre of attention. Diana resented this and later said she felt 'excluded totally', and little William Arthur Philip Louis, sensing his mother's mood, cried throughout.

The broadcast that Christmas commemorated the fiftieth anniversary of the first Christmas message. The theme was the sea, which was a subtle way of dealing with a year in which British troops had gone to war in the Falklands supported by the Royal Navy, which had been depleted as the government looked to reduce its military expenditure. It was also used to highlight the means by which the Commonwealth had been brought together:

> It is fifty years since the BBC External Service was started and my grandfather King George V made the first Christmas broadcast from Sandringham. Today I am speaking to you from the library at Windsor Castle, in a room which was once occupied by Queen Elizabeth I. This is my home, where for many years my family and I have celebrated Christmas ...
>
> Earlier this year in the South Atlantic the Royal Navy and the Merchant Navy enabled our sailors, soldiers and airmen to go to the rescue of the Falkland Islanders 8,000 miles across the ocean; and to reveal the professional skills and courage that could be called on in defence of basic freedoms.

Until 1974, Sandringham was always the roof under which the royal family gathered for the Christmas celebrations. But as more children were born to younger members of the royal family, the Norfolk house became just too small to accommodate the expanding family. Only Windsor Castle, with all its turrets, towers and hundreds of rooms, had sufficient space for everyone. Sandringham, one of the Queen's private residences, was bought for the Prince of Wales (later King Edward VII) in the nineteenth century for £220,000 from the revenues of the Duchy of Cornwall. It was then a very large house of 365 rooms, but the present Queen deemed it too expensive and impractical to maintain so many rooms and in the Seventies ordered 91 to be demolished. The family now occupy only a small part of the main building, which has comfortable but fairly cramped accommodation.

A royal Christmas has to have space for nannies, chefs, dressers, pages, footmen and valets, as the royal family always travel in the Edwardian style with all their creature comforts. Sandringham has its own resident domestic staff and when the Queen took the court to Windsor for the first time, the move caused great disappointment to the Sandringham retainers. But since the Queen dislikes change she worked out a compromise. She used to leave Buckingham Palace on 22 December for Christmas at Windsor and then, with her immediate family, move to Sandringham for New Year. When Windsor Castle was refurbished and rewired at the end of the Eighties, Sandringham once again became the only venue for Christmas and New Year. Despite talk of returning to Windsor Castle, it has remained so ever since.

In 1983, President Reagan returned the overwhelming hospitality he had received from the Queen at Windsor Castle with a little rustic California-style welcome of his own during the state visit to the United States. Unfortunately, the weather was so bad that when the royal couple reached the Reagan ranch, instead of riding over the range and looking at magnificent views on horseback, they had to stay inside by a roaring fire. The visit became known as the 'scuba tour', because of the incessant rain which threatened to wash the mountainsides away.

At least the Queen and Prince Philip had the royal yacht *Britannia* as their floating palace, and there was no better sight than to behold her tied to some foreign quayside 'dressed' in all her glory. The rough seas prevented the ship being used to her full potential, as the stabilisers were not very effective. In fact, the *El Niño* storm was guaranteed to make the royal yacht uncomfortable, and she was forced to remain at anchor at Long

Beach while the Queen and Prince Philip flew to San Francisco. But British to the end, *Britannia* still played host to a fantastic party for the Reagans.

During a state banquet in San Francisco, the Queen joked about the conditions they had had to put up with:

> I know before we came we had exported many of our traditions to the United States. But I had not realised before the weather was one of them. We have seen some magnificent technological achievements – the space shuttle, which has begun to turn the adventure of space exploration into the equally adventurous but more tangible reality of scheduled space travel; Silicon Valley, which has brought the world of yesterday's science fiction into today's home, office and classroom – and into Buckingham Palace. This image of the United States at the forefront of technical invention is one of which you are rightly proud.

Once again, she had highlighted her own excitement and interest in the latest scientific developments which were to become synonymous with Silicon Valley in the future.

During this visit the Queen also made stops at Palm Springs, Los Angeles, Sierra Madre, Santa Barbara, Sacramento, Stanford, Palo Alto, Yosemite and Seattle. In her address to the Los Angeles City Council, she officially thanked the American people for their support during the 1982 Falkland Islands war. The Queen reminded Los Angeles residents that her northward journey from San Diego paralleled a similar trip made 400 years previously by Sir Francis Drake who, she said, 'Unsuccessfully claimed this territory as Nova Albion for the first Queen Elizabeth and for the Queen's successors forever. I am happy, though, to give you an immediate assurance, Mr Mayor, that I have not come here to press the claim.'

At Christmas that year, the Queen returned to her theme of progress, inspired by the trip to Los Angeles, where she had seen the space shuttle *Columbia* and inspected an *Apollo* space capsule in which the astronauts travelled. Space travel has always fascinated her and she is an expert on the night sky and the constellations.

One of the tasks of that space shuttle was to launch an Indian telecommunications and weather satellite and last month I was able to see how this operated during our visit to an Earth Station in New Delhi ... All this astonishing and very rapid development has changed the lives of almost everyone ... But in spite of all the progress that has been made the greatest problem in the world today remains the gap between rich and poor countries ... What we want to see is still more modern technology being used by poorer countries to provide employment and to produce primary products and compo-nents, which will be bought in turn by the richer countries at competitive prices.

As a prediction for how the global economy would develop over the next generation, it was hard to beat.

The biggest changes that were occurring were, however, within the Queen's own family and their difficulties in adapting to the times. They were still expected to be royal and behave like royalty and at the same time be ordinary enough to have a drink in a pub. They were no longer cocooned, but exposed and indeed often overexposed. In an interview with the *Observer* newspaper, Prince Philip tried to explain what it was like living above 'the shop' at Buckingham Palace. 'We didn't choose this house we didn't build this house, we simply occupy it like a tortoise occupies a shell,' he said firmly. 'We go to State occasions all dressed up but we wouldn't dress up like that if the occasion were not a State occasion – the State occasions are part of the living theatre of the monarchy. People expect us to be all things to all men and to all kinds at all times.'

In September 1984, when the Queen was on her Balmoral break with the Duke and members of her family, the Princess of Wales gave birth to her second child. She had a difficult pregnancy; she was tired, overwrought and felt thoroughly miserable. She was not, she said, 'made for the production line'. The Queen had been aware for a while that her daughter-in-law was finding it difficult to adapt to the pressures of her royal role, but assumed she would eventually find her feet. And, to outward appearances at least, that is what Diana seemed to be doing. She carried on performing her royal duties until July, to the admiration of people she met. This was in marked contrast to the way things had happened during the Queen's pregnancies, when she had kept a low public profile. Diana's relaxed, informal approach in public gave a new dimension to the royal family, and her popularity at this time was unparalleled.

At 4.20pm on Saturday 15 September Diana gave birth to a boy. His name was announced from the steps of the Lindo Wing as Prince Henry Charles Albert David and he would be known as Harry. Four days before Christmas, he was christened in St George's Chapel, Windsor. Lord Snowdon, who took the official photographs after the ceremony, had an almost impossible task. William was trying to get all the attention and kept tugging at the ancient Honiton lace christening robe his brother was wearing and protesting loudly when he was not allowed to hold the baby. Snowdon's assistant recalled his spoilt behaviour: 'Every time he did something naughty they roared with laughter. No one admonished him and he was a thorough pest.'

The christening was shown in the Christmas broadcast that year, with rare footage of William chasing his cousin Zara Phillips round the legs of the Archbishop of Canterbury. In another sequence, Diana was seen trying to explain to William how many generations of royalty had worn the robe he had tried to tear to pieces. 'Great Granny was christened in it,' she said. Charles quickly interjected, 'And I was christened in it.' He was trying to cover up for his wife's mistake, for the great-granny in question was the Queen Mother who, like Diana, was an earl's daughter and therefore had not worn the regal robe at her christening. During her speech, the Queen said:

> The happy arrival of our fourth grandchild gave great cause for family celebrations. But for parents and grandparents, a birth is also a time for reflection on what the future holds for the baby and how they can best ensure its safety and happiness. To do that, I believe we must be prepared to learn as much from them as they do from us ... We must retain the child's readiness to forgive with which we are all born and which it is too easy to lose as we grow older. Without it, divisions between families, communities and nations remain unbridgeable. We owe it to our children and grandchildren to live up to the standards of behaviour and tolerance which we are so eager to teach them.

This period was to be one of the more challenging times in the Queen's reign. Between 1984 and 1985 the miners' strike was an almost daily item on the news, as the government of Margaret Thatcher tried to clamp down on union activity. It was portrayed by both sides as a battle for survival. It was also a period when the terrible famine in Ethiopia shocked everyone, following Michael Buerk's famous report on the situation in October 1984. In such an atmosphere, the Queen's speech in 1985 tried to soothe troubled waters:

> All this year we seem to have had nothing but bad news with a constant stream of reports of plane crashes, earthquakes, volcanic eruptions and famine – and as if natural disasters were not enough, we hear of riots, wars, acts of terrorism and generally of man's inhumanity to man. It used to be said that 'no news is good news' but today you might well think that 'good news is no news'. Yet there is a lot of good news and some wonderful things are going on in spite of the frightening headlines.

'They come from all walks of life,' she said, describing the people who are honoured at Buckingham Palace investitures. 'And they don't blow their own trumpets; so unless, like me, you are able to read citations describing what they have done, you could not begin to guess at some of the remarkable stories that lie behind their visits to the Palace.' It was the perfect message for such troubled times, all the more powerful because it showed how small local good deeds do get noticed at the highest level.

In the 1992 documentary *Elizabeth R*, the Queen would explain how she handles the brief chats allotted to each recipient: 'One mustn't have a long conversation, because you would never finish,' she explained. 'You hope you are going to get the answer you want, but it doesn't always happen. I am absolutely fascinated by the people that come – all the things they have done ... The system does discover people who do unsung things ... People need that sort of thing. It's a very dingy world otherwise.'

On 21 April 1986, the Queen marked her sixtieth birthday and the nation seemed genuinely delighted to share in her birthday celebrations. The Queen is surprisingly humble and unsure if her subjects want to partake in all the anniversaries she feels are put upon them. The *Fanfare for Elizabeth*, which was staged in honour of her birthday at the Royal Opera House in Covent Garden, and televised by ITN, was one such event. The audience, consisting of politicians, friends and every member of the Queen's immediate family, were specially invited and dressed in their evening finery. The Queen Mother wore yellow taffeta and lace; Princess Margaret wore coral silk and Princess Diana the Princess of Wales, a spotted, ruched dress of blue and red. The Queen wore Queen Mary's diamond tiara, long gloves, a white fur stole and a blue gown.

That morning there had been a service of thanksgiving in St George's Chapel, Windsor, attended by forty-four members of the royal family and Sarah Ferguson, Prince Andrew's fiancée, the daughter of Major Ronald Ferguson, friend and unofficial polo manager to both Prince Philip and later Prince Charles. Four-year-old Prince William was a last-minute addition and spent the service agog with excitement, bobbing up and down in the pew he shared with his parents. According to a member of staff, he was fascinated by how the horses pulling the carriage managed to trot and 'plop' all at the same time, and regaled anyone who would listen with his vocal rendition of that moment. Later that afternoon, the Queen returned to Buckingham Palace, where children from all over the country and the Commonwealth sang her a specially composed birthday song from the courtyard and plied her with bunches of daffodils.

In her Christmas speech that year, the Queen did not mention her historic visit to China, or even the banquet in the Great

Hall of the People in Peking, which had been one of her most high-profile trips. She obviously considered it too political and preferred to stick to talking about how important it was to care for children. However, on another occasion, she did say that the Hong Kong settlement of 1984 was largely responsible for 'the fact that, today, relations between the United Kingdom and the People's Republic of China are closer than they have ever been'.

The speech also made brief mention of the wedding of Prince Andrew and Sarah Ferguson on 23 July 1986. London is brought to life by the rites of passage of a royal wedding. The mood lightens and the spirits rise. There is a feeling of expectancy in the air and even die-hard republicans feel unexpectedly cheerful as they witness the ancient spectacle of the marriage of a monarch's son. The crowds had been gathering for two days, a trickle that became a stream that became a flood, and by nightfall of 22 July 100,000 people had been drawn into the heart of London.

On the wedding day, the Queen chose a particularly stunning outfit designed by her Hartnell-trained couturier, Ian Thomas. It had prompted a rare compliment from Prince Philip, who came into her dressing room during one of the fittings. According to Thomas, she had blushed with pleasure. She may not have felt quite so happy with Prince William's behaviour as a sailor-suited page at the wedding in Westminster Abbey. He jiggled and fiddled throughout the ceremony and the Queen kept glancing disapprovingly in his direction. She had been taught to sit still when she was far younger than the four-year-old Prince William – and to keep a straight back. As far as she could see, he had not yet been taught either, let alone any kind of discipline.

It was, however, an exceptionally happy day. The Queen liked her new daughter-in-law and was delighted with the match. The feeling was mutual and Sarah often spoke of their 'special bond'. They both loved horses, dogs, country life and, of course, Prince Andrew – and to this day the Queen keeps in touch with Fergie, as she had been dubbed by the press, despite some of the troubles she has been involved in. She prefers to remember the happier times and the wedding was certainly one of those. 'Even the horses in their stables seem to be aware that something quite special is happening – as they were on that happy day back in July when my son and daughter-in-law were married, and they drew the carriages through the cheerful crowds thronging the London streets,' she recalled in her Christmas message.

The speech was directed by David Attenborough for the first time and filmed in the Royal Mews at Buckingham Palace. The occasion was the annual carol service for the families of the coachmen, grooms and chauffeurs who live there. The Queen walked through the seventeenth-century state stables designed by John Nash, which today house the coaches, and chatted to the children as she went. She then read her message smoothly and professionally from the autocue set up between the two lines of tethered horses. She was clearly happy to be surrounded by horses and, as Attenborough's first attempt at filming there had resulted in one of the horses lifting their lip in distaste in the background, there was much laughter and they had to do a retake.

Just two days before Christmas, Buckingham Palace had announced that Her Majesty would no longer be riding side-saddle at the annual Trooping the Colour ceremony. Not because of security or a possibility of injury, but because her horse Burmese was retiring at the age of twenty-four. The Queen did not want to start again with a new horse. She would be sixty-one herself the following year and thought it more appropriate to travel by carriage instead. It was the end of a tradition she had enjoyed since she was Princess Elizabeth and had taken the salute for the first time in 1951 at the age of twenty-five.

After the family high point of the Duke and Duchess of York's wedding, the behaviour of the Queen's other children began to cause her some concern as the decade drew to an end. Prince Edward dropped out of the Royal Marines in January 1987, much to the horror of his siblings, who thought that after lengthy discussion they had persuaded him to stay and complete his training.

Instead, he began a career working in the theatre, and that summer he produced the charity TV show *It's a Royal Knockout*, in which members of his family, dressed in period costume, competed in a tournament with celebrities at Alton Towers theme park. It was undignified, loud and brash. To make things worse, Edward was in a truculent mood; he lost his temper and flounced out of the ensuing press conference. Although the various charities made money out of the broadcast, it was considered such a disaster that it is still talked of today as one of the greatest PR gaffes the royal family have made.

For the Queen and Prince Philip, who were celebrating their fortieth wedding anniversary, and the Queen Mother, who was about to celebrate her eighty-seventh birthday, it was a sorry state of affairs. The Queen Mother was incensed and told Andrew, Edward and Anne that she had spent years building the reputation of the monarchy with the King, only to have them try to destroy it in one evening. Her underlying fear was that everything her daughter had strived to build since the beginning of her reign by hard work and duty could so easily be erased by the behaviour of her own grandchildren and the over-vigilant press attentions they attracted.

As the Queen's confidant, the Right Reverend Michael Mann, former Dean of Windsor, explained: 'For the best reasons in the world, younger members of the royal family wanted to make the monarchy more approachable. I think the supreme example of that was when they all participated in *It's a Knockout*. It was making it a soap opera.'

It was not in the Queen's nature to become a participant in other people's troubles, especially those of her own children. She found it hard enough dealing with her own and, like her mother before her, preferred to overlook a problem rather than confront it, in the belief that if she ignored it long enough it would go away. But she listened: to Diana's tearful accounts of the state of her marriage; to Princess Anne's horror over love letters addressed to her bring stolen from Buckingham Palace and offered for sale; to Prince Charles's despair at Diana and his reunion with his old lover, Camilla Parker Bowles. The Queen, aware of the broader picture, did what she always did and counselled patience. She told Diana what she told her own children, 'Just wait and see what happens.'

In her Christmas speech the only reference she made to her personal troubles was when she mentioned it was pointless regretting the passage of time. 'Growing older is one of the facts of life, and has its own compensations,' she said. 'Experience should help us to take a more balanced view of events and be more understanding of the foibles of human nature.' She also spoke of the hundreds of letters she received every day from members of the public, not all of them kind. She explained they were sometimes 'full of frank advice for me and my family and some of them do not hesitate to be critical'.

She also added: 'It is only too easy for passionate loyalty to one's own country, race or religion, or even to one's favourite football club, to be corroded into intolerance, bigotry and ultimately into violence. We have witnessed some frightening examples of this in recent years.' It was a period when football hooliganism was a cause for particular concern to many in society, and doubtless had cropped up in some of those letters she had received.

On 8 August 1988, the Queen and Prince Philip were overjoyed when Sarah and Andrew had their first child – and their fifth grandchild. She was named Princess Beatrice after Queen Victoria's youngest daughter. The Queen was at Balmoral as usual at that time of year, but four days after the birth Sarah made the effort to travel to Scotland so the Queen and Philip could see the baby before Andrew returned to his ship in the Philippines.

That year was one of significant anniversaries: 400 years from the defeat of the Spanish Armada, 300 from the arrival of King William and Queen Mary in England in 1688, and 200 from the establishment of the colony of Australia. All were mentioned in her speech, and marked by various events during the year.

Having grandchildren of her own made the Queen more conscious of the kind of world that they would one day inherit. She used her final Christmas message of the eighties, delivered during a Save the Children Fund charity concert at the Royal Albert Hall, to send a special message to the children of the Commonwealth to respect and take care of the world.

The speech had been partly inspired by Prince Philip, who believed the government had been slow to move on the issue of pollution. On his advice, the Queen had ordered all cars in the Royal Mews to be run on lead-free petrol. To emphasise her support, the Queen had watched a display of 10,000 green balloons released from the mews to promote the use of lead-free petrol. When the Queen spoke from the podium on stage at the Royal Albert Hall in 1989 she felt confident she had 'done her bit':

Many of you will have heard of the greenhouse effect, and perhaps you've heard too about even more urgent problems caused by the pollution of our rivers and seas and the cutting down of the great forests. These problems don't affect just the countries where they are happening and they make neighbourly cooperation throughout the world a pressing necessity ... It is not too late to reduce the damage if we change attitudes and behaviour.

It would be splendid to think that in the last years of the twentieth century, Christ's message about loving our neighbours as ourselves might at last be heeded. If it is, they'll be good years for you to grow up in. If we can reduce selfishness and jealousy, dishonesty and injustice, the nineties can become a time of peace and tranquillity ... for children and grown-ups, and a time for working together for the benefit of our planet as a whole.

And, on that hopeful note, the Queen looked forward to the decade ahead, little realising that it was about to throw up some of the most serious challenges of her reign.

Chapter 7

THE DIANA YEARS

1992 is not a year on which I shall look back with undiluted pleasure. In the words of one of my more sympathetic correspondents, it has turned out to be an 'Annus Horribilis'.

SPEECH AT GUILDHALL,
LONDON, 24 NOVEMBER 1992

The years from 1990 to 1999 were the most exacting, difficult and draining of the Queen's reign. As soon as she had overcome one problem, another – seemingly more horrendous than the one before – replaced it. Nothing in her life had prepared the Queen for the troubles that overwhelmed her family in the years leading up to her annus horribilis in 1992. In the past, she had had to deal with bereavements, her sister's personal problems and her husband's alleged infidelities. Up until that year, she had sat in counsel with nine prime ministers and visited most of the world's countries. Over the span of forty years she had met nearly all the great leaders of the age – some good, many bad, a few utterly deranged – and handled them all with grace and finesse. In that time, she had shown herself to be a woman of will, determined to carry out her duties in her own way and according to her own beliefs. She had seen the influence of the monarchy eroded, but had steadfastly maintained her personal authority.

The 1990s saw some enormous changes for her, on every level. Three of the Queen's four children separated and subsequently divorced, while a fire devastated her beloved home, Windsor Castle. The popularity of the monarchy, the institution to which she had devoted her life, waned; despite the fact that Buckingham Palace was opened to the public and she began paying tax on her personal income for the first time. Above all, there was the media havoc wreaked by the popularity and eventual tragic death of Diana, Princess of Wales.

The period started with a financial overhaul, which included reforms on the way Buckingham Palace was run. Her Majesty's income and wealth were arousing great interest at the beginning of the 1990s, and one of Margaret Thatcher's last actions as prime minister was to put the civil list on a sounder footing, with the Queen agreeing to meet more of the costs out of her own income. In 1992, she volunteered to start paying income tax and capital gains tax, with some critical tabloids claiming she was saving as much as £256 million on income tax. The settlement was in the nick of time, as public and political opinion, already strained by reports of the extravagance of its younger members, had been losing sympathy with the royal family on the issue of money. The Queen was said by various publications to be the richest woman in the world, and it was claimed that shrewd investments had raised her untaxed income by 20 per cent in one year alone.

As always, the subject of royal finances was a confusing one. The palace pointed out for the umpteenth time that the Queen owning something did not necessarily mean that she could sell it and pocket the cash. To many ordinary taxpayers, the distinction between disposable wealth and being a custodian of so much property hardly mattered, but because of the behaviour of the younger members of the royal family it was brought sharply into focus. Many decided the House of Windsor was 'an expensive luxury', and in 1991 the issue became more prominent, partly because of the short-lived Gulf War.

The media said the royal family should be setting a better example at a time of national emergency and objected to photographs of Viscount Linley in drag at a party, 'Fergie spending £5 million on a house that's always empty' and Prince Andrew playing golf on 'sunny Spanish links'.

Following the invasion of Kuwait by Saddam Hussein's Iraq on 2 August 1990, the prospect of war became very real. For new prime minister John Major, who succeeded Margaret Thatcher in the autumn, it was an enormous initial challenge. Unsurprisingly, with war imminent, in her Christmas broadcast of 1990 the Queen paid tribute to the role of the armed services in the Arabian Gulf:

> The servicemen in the Gulf who are spending Christmas at their posts under this threat are much in our thoughts. And there are many others, at home and abroad, servicemen and civilians, who are away from their own firesides. Wherever they are, may they all, when their duty is done, soon be reunited with their families safe and sound.

She continued by giving a strong moral message, whether it was dealing with the ongoing problem of terrorism in Northern Ireland or dictators such as Saddam, drawing inspiration from the lessons learnt from the celebrations of the fiftieth anniversary of Dunkirk and the Battle of Britain that year:

Nowadays there are all too many causes that press their claims with a loud voice and a strong arm rather than with the language of reason. We must not allow ourselves to be too discouraged as we confront them.

In January, allied forces began the first Gulf War to reclaim Kuwait from Iraq in Operation Desert Storm, and within a few weeks the country was liberated, with forty-seven British troops killed in action. Later that year, the Queen was given the rare honour of addressing the United States Congress, in recognition of Britain's role in support of the US.

Meanwhile, the fall of the Berlin Wall in 1989 had initiated a series of changes across Eastern Europe, and in her speech in 1991, the Queen welcomed these moves in one of her more political Christmas addresses:

The 'Cold War' sustained an atmosphere of suspicion, anxiety and fear for many years. Then, quite suddenly, everything began to change, and the changes have happened with bewildering speed. In 1989 the Berlin Wall came down. Since then the rest of the world has watched, fascinated, as oppressive regimes have crumbled under popular pressure. One by one, these liberated peoples have taken the first hesitant, and sometimes painful, steps towards open and democratic societies. Naturally, we welcome this, and it may be that we can help them achieve their aims.

A few had predicted that the Queen would use her Christmas broadcast that year to declare her intention to step down in favour of her eldest son, as she had reached the age of sixty-five. It never happened, of course, but her message concluded on a serious note, stressing her own continuity in such a momentous period:

Next February will see the fortieth anniversary of my father's death and of my Accession. Over the years I have tried to follow my father's example and to serve you as best I can. You have given me, in return, your loyalty and your understanding, and for that I give you my heartfelt thanks. I feel the same obligation to you that I felt in 1952. With your prayers, and your help, and with the love and support of my family, I shall try to serve you in the years to come.

Because of the general sense of apathy surrounding the monarchy, the Queen decided that the fortieth anniversary of her accession, 6 February 1992, was to be suitably low key. She discouraged any festivities and a plan to erect a fountain in Parliament Square was dropped at her request. The milestone was marked, however, by a BBC documentary, *Elizabeth R*, which showed a relatively informal monarch at work in her various homes, preparing speeches, making official visits and with her family at Balmoral. The 110-minute film, produced and directed by Edward Mirzoeff, was extremely well received, and attracted a huge audience of 17.85 million, making it one of the most-watched programmes of the year, and when it was released on video, it sold extremely well.

However, by then, the year had already provided the first of its major problems. In January, the Queen was confronted by her favourite son Prince Andrew and his wife telling her that their marriage was all but over. The meeting was brief and painful and Sarah later wrote: 'She asked me to reconsider, to be strong and go forward.' To placate the Queen, the Yorks agreed to delay any final decision for six months. But this patchwork solution did not last, as later in January embarrassing photographs of the Duchess of York with Steve Wyatt, an American millionaire, were published, leading to a legal separation in March.

Princess Anne's separation from Mark Phillips was formalised and the couple divorced in April. In May, Sarah was seen to pack up and leave the marital home, Sunninghill, with her daughters Princesses Beatrice and Eugenie. But of far greater constitutional significance was the fact that the 'War of the Waleses' occupied many of the newspaper front pages.

In the current climate, with the success of the Duke and Duchess of Cambridge's marriage and the general upsurge in popularity of the royal family, it is hard to remember just how bad things were in the 1990s. There was no direct criticism of the Queen, but Charles and Diana's disintegrating relationship and the increasingly outlandish antics of the Duchess of York eroded the brand of royalty. When the Queen and the Duke of Edinburgh visited Australia in 1992, they received a lukewarm reception compared with earlier visits. Prince Philip, ever the keeper of family affairs, told Diana and Sarah (in the nicest possible terms to the former but rather more vehemently to the latter) that their behaviour was damaging the institution of the monarchy, which the Queen had strived her whole life to uphold.

According to Robert Lacey, author of *Royal: Her Majesty Queen Elizabeth II*, 'the turning point in the history of the modern monarchy occurred in a transport café in North Ruislip in the summer of 1991'. There, an old friend of Diana, Dr James Colhurst, told journalist Andrew Morton about her 'catalogue of marital grievances and proposed that this should form the basis of a book, which Morton would write with the covert assistance of Diana, alongside the on-record testimony of her family and friends, whom she would authorise to speak'.

On 7 June 1992, when the book was first serialised in the *Sunday Times*, no detail of the agony that was the Waleses' marriage was spared. The Queen, still clinging to the delusion that the situation could be salvaged, authorised her private secretary Robert Fellowes (who also happened to be Diana's brother-in-law) to speak to the Princess, so the palace could deny her complicity in the book.

Diana told him it was nothing to do with her, and Fellowes and the Queen believed her. But by midweek the truth was out, and Diana was proven to be an accomplice; Fellowes did the honourable thing and offered the Queen his resignation. She refused it on the grounds that it was her daughter-in-law and not her private secretary who was guilty of misleading her.

In most families this would have sparked an explosive bout of rows and recriminations and most likely an immediate end to the marriage, but the royal family is governed by its own needs and even at this juncture the Queen had the vain hope that, given time, the situation could be resolved.

Trooping the Colour took place on the Saturday after the first *Sunday Times* instalment, and Diana had to stand beside her mother-in-law on the balcony of Buckingham Place looking as if absolutely nothing were amiss. The following week she was at Royal Ascot with the rest of the royal family, but the tension was there for all to see. Prince Philip snubbed Diana in full view of everyone in the Royal Enclosure, but at least she was there. Fergie wasn't. She had been banished to social Siberia and made the cardinal error of embarrassing the Queen when, having not been invited to join the royal party, she stood with her daughters and watched the royal procession go past in Windsor Great Park on the way to the races. To make matters worse, she made Prince Andrew stand with her the next day and repeat the performance as a show of 'solidarity'.

The Prince and Princess of Wales had already had a summit meeting with the Queen and Prince Philip at which Charles's parents had tried in vain to explain how they understood the problems a marriage can go through. When the question of a separation was raised, the Queen insisted, as she had done with Princess Margaret when her marriage was collapsing, that they make yet another attempt to resolve their differences. It was the monarch talking, not the mother, but it only made the situation even more unpalatable.

Instinct suggested that the Waleses had long passed the point of reconciliation and should be allowed to go their separate ways. Yet even at such a late stage, this remained in the realms of the unthinkable for a sovereign whose throne rested on the foundation of a dutiful and – above all united – family. Unwilling to face up to the constitutional implications of a separation, the Queen instead ordered her favourite solution for Charles and Diana – a six-month cooling-off period.

If July provided a respite, August brought the Queen a double dose of trouble. Balmoral is Her Majesty's holiday home and, although the court is officially in Scotland and she works on her state boxes every day, the tranquillity of the Highlands allows the Queen some time to herself. She loves it. Nothing is allowed to disturb the peace of her Scottish break, but quite often something does. In this case it was photographs of a topless Duchess of York sunbathing beside a pool in the South of France, with her 'financial advisor' John Bryan kneeling at her feet, sucking her toes. The unfortunate Fergie, although separated from Prince Andrew, was staying at Balmoral with her daughters when the story broke in the *Daily Mirror*.

The Queen, Sarah recalled, was 'furious'. She did not scream or shout; that is not her way. Rather, she was cold and abrupt as she berated her daughter-in-law for exposing the monarchy to such ridicule. 'Her anger wounded me to the core,' Fergie said later, but for the sake of the children she was forced to spend three more humiliating days at Balmoral before returning to her rented home at Wentworth.

By the week's end it was Diana's turn to come under the lash – with far greater consequence to the royal family. In response to the *Daily Mirror*'s scoop, the *Sun* decided the time had come to publish the transcript of a three-year-old telephone conversation between the Princess and her friend James Gilbey. He called her 'Squidgy' constantly during the twenty-three-minute recording, which contained Diana's disparaging observations about the royal family and her husband.

In a tearful conversation, Diana tried to persuade the Queen that she was being set up and hinted darkly that she believed some of her mother-in-law's courtiers were conspiring to discredit her. The Queen dismissed this for the nonsense it was – her much-tried patience with Diana was running out, but she still clung to the hope that things might change and the marriage be salvaged. Prince Charles shared those hopes, and plans went ahead for the couple's scheduled trip to Korea in the autumn. It was, as many predicted, a disaster, as it became clear they were a couple who could no longer stand the sight of each other. The tensions in their relationship were compounded when, in November, the transcript of yet another illicit recording, the 'Camillagate' tape, was published. In this, the most sensational recorded conversation so far, the Prince of Wales spoke to his mistress touchingly and absurdly, and with reckless indiscretion.

If the Queen's subjects imagined that the royal family discussed these scandals openly, they were mistaken. That is not the royal way, although perhaps it should have been. Despite the fact that things were not comfortable at Balmoral that summer, Princess Margaret assured a friend that the Queen kept off the topic and the guests did not raise it.

'We all had to come down to breakfast anyway,' Princess Margaret said.

The Queen's children have described how difficult it is to get their mother to discuss anything unpalatable. Like the Queen Mother, she has always compartmentalised things and avoided moral confrontation. Had she been a different character, she might have tackled the problem of Charles and Diana far earlier and found a solution, but she was – and still is – wary of interfering in her children's private affairs. She was as surprised as anyone, for instance, when Princess Anne announced she was separating from Mark Phillips in 1989. By April 1992 they were divorced and, by the following December, Anne had married the Queen's former equerry, Tim Laurence, then a commander in the Royal Navy.

Although the Queen preferred to take a back seat as far as the private lives of her children were concerned, she was thrust into the drama between Charles and Diana. It was yet another row over their sons, who might perhaps have helped bring them together, which finally brought down the curtain on the Waleses' marriage. Back from Korea, Charles arranged a shooting weekend at Sandringham to coincide with William and Harry's exeat from Ludgrove, their prep school. Diana refused to go and informed Charles she was taking the boys to Windsor instead. Charles snapped and telephoned the Queen. When she again pleaded patience, he abandoned the training of a lifetime and shouted down the line at his mother. 'Don't you realise? She's mad, mad, and mad!' And he slammed the receiver down.

A state visit to Germany saw the Queen pelted with eggs when she toured Dresden, which had been heavily bombed during the war. But much worse was to follow when, on 20 November 1992, Windsor Castle was engulfed by flames. The fire was started by a restorer's lamp, which set a curtain alight. It quickly spread through the private chapel and devoured St George's Hall. Prince Andrew organised the rescue of many treasures, but great parts of the building itself were consumed by the blaze, with more than a hundred rooms damaged. A corner of Windsor Castle, the symbol of the monarchy for almost a thousand years, had all but been reduced to smouldering rubble. It was the Queen and the Duke of Edinburgh's forty-fifth wedding anniversary that day, but Philip was overseas at the time so missed the fire.

Four days later, the Queen was at Guildhall in the City of London for a luncheon to mark the fortieth anniversary of her accession. The occasion came just after John Major had announced she was going to pay tax on her private income, telling the House of Commons that the initiative had come from the monarch herself, the decision having been made the previous summer. In the circumstances of all that had happened that year, it was hardly the time for celebration as the Queen, with Philip back at her side, and in a voice hoarse with flu and emotion, made her famous 'Annus Horribilis' speech.

However horrible her year might have been, she managed to inject a note of levity when she said:

A well-meaning Bishop was obviously doing his best when he told Queen Victoria, 'Ma'am, we cannot pray too often, nor too fervently, for the Royal Family.' The Queen's reply was: 'Too fervently, no; too often, yes.' I, like Queen Victoria, have always been a believer in that old maxim 'moderation in all things'.

But perhaps the most significant part of the speech came in the Queen's recognition of the criticism that had been directed at her, and in her acknowledgement that the monarchy had to adapt to the changing circumstances:

There can be no doubt, of course, that criticism is good for people and institutions that are part of public life. No institution – City, Monarchy, whatever – should expect to be free from the scrutiny of those who give it their loyalty and support, not to mention those who don't.

But we are all part of the same fabric of our national society and that scrutiny, by one part of another, can be just as effective if it is made with a touch of gentleness, good humour and understanding. This sort of questioning can also act, and it should do so, as an effective engine for change.

There was even worse to come, as the Queen already knew. On 9 December 1992, the prime minister stood up in the House of Commons and made a statement. 'It is announced from Buckingham Palace that, with regret, the Prince and Princess of Wales have decided to separate,' he said. 'The decision has been reached amicably, and they will continue to participate fully in the upbringing of their children ... The Queen and the Duke of Edinburgh, though saddened, understand and sympathise with the difficulties which have led to this decision.'

The Queen was at Wood Farm on the Sandringham estate with only a handful of staff when the announcement was made. She did not watch John Major on television. Instead, she did what she often does when agitated: she took her corgis for a walk through her Norfolk estate. When she returned, a member of her staff said how sorry he was to hear the news. The Queen replied: 'I think you'll find it's all for the best.'

In her Christmas speech from Sandringham, the Queen spoke nostalgically of the past. But even that was not without some drama, as two days before it was broadcast, the *Sun* published the text. The Queen subsequently sued the paper for breach of copyright, and donated the damages she received to charity.

I first came here for Christmas as a grandchild. Nowadays, my grandchildren come here for the same family festival. To me this continuity is a great source of comfort in a world of change, tension and violence. The peace and tranquillity of the Norfolk countryside make me realise how fortunate we are, and all the more conscious of the trials and sorrows that so many people are suffering, both in this country and around the world.

Like many other families, we have lived through some difficult days this year. The prayers, understanding and sympathy given to us by so many of you, in good times and bad, have lent us great support and encouragement. It has touched me deeply that much of this has come from those of you who have troubles of your own.

As some of you have heard me observe, it has, indeed, been a sombre year.

The Queen recognised that 'there is no magic formula that will transform sorrow into happiness', but hoped that 1993 would bring better news. There was some progress, with an interim constitution agreed in South Africa that year, marking the beginning of the end of apartheid – an event noted in her 1993 Christmas broadcast.

But, if she was exhausted by the events of 1992, the next few years provided little respite from the fallout from Charles and Diana's separation. In the autumn of 1994, an authorised biography written by journalist and broadcaster Jonathan Dimbleby appeared, to mark the twenty-fifth anniversary of Charles's investiture as Prince of Wales. Its publication was preceded by a lengthy BBC interview with the Prince. The book aroused interest as it gave a full account of Charles's relationship with Camilla Parker Bowles, but more upsetting for the Queen were the details, albeit brief, of how Charles saw his relationship with his parents. The Queen was presented as cold; Prince Philip as a bully. To compound matters, the book was serialised in the *Sunday Times* at the same time as Her Majesty's historic first state visit to Russia as the guest of President Boris Yeltsin.

In spite of the trials and tribulations the Queen was enduring, she ploughed on stoically with a full programme of official duties. In 1994, together with other members of the royal family, she travelled to France for the fiftieth anniversary of the D-Day landings. In her 1994 Christmas broadcast, she said:

I shall never forget the events in Normandy last June, when the representatives of the wartime allies commemorated the fiftieth anniversary of the D-Day landings ... As Prince Philip and I stood watching the British veterans march past on the beach at Arromanches, my own memories of 1944 were stirred – of how it was to wait anxiously for news of friends and relations engaged in that massive and hazardous operation ... and of the gradual realisation that the war really was at last coming to an end.

Since those D-Day commemorations, Prince Philip and I have been to Russia. While we were in St Petersburg, we had the opportunity to honour the millions of patriotic Russians who died fighting the common enemy. To see British and Russian veterans standing together, in memory of the sacrifices of their comrades-in-arms, was a moving experience. I never thought it would be possible in my lifetime to join with the Patriarch of Moscow and his congregation in a service in that wonderful cathedral in the heart of the Moscow Kremlin.

The Queen was so concerned by the effect that Diana and Charles's media battle was having on the institution of the monarchy that she managed to convince herself that few would turn up at Buckingham Palace in May 1995 for the fiftieth anniversary of VE Day, the end of the Second World War in Europe. Throughout the early morning she kept looking out of the window, anxiously checking to see if anyone was there. But by the time she made her balcony appearance with the 94-year-old Queen Mother and Princess Margaret, the area in front of Buckingham Palace was packed with people.

'Her Majesty was thrilled,' a member of her staff revealed later. 'When she went on to the balcony she remained stony-faced for fear of showing too much emotion. She was actually close to tears.'

The commemorations seemed to revive the bond between monarchy and people. The sight of three elderly women, in contrasting colours, standing together as they had stood five decades earlier, was deeply affecting and the Queen was touched and reassured by the public response.

In many ways, the year provided plenty of good news. As well as the commemorations for the end of the war, there were encouraging signs that peace was finally coming to Northern Ireland; while a trip to South Africa, where the Queen met Nelson Mandela, showed how long-term disputes could be overcome if the right people stood up for change. Unsurprisingly, she chose to focus on this theme in her Christmas address: 'It is the ordinary men and women who, so often, have done more than anyone else to bring peace to troubled lands.'

But while these disputes all seemed to be coming to a positive resolution, there was one that wasn't. Despite her misgivings over her daughter-in-law, the Queen had continued to be accommodating with Diana. While Prince Philip raged, the Queen stuck to her guns and continued to insist that the Princess needed support, not condemnation. She knew Diana's glamour and hands-on charity work had won her international approval, but subsequent events proved too much even for the Queen.

Diana had been outraged by her husband's Dimbleby interview, which she saw as a riposte to the Morton book and, as such, a deliberate attempt to discredit her. In fact, Charles had been very careful not to voice any criticism of his wife. The accompanying biography, however, made it quite clear that many of the Prince's coterie regarded her as mentally unstable. It was a charge she was determined to refute, and to do that she too chose the medium of television.

In an hour-long interview broadcast on BBC *Panorama* on 20 November 1995, watched by the largest television audience the programme had ever had, with almost 22.8 million tuning in, she admitted adultery with James Hewitt, indicated she did not expect Charles to be King, and offered her elder son as an alternative. And she said she would like to be 'queen of people's hearts'.

On the night of the broadcast, the Queen attended the Royal Variety Performance; it was her forty-eighth wedding anniversary. In the days after the interview, which took everybody including the Queen by surprise, she consulted the prime minister, the Archbishop of Canterbury and senior royal staff. Then in December she made a pre-emptive strike – writing letters to both the Prince and Princess giving it as her own opinion, with her husband's support, that an early divorce was desirable. On 28 August 1996, Charles and Diana were finally divorced. The fairy tale that had become a gothic nightmare was almost at its end. Diana, Princess of Wales, as she was now to be known, had just one year and three days left to live.

The Queen, who had celebrated her seventieth birthday on 21 April 1996, carried on as before. She might have led a more solitary existence than in the past, as a number of her friends had 'gone to greener pastures', as the Queen Mother was fond of saying. Patrick Plunket had died in 1975 and Rupert Neville in 1982. In September 1993, Margaret 'Bobo' MacDonald – nursemaid at 145 Piccadilly and then royal dresser, companion, confidante and friend for sixty-seven years – died at the age of eighty-nine. However, her mother, one of the pillars of her life, had a successful hip operation in 1995 and seemed indestructible. When her husband was away, the Queen frequently dined alone, but the continuing domestic crises brought her closer to Princess Anne, and the two women were often seen walking together in the palace garden deep in conversation. For the first time, the Queen now began to listen to someone other than her husband on family matters and valued her daughter's forthright opinions.

In March 1996, they travelled together to Dunblane to visit the families of fifteen schoolchildren and their teacher who had been shot in a massacre. The Scottish press recorded the Queen weeping openly and turning to Princess Anne for support as she spoke to the parents of the victims. A few days later, the Queen and Prince Philip paid successful state visits to Poland and the Czech Republic.

Despite the problems that she faced during the first part of the decade, the Queen steadfastly got on with her job and put on a brave face to the outside world. In her Christmas address of 1996, she chose to give a personal memo of events as she had seen them throughout the year, such as the Maundy service at Norwich cathedral in March, Trooping the Colour in June and the State Opening of Parliament in October:

So, the past, with its traditions, has its lessons for us in 1996. And this year, in our travels, Prince Philip and I have also been looking to the future. I and all my family have always felt that one of our most important duties is to express, in our visits overseas, the goodwill of our country towards friends abroad, near and far ...

And I shall never forget the State Visit of President Mandela. The most gracious of men has shown us all how to accept the facts of the past without bitterness, how to see new opportunities as more important than old disputes and how to look forward with courage and optimism. His example is a continuing inspiration to the whole Commonwealth and to all those everywhere who work for peace and reconciliation.

This, I know, has been a difficult year for many families. Discord, sickness, bereavement, even tragedy have touched all too many lives. We recall, with sadness and bewilderment, the horror of Dunblane and Port Arthur [Tasmania, where thirty-five people were killed by a random gunman]. We watch anxiously as violence threatens again to disrupt the lives of the people of Northern Ireland.

In difficult times, it is tempting for all of us, especially those who suffer, to look back and say 'if only'. But to look back in that way is to look down a blind alley. Better to look forward and say 'if only'.

It was an important message from the Queen, after such a difficult period, especially in the aftermath of the divorce of Charles and Diana. Her point was that it is impossible to change what has happened; all that can be done is to take on the challenges and opportunities that lie in the future and do one's best.

As her words suggested, Nelson Mandela enjoyed a warm friendship with the Queen, flouting royal custom and addressing her by her first name. Throughout his life he always referred to Her Majesty as 'my dear friend Elizabeth'; their friendship was so close that protocol was cast aside. She returned the compliment, with letters to him signed off: 'Your sincere friend, Elizabeth R.' – it was truly a relationship based on mutual respect.

If the Queen had hoped that things would improve, 1997 would bring one of the biggest crises of her whole reign. At the beginning of August, Her Majesty boarded the soon-to-be decommissioned royal yacht *Britannia* for the last of the Western Isles cruises. With sixteen members of her family on board, she was looking forward to the cruise, followed by a peaceful two months in Scotland.

The court was in residence at Balmoral when the Queen's acting private secretary, Robin Janvrin, received a call from the British Embassy in Paris to say that Diana, Princess of Wales, had been involved in a car crash. He looked at his watch and saw it was shortly before 1am on Sunday 31 August. The severity of the accident was unclear at first, but Janvrin immediately informed the Queen and Prince Charles, who was also at Balmoral at the time with his sons. The Prince resolved to travel to France to be at her side, but as a flight was being arranged Janvrin took another call, this time informing him that the Princess was dead. It was 4am.

Upset though she was (her first reaction, according to someone who was with her at the time, had been that someone had 'greased the brakes' to get rid of the Princess), the Queen decided it should be business as usual and the whole family went to church at nearby Crathie that morning. William and Harry, who had been told of the tragedy by their father, agreed to go too. After that, the boys were kept completely out of the public eye so that they could mourn in private.

The funeral, the Queen said, should be a family affair at Windsor, followed by interment in the royal burial ground at Frogmore; Robert Fellowes agreed. The situation was, however, being wrested from her control, as the crowds of mourners who gathered in London as the days progressed were perilously close to turning into a mob. Repeating tabloid sentiments, they wanted to know why no flag was flying at half-mast from Buckingham Palace; why no royal tributes to the Princess had been forthcoming; and, above all else, why the royal family had chosen to remain in Scotland instead of returning to the capital to join in the nation's mourning.

The Queen, reflecting on her comments the previous Christmas, had focused on what was most important for the future: looking after the two young Princes. But this was not the way a large proportion of the public saw it. They believed the royal family was snubbing the death of a hugely popular figure, perhaps because she had stood up to the fusty old traditions of the monarchy and embarrassed the heir to the throne. To many, it had appeared as though the new prime minister, Tony Blair, had judged the mood of the nation far more accurately, but his approach was not one the Queen could adopt.

The Queen finally returned to London on 5 September, the eve of Diana's funeral. She was driven straight to Buckingham Palace where, with Prince Philip at her side, she left the safety of her car and went to mingle with the heaving throng gathered outside the flower-covered railings. Dressed in black, she walked down the line of mourners in total silence until an eleven-year-old girl handed her five red roses. 'Would you like me to place them for you?' asked the Queen.

'No, Your Majesty,' replied the girl. 'They are for you.'

'You could hear the crowd begin to clap,' recalled an aide. 'I remember thinking: "Gosh! It's all right."'

The Queen was more her usual self by the time she made a live television broadcast that evening. With the composure that comes from a lifetime's training, she addressed the nation 'as your Queen and as a grandmother', paying tribute to Diana, explaining the royal family's decision to stay in Scotland and promising a new beginning:

> She was an exceptional and gifted human being. In good times and bad, she never lost her capacity to smile and laugh, nor to inspire others with her warmth and kindness. I admired and respected her – for her energy and commitment to others, and especially for her devotion to her two boys. This week at Balmoral, we have all been trying to help William and Harry come to terms with the devastating loss that they and the rest of us have suffered ...
>
> I for one believe there are lessons to be drawn from her life and from the extraordinary and moving reaction to her death. I share in your determination to cherish her memory ... I hope that tomorrow we can all, wherever we are, join in expressing our grief at Diana's loss, and gratitude for her all-too-short life. It is a chance to show to the whole world the British nation united in grief and respect.

Some seven years later, at the opening of the Diana memorial fountain in London's Hyde Park, the Queen remembered Diana in rather more eloquent and emotional terms:

> It is sometimes difficult to believe that it is now nearly seven years since we heard the news that Diana, Princess of Wales, has been killed in a car crash in Paris. Certainly the days that followed are etched on my memory as we as a family and nation came to terms with the loss, united by an extraordinary

sense of shock, grief and sadness. By any standard Diana's tragic death held the attention of the world. Central to this remains the extraordinary effect Diana had on those around her. Her drive to empathise with those in difficulty, hardship or distress, her willingness to embrace a new cause, her shrewd ability to size up all those she met, allowed her not only to touch people's lives but to change them.

The funeral proved difficult for the Queen, as not only was she genuinely upset at the loss of Diana, but she was also obliged to sit opposite her godson, Earl Spencer, in Westminster Abbey while he articulated his extraordinary address with its veiled threats. He said he would do everything he could to make sure William and Harry's souls were 'not simply immersed by duty and tradition, but can sing openly as you [Diana] planned'.

The year ended on a happier note when the Queen and Prince Philip celebrated their golden wedding anniversary. This time, it was Prince Philip's turn to praise his family for their achievements, and he revealed the secret of his long and happy marriage when he said, 'You can take it from me, the Queen has the quality of tolerance in abundance.' Besides a service of thanksgiving at Westminster Abbey, a royal gala at the Festival Hall and a lunch at Guildhall, the Queen gave a dinner dance at the newly restored Windsor Castle.

Earlier on the day of their anniversary, Tony Blair hosted a 'people's banquet' at the Banqueting House in Whitehall, with a cross-section of people invited at the Queen's request. Recalling the changes in the last fifty years, the Queen said:

Think what we would have missed if we had never heard of the Beatles, or seen Margot Fonteyn dance; never have watched television, used a mobile phone or surfed the Net or, to be honest, listened to other people talking about surfing the Net. We would never have heard someone speak from the Moon; never have watched England win the World Cup or Red Rum three Grand Nationals. We would never have heard that Everest had been scaled, DNA unravelled, the Channel tunnel built, hip replacements become commonplace.

It was an eclectic and revealing personal list of key moments during that period. The Queen struck a more personal note when she added, 'Above all, we would have never known the joys of children and grandchildren.' She also paid a warm and touching tribute to Prince Philip. 'He is someone who doesn't take easily to compliments but he has, quite simply, been my strength and stay all these years, and I, his whole family, and this and many other countries, owe him a debt greater than he would ever claim or we shall ever know.'

There was also a fascinating passage in the speech where the Queen shared her thoughts on the different problems faced by monarchs and prime ministers. She reminded Tony Blair that he was 'born in the year of my Coronation', perhaps a subtle reminder of the depth of her experience, in contrast to the few months he had been in power, and added:

Each, in its different way, exists only with the support and consent of the people. That consent, or the lack of it, is expressed for you, Prime Minister, through the ballot box. It is a tough, even brutal, system but at least the message is a clear one for all to read. For us, a Royal Family, however, the message is often harder to read, obscured as it can be by deference, rhetoric or the conflicting currents of public opinion. But read it we must.

It appeared to be a frank acknowledgement that she had heard, and accepted, the criticisms that had come her way during the year, and that she had learnt from them.

That same evening, despite the grandeur of the setting, the party at Windsor Castle was said to be the most relaxed and informal gathering of European royalty that anyone could remember, which was exactly what the Queen had hoped for.

Sixty guests, including heads of state, kings, queens, princes and princesses, were invited to dinner in the State Dining Room. The younger members of the family had their own party at Ascot racecourse, then they all joined together back at the castle. The Queen Mother, who had been on her feet for most of the day, was finally driven home to Royal Lodge well after midnight, while the last of the revellers didn't leave until 3am.

In her Christmas broadcast she referred to the tragic events of August 1997 as well as her golden wedding anniversary:

At the Christian heart of this United Kingdom stands Westminster Abbey, and it was right that it provided the setting for two events this year – one of them almost unbearably sad, and one, for Prince Philip and me, tremendously happy.

Joy and sadness are part of all our lives … This interweaving of joy and woe has been very much brought home to me and my family during the last months. We all felt the shock and sorrow of Diana's death.

The speech also marked the continuing evolution of the nation and its old colonial past. That year had seen Hong Kong handed over to the Chinese, and the Queen commented on how 'we should be proud of the success of our partnership in Hong Kong and in how peacefully the old Empire has been laid to rest'. The Blair government had come to power offering devolution to Scotland and Wales, and both nations had voted in referendums to set up their own national assemblies, and the Queen responded to this by saying: 'Unity and diversity can go hand in hand. Recent developments at home ... should be seen in that light and as proof that the kingdom can still enjoy all the benefits of remaining united.'

Towards the end of 1998, the Queen faced an unprecedented outburst during her speech at the state opening of parliament. As the monarch outlined her government's plan to ban most hereditary peers from sitting in the House of Lords, she was interrupted by shouts of 'hear hear' from Labour MPs. It was a considerable act of discourtesy and the first time in living memory that the sovereign's address had been interrupted. The speech is the pinnacle of the unique constitutional relationship that exists between Crown and parliament and is traditionally heard in silence, as a mark of respect if nothing else. The royal family have made it clear they no longer expect people to bow or curtsey to them, unless they want to do so, but rude interruptions are strictly taboo.

In her Christmas speech of 1998, the Queen spoke of signposts in her life and the different generations giving advice to each other:

My mother has much to say to me. Indeed her vigour and enjoyment of life is a great example of how to close the so-called generation gap. She has an extraordinary capacity to bring happiness into other people's lives. And her own vitality and warmth is returned by those whom she meets ... But with age does come experience and that can be a virtue if it is sensibly used ... It is hard to believe that half a century has passed since our son Charles was christened and now, last month, he has celebrated his fiftieth birthday. It was a moment of great happiness and pride on our part in all he has achieved during the last three decades.

As the decade, and indeed the millennium, drew to a close, the increasing informality of her Labour government occupied Her Majesty's thoughts. At the end of 1999, she was obliged to hold hands (rather than the traditional linking of arms) with Tony Blair and sing 'Auld Lang Syne' at the Millennium Dome, which she had officially opened just before midnight. She understood that she had to move with the times, but some elements of what that entailed didn't come easily to her.

There was some happiness to end the distressing decade of the 1990s, however, when the Queen's youngest son, Prince Edward, married his long-term girlfriend Sophie Rhys-Jones on 19 June 1999 at St George's Chapel, Windsor. There were no grand processions: the late-afternoon ceremony was followed by a carriage drive through Windsor by the newlyweds and a reception in the state apartments. It was low-key for a royal wedding, compared to how each of Edward's elder siblings had celebrated their marriages, but it was considered fitting for the times. After all the challenges the royal family had faced in the 1990s, and with the modernising approach of Tony Blair's New Labour project, grand weddings seemed as though they had had their day. However, to many people's surprise, the dawning of the twenty-first century would not see a further erosion of the grandeur of the royal family. Instead, there would be a rebirth, as the stability of the monarchy came to be contrasted with the impermanence of politicians.

In her final Christmas broadcast of the millennium, filmed in the White Drawing Room at Windsor Castle, the Queen stressed the 'importance of history' when she said: 'We can make sense of the future – if we understand the lessons of the past. Winston Churchill, my first Prime Minister, said that "the further backward you look, the further forward you can see."'

Perhaps unsurprisingly, there was no mention of Diana in the Christmas broadcast, even though, two years after the event, Diana's dramatic end was still unresolved. That is one piece of the past the royal family would like to distance themselves from. The monarchy survived the abdication crisis of 1936 by retreating into itself and becoming worthy and dull. Diana gave it back its glamour – with dire results. She captured the imagination of millions, and in her brief, spectacular reign she swept away the preconceptions and expectations of what the royal family was like and how they really conducted themselves. By putting her marital unhappiness on to the national agenda, she called into question the relationship between the established Church of England and the Crown. By challenging the probity of the palace courtiers, and the civil service which serves the head of state, she cast doubt on the integrity of the monarchy itself.

The Queen, however, preferred to look forward again, staying true to her mantra that it was only the future that could be changed, not the past:

> This December we are looking back not just on one year, but on a hundred years and a thousand years. History is measured in centuries. More than ever we are aware of being a tiny part of the infinite sweep of time when we move from one century and one millennium to another.

Chapter 8

THE NEW MILLENNIUM

*For if a Jubilee becomes a moment to
define an age then for me we must speak of
change – its breadth and accelerating pace
over the years ... Change has become a
constant; managing it has become an
expanding discipline. The way we embrace
it defines our future.*

GOLDEN JUBILEE SPEECH, PALACE
OF WESTMINSTER, 30 APRIL 2002

In her final Christmas address of the last millennium, the
Queen had stressed the importance of history and the sheer
rate of change which seemed to be sweeping it away, along with
everything that was familiar and comforting. She was not simply
speaking for herself. Buckingham Palace stood in its pale magnificence in the heart of London, the enduring symbol of royal
authority. Windsor Castle, the family seat of royalty since the
reign of William the Conqueror a millennium ago, had been
restored to its ancient splendour after the fire. The aftershocks
following the death of Diana, which for one clamorous week

threatened to engulf the House of Windsor, had abated and the new millennium had dawned.

The Queen did not like many of the changes being forced upon her. She is constitutionally required to remain above politics, but it is no secret that she was apprehensive about much of what was being done by the Labour government which still, in theory, acted in her name. She disapproved of the abolition of the 700-year-old right of the hereditary peers to sit in the House of Lords, seeing it as a move against the hereditary principle in general. Although there was no call from the government for this principle to be extended to the monarchy, the Queen feared that the change could eventually lead to the palace gates.

She regarded the suggestion that the homeless should be housed in flats above Admiralty Arch as the kind of cheap-gesture politics of which Tony Blair was fond. She was irritated at the way he had been late for their traditional weekly meetings and on occasion even cancelled them, seeing it as a slight to her constitutional position. Sir Winston Churchill, who she often quoted, was one of her favourite prime ministers. Tony Blair was not. She found him obsequious and most distressingly out of touch with rural England and its inhabitants.

In his autobiography, *A Journey*, Blair describes the prime minister's traditional Balmoral weekend with the Queen in unenthusiastic terms: 'I found the experience of visiting and spending the weekend a vivid combination of the intriguing, the surreal and the utterly freaky,' he wrote. And then, as if he had never heard that royalty have staff, he condescendingly added: 'There are footmen – in fact very nice guys but still footmen.'

The account continued as follows: 'The blessing was the stiff drink you could get before dinner. Had it been a dry event, I don't believe I could have got through the weekend.' It was a highly disrespectful description from a man who was used to dealing with world leaders, dictators and tyrants. Traditionally, the prime minister's weekend at Balmoral was a three-day affair, with a formal dinner on Friday, a barbecue on Saturday – where the Queen does the washing-up afterwards – and a lunch after church on Sunday. More recently, prime ministers have arrived on Saturday in time for their private audience with the Queen, which is followed by a barbecue and then lunch after church on Sunday.

In March 2000, the Queen and Prince Philip set off for Australia, which had voted in their recent referendum to keep Her Majesty as their Queen and head of state. In a historic speech at Sydney Opera House, she confirmed Australia's constitutional future was entirely a matter for them:

I have always made it clear that the future of the monarchy in Australia is an issue for you, the Australian people, and you alone to decide by democratic and constitutional means. It should not be otherwise.

As I said at the time, I respect and accept the outcome of the referendum. In the light of the result last November, I shall continue faithfully to serve as Queen of Australia under the Constitution to the very best of my ability, as I have tried to do for these past forty-eight years ... That is my duty. It is also my privilege and my pleasure. I cannot forget that I was on my way to Australia when my father died. Since then and since I first stepped ashore here in Sydney in February 1954, I have felt part of this rugged, honest, creative land. I have shared in the joys and the sorrows, the challenges and the changes that have shaped this country's history over these past fifty years.

Back home that summer it was time for more celebrations. The invitation from the Master of the Household summoned 900 guests to Windsor Castle to celebrate the decades of Queen Elizabeth the Queen Mother; Princess Margaret, Countess of Snowdon; the Princess Royal and the Duke of York. The party lived up to its billing, but guests were left in little doubt that the real belle of the ball was the Queen Mother, who celebrated her one hundredth birthday on 4 August.

As she walked among the assembled throng on her way from dinner, without the aid of a wheelchair – she gave that to Princess Margaret, who was still suffering from having scalded her feet while getting into a bath – the guests parted like the Red Sea to let her through. Wearing diamonds and a mint green evening gown, she had a witty word for everyone she met and, despite having attended Trooping the Colour the previous weekend followed by the Garter ceremony and two full days' racing at Royal Ascot, she stayed at the party until 1.15am. For once she resisted the temptation to dance, but was serenaded by her old friend Lester Lanin's band, flown in from New York, and Graham Dalby and the Grahamophones, who played her favourites: 'A Nightingale Sang in Berkeley Square' and 'In the Mood'.

If the Queen Mother and Princess Margaret didn't dance, the Queen made up for them both. From the moment she and Prince Philip took to the dance floor in the Waterloo Chamber, she danced on and on, changing partners with each tune and eventually ending up with two partners at the same time. All three convulsed with giggles as the contents of someone's handbag spilled out over the floor. The party finished at 3am when the Queen and Prince Philip stood in a semi-formal receiving line as guests gave their grateful thanks for what they all agreed was a magical evening.

If that was a private event, the next one most definitely wasn't. A crowd of over 40,000 gathered outside Buckingham Palace to see the balcony appearance of the Queen, Princess Margaret and the Queen Mother to celebrate the latter's birthday. The Queen had delivered her mother a handwritten card instead of the customary telegram, which was opened with a suitable flourish by an equerry's sword. An occasion such as this did much to restore the popularity of the monarchy, after all the convulsions of the 1990s.

It had been a happy year and by the autumn the Queen was off again, this time on a state visit to Italy. It was her third and last meeting with Pope John Paul II, and as they parted the pontiff clasped her hand emotionally with a double handshake. Much to the Queen's delight, the Italians liked her sense of style, which was praised by the notoriously critical fashion writers who named her 'one of the most elegant women in the world'.

In her Christmas speech, the Queen reminded us of her own strong Christian beliefs:

> But as this year draws to a close I would like to reflect more directly and more personally on what lies behind all the celebrations of these past twelve months. Christmas is the traditional, if not the actual, birthday of a man who was destined to change the course of our history. And today we are celebrating the fact that Jesus Christ was born two thousand years ago; this is the true millennium anniversary.

The celebrations of the previous year almost eclipsed the Duke of Edinburgh's eightieth birthday in June 2001, which at his request was a much lower-key affair. For the first time during Royal Ascot the following week, there was no carriage procession for the two opening days, as the horses and carriages were needed for the State Opening of Parliament for Tony Blair's new government, following his convincing election victory.

But such domestic and formal considerations were shattered on 11 September – the day the terrorist group Al-Qaeda attacked the World Trade Center in New York. At the time, the Queen was at Balmoral on her extended Scottish sojourn. It was early afternoon when she received news of what had happened and, like millions of others around the world, followed the unfolding drama on television. Prince Philip was with her, but Prince Charles was already down south preparing for a series of official engagements.

The Queen was quick to react and expressed her 'growing disbelief and total shock' at what she saw. The American national anthem was played at Buckingham Palace for the Changing the Guard ceremony and traffic in the Mall came to a standstill as a tribute. Three days after the attacks, the Queen attended a sombre service at St Paul's Cathedral. On the advice of the prime ministers of Australia and New Zealand, she decided to postpone her tour of both those countries.

In the same week, her childhood friend and racing manager, Lord Carnarvon, died from a heart attack and she attended his funeral at his family estate, Highclere, the setting for the TV series *Downton Abbey*.

Unsurprisingly, the Queen dealt with the 9/11 attacks in her Christmas speech, but she did not forget another crisis closer to home. That year had seen much of the countryside closed off following an outbreak of foot and mouth. A countrywoman to her core, she made sure that she addressed the topic in her speech, showing that the rural community had not been forgotten by her:

This country has not been spared, with the floods this time last year, and foot and mouth, which has had such devastating consequences for our farmers and rural communities. They and others whose livelihoods have been affected continue to suffer hardship and anxiety long after the newspaper headlines have moved on.

The Queen also struck a fresh note when she said: 'We all have something to learn from one another, whatever our faith ... whatever our background, whether we be young or old, from town or countryside.' She had not previously highlighted the difference between town and country, but it was one that was increasingly felt in rural areas, where people believed the government did not even try to understand their ways. Another traditional country pursuit, fox hunting, was under threat at the time, and this added to the sense of persecution felt by many.

By the end of the year, it was becoming clear that two of her closest family members were ailing. The Queen Mother was able to come to Sandringham for Christmas, despite a broken collarbone, but the 71-year-old Princess Margaret was too frail to travel. She remained bedridden at her Kensington Palace home, having suffered a series of strokes.

The year 2002 was meant to be a special one as the Queen celebrated her eagerly anticipated Golden Jubilee, but unfortunately it got off to the most tragic start. Early in the morning of Saturday 9 February, a notice was hung on the railings of Buckingham Palace. Its content was stark: 'The Queen, with great sadness, has asked for the following announcement to be made immediately. Her beloved sister Princess Margaret died peacefully in her sleep this morning at 6.30am in the King Edward VII hospital. Her children Lord Linley and Lady Sarah Chatto were at her side. Princess Margaret suffered a further stroke yesterday afternoon. She developed cardiac problems during the night and was taken from Kensington Palace to the King Edward VII Hospital at 2.30am. Lord Linley and Lady Sarah were with her, and the Queen was kept fully informed throughout the night. Queen Elizabeth the Queen Mother and other members of the royal family are being informed.'

The Queen had just returned to London from Sandringham the previous afternoon and had to break the sad news to the Queen Mother by telephone. She was not well enough to travel having had another fall. Later she flew to Royal Lodge by helicopter. On Friday 15 February, exactly fifty years to the day since George VI's funeral in the same place, the family gathered at St George's Chapel for the private service, after which the Princess's body was cremated according to her wishes.

Seven weeks later, at 5.45pm on Saturday 30 March – Easter weekend – the palace announced that the Queen Mother had died peacefully at Royal Lodge that afternoon with her daughter by her side. The Queen had been out riding in the grounds of Windsor Castle when she was informed of her mother's worsening condition. Still dressed in a blue riding jacket and headscarf, she was driven straight to Royal Lodge where her cousin Margaret Rhodes, her mother's personal chaplain, Canon John Ovenden, and her loyal dresser Jackie, plus two doctors, were all in attendance.

In his Easter Sunday sermon, the Archbishop of Canterbury, Dr George Carey, said: 'Our thoughts and prayers this morning are with the entire royal family, but especially with the Queen, who has lost first a sister and now a much-loved parent in a matter of weeks.'

In accordance with her wishes, Queen Elizabeth's coffin was carried to her personal place of worship, the Royal Chapel of All Saints in Windsor Great Park, where the royal family gathered for a private evensong service. It was then taken to the Queen's Chapel at St James's Palace in central London before being carried in a ceremonial procession to Westminster Hall, where she lay in state for three days, as befitting a Queen Empress. Over 200,000 people filed past her coffin before her funeral on 9 April. The numbers caught everyone by surprise: people knew how popular the Queen Mother was, but no one had anticipated this sort of response.

Speaking from Windsor Castle on the eve of the funeral, the Queen urged the public not just to mourn her mother, but to celebrate her life. The Queen's address was filmed in front of a window with the picturesque backdrop of the Long Walk, which was originally planted in the time of King Charles II.

Ever since my beloved mother died over a week ago, I have been deeply moved by the outpouring of affection which has accompanied her death.

My family and I always knew what she meant for the people of this country and the special place she occupied in the hearts of so many here, in the Commonwealth and in other parts of the world. But the extent of the tribute that huge numbers of you have paid my mother in the last few days has been overwhelming. I have drawn great comfort from so many individual acts of kindness and respect.

Over the years I have met many people who have had to cope with family loss, sometimes in the most tragic of circumstances. So I count myself fortunate that my mother was blessed with a long and happy life. She had an infectious zest for living, and this remained with her until the very end. I know too that her faith was always a great strength to her.

At the ceremony tomorrow I hope that sadness will blend with a wider sense of thanksgiving, not just for her life but for the times in which she lived – a century for this country and the Commonwealth not without its trials and sorrows, but also one of extraordinary progress, full of examples of courage and service as well as fun and laughter. This is what my mother would have understood, because it was the warmth and affection of people everywhere which inspired her resolve, dedication and enthusiasm for life.

I thank you for the support you are giving me and my family as we come to terms with her death and the void she has left in our midst. I thank you also from my heart for the love you gave her during her life and the honour you now give her in death.

After the sadness of losing both her mother and sister within two months of each other, the Queen still had her Golden Jubilee tour to undertake in celebration of the fiftieth anniversary of her accession. There was no escaping the number of speeches and addresses she was going to have to give – she was used to them – but from April, when she addressed both Houses of Parliament, until the end of the year she had over two dozen to deliver.

'It is right that the first major event to mark my Golden Jubilee this summer is here in the Palace of Westminster,' she read as she addressed both Houses on 30 April, embracing one of her favourite issues, that of change, and mentioning 'the dark threat of terrorism' that was to define the remaining years of her reign.

'For if a Jubilee becomes a moment to define an age, then for me we must speak of change – its breadth and accelerating pace over the years ... Change has become a constant; managing it has become an expanding discipline. The way we embrace it defines our future.'

The Golden Jubilee weekend culminated in two public

concerts held in the gardens of Buckingham Palace, and on 4
June the Queen rode to St Paul's Cathedral in the Gold State
Coach for a service of thanksgiving. During lunch at Guildhall,
the Queen made a speech thanking the nation for their support
throughout her reign.

> Although this weekend comes halfway through my Jubilee
> year, as far as we are concerned, it bears no relation to a rest
> at 'half time' ... It has been a pretty remarkable fifty years by
> any standards ... I take this opportunity to mention the
> strength I draw from my own family. The Duke of Edinburgh
> has made an invaluable contribution to my life over these
> past fifty years ... I want to express my admiration for the
> Prince of Wales and for all he has achieved for this country.

It was not the first time she had praised her 54-year-old son,
but it was the first time since the years of drama with Diana and
was significant because of this if nothing else.

Although the speech was largely a matter of giving thanks,
there was one intriguing passage where the Queen raised a point
that was clearly important to her to emphasise, given the growing concerns at the breakdown of neighbourly behaviour:

> At every stage along the way, Prince Philip and I have been
> overwhelmed by the crowds waiting for us and deeply moved
> by the warmth of their welcome ... I am quite convinced that
> these local celebrations have helped to remind people of the
> value of such neighbourhood events in building a genuine
> community spirit.

The culmination of four days of unprecedented celebration
came when a crowd of more than a million roared their

appreciation to the tiny figure in vivid coral that appeared on the Buckingham Palace balcony later that day. Three times the roar brought the Queen and Prince Philip back, as the huge mass of spectators serenaded her with 'Land of Hope and Glory'. It appeared to be all over, but as the crowds were fighting their way up Constitution Hill, the band started playing 'God Save the Queen' and they turned and started running back. It was over, but not for the Queen, who still had many more places to visit on her jubilee tour before the official celebrations came to an end. After the low point just five years earlier, it was an occasion that showed not only the enduring strength of the monarchy, but the huge personal popularity of the Queen.

The routine business of her life continued and, helped by Prince Philip's support and jocular chiding which kept up her spirits, they travelled around the United Kingdom. In July, they paid a visit to the industrial West Midlands, and the Queen made a speech at the opening of Millennium Point in Birmingham where she spoke of the nuts and bolts of Britain's Industrial Revolution. She went on to say: 'Tomorrow, in contrast, we will visit the Royal Show, which is the largest outdoor rural business event of its kind in the world. Prince Philip will also sample what can safely be described as a distinctive flavour of the region at the Marmite factory, which is celebrating its centenary.'

One of the Queen's favourite moments came when they visited the National Space Centre in Leicester towards the end of their tour of the UK in August. The centre is a tourist attraction, but also houses experts and a full space communications team, which interested the Queen as she has long been fascinated by the planets, astronomy and space travel, subjects that have frequently cropped up in her speeches. 'Over this summer I have travelled widely,' she said in her address, 'but I hope

I will be forgiven for having limited my tour to the earth's surface.'

After the euphoria of the jubilee and an extremely welcome summer sojourn for the Queen and Prince Philip at Balmoral, the trial of the late Diana, Princess of Wales's butler Paul Burrell heralded the beginning of the autumn troubles. The court case, which started on 14 October at London's Old Bailey, was unpleasant for the royal family, as it threatened to reveal intimate details of their private lives and once again raised the ghost of Diana.

The Queen was in Canada when the trial began. Paul Burrell had once been her own personal page, and during the years he worked at Buckingham Palace the Queen had grown fond of him. He eventually left the palace to join the staff of the Prince and Princess of Wales at Highgrove, where he was equally popular. Burrell stood accused of stealing over 300 personal effects from Kensington Palace on or before June 1998. Six of them were allegedly stolen from Prince Charles, twenty-one from Prince William and 315 from Princess Diana, for whom he was working. Among the items were photographs, private letters, photograph albums, personal belongings such as handbags and designer clothes, CDs, a ceremonial sword, and a notepad with details of landmine victims in Diana's hand. Burrell, who worked for Diana for ten years until her death, was first arrested in January 2001 as part of a police inquiry that lasted over a year. The royal family have always had close relationships with their staff and Diana was no exception. After her divorce, she relied on Burrell to look after her and he was privy to many of her closest secrets.

Even though the Queen treats her personal staff like an extended family, listening to their problems and caring for their welfare, she cannot afford to get involved in their scandals and never has. Royal staff are frequently the recipients of cast-off gifts – but the fact that Burrell's case was heard in the Old Bailey, the scene of many a murder trial, meant the police had decided to take the charges against him extremely seriously. The trial went on creating a sensation every day until suddenly it was halted when the Queen remembered she had met with Burrell, at his request, in the weeks after the death of Diana five years previously. She had spent over an hour listening to him, during which time he had told her he was looking after some of Diana's papers for safekeeping.

The significance of the Queen's shock information was said to have struck her after she had returned from Canada, where she had been travelling as part of her jubilee tour when the trial began. She mentioned to Prince Philip and Prince Charles that she recalled the meeting as all three of them shared a royal limousine on the way to St Paul's Cathedral – close to the Old Bailey – for a memorial service for the victims of the Bali nightclub bombings, which killed 202 people, including eighty-eight Australians and twenty-seven Britons, in Kuta, a popular tourist spot on the Indonesian island.

Believing his mother's information was relevant to the trial, the Prince swiftly alerted his private secretary, Sir Michael Peat, who in turn instructed royal lawyer Fiona Shackleton to inform the police. The eleventh-hour intervention came at a critical point in the trial, which was scheduled to last six weeks. Burrell was on the verge of giving evidence and was expected to spend about two days in the witness box, explaining why he had kept so many items in the loft, study, living room and under the stairs of his Cheshire house. Burrell was fighting for his life as a free man and would have certainly had to divulge embarrassing personal information that members of the royal family, and Prince Charles in particular, would have loathed to be on public record.

The Queen's speech through the years.

1987, the year of her fortieth wedding anniversary.

1998, when she commended the work of the Queen Mother and Prince Charles.

2012, a spectacular year, highlighted by her Diamond Jubilee and the London Olympics.

Certain themes crop up regularly in the Queen's Christmas speeches, especially her faith, the Commonwealth, and the role of women in society.

The Queen leaves the church at Sandringham on Christmas Day 2014.

PA

Visiting South Africa during a Commonwealth Heads of Government Meeting in 1999.

Getty

Getty

Awarding an honorary damehood to Angelina Jolie in October 2014 for her global charity work.

Other interests of the Queen are less regularly referenced.

The Queen is presented with the trophy by Prince Andrew after her horse Estimate won the Gold Cup at Royal Ascot in 2013.

The Queen has always been very hands-on when it comes to looking after her corgis.

Princess Anne and the Countess of Wessex join the Queen as she marks the centenary of the WI at the Royal Albert Hall in June 2015.

Nelson Mandela on a state visit to the UK in 1996. She described him as 'the most gracious of men'.

Michelle Obama and the Queen share a quiet moment during President Obama's state visit in 2009.

Pope Benedict XVI was received by the Queen at the Palace of Holyroodhouse during the first ever state visit of a pontiff.

The Queen meets Sir Peter Cosgrove, the new governor general of Australia, at Balmoral in 2014.

A symbolic moment as the Queen greets Ireland's president Mary McAleese in May 2011 – it was the first visit to Ireland by a British monarch in a hundred years.

The Queen and Prince Philip survey the mass of flowers piled up outside Buckingham Palace after the death of Diana, Princess of Wales in 1997.

The Queen leaves hospital after having an operation on her torn knee cartilage in 2003. She continues to enjoy excellent health for her age.

Family matters. (Above left) The Duchess of Cambridge with the Queen in Leicester at the start of the nationwide Diamond Jubilee tour. (Above right) The Queen and Camilla enjoy the Royal Windsor Horse Show in May 2015. (Left) Prince Harry can't keep a straight face during the Sovereign's Parade at Sandhurst in 2006. (Below right) The next three generations join the Queen on the balcony at Buckingham Palace after Trooping the Colour in June 2015.

Her Majesty and her constant companion Prince Philip who she described as her 'strength and stay all these years'.

At the end of that year, the Queen delivered an especially heartfelt and personal Christmas message:

> As I look back over these past twelve months, I know that it has been about as full a year as I can remember … Many of you will know only too well from your own experience the grief that follows the death of a much-loved mother or sister. Mine were very much part of my life and always gave me their support and encouragement …
>
> Our modern world places such heavy demands on our time and attention that the need to remember our responsibilities to others is greater than ever. It is often difficult to keep this sense of perspective through the ups and downs of everyday life – as this year has constantly reminded me.

The Queen must have been more stressed than she realised, as she slipped and strained a knee ligament while on a private visit to stables in Newmarket. This meant she had to use a walking stick and was not able to take her usual morning ride. After the New Year, she was admitted to hospital for what was described as routine keyhole surgery on her right knee. A mere twenty-four hours later she left hospital and returned to Sandringham. She enjoys remarkable health and it was only the second time in twenty-one years that she had to have an overnight stay in hospital.

As head of the armed forces of the United Kingdom, the Queen has always taken an active and protective interest in those deployed overseas at times of war. During her reign, she has seen methods of warfare change and the number of her armed forces dramatically reduced – when she ascended to the throne, national service was still in operation. The Queen is unable to interfere on the question of defence spending and the amalgamation of so many of her regiments, but she can offer support. Even in the technological age, people look to the Queen for moral guidance, as she is above politics and has no need to engender personal popularity as a prime minister does. So when Britain joined the United States and invaded Iraq in the early hours of 20 March 2003 to topple the tyrant Saddam Hussein, the Queen issued the following statement from Buckingham Palace:

> At this difficult moment in our nation's history, I would like to express my pride in you, the British service and civilian personnel deployed in the Gulf and in the vital supporting roles in this country and further afield. I have every confidence in your professionalism and commitment as you face the challenges before you. Especially for those of you now waiting to go into action, may your mission be swift and decisive, your courage steady and true, and your conduct in the highest traditions of your service both in waging war and bringing peace.
>
> My thoughts are with you all, and with your families and friends who wait at home for news and pray for your safe return.

For the first time in her life, the Queen was managing the sensitive issue of a potentially long-drawn-out foreign war in a country alleged to be harbouring weapons of mass destruction. She was without the comforting presence of her mother or sister to advise her, and was dealing with a prime minister with whom she had little in common, but she was too well trained to let any personal feelings show. By 9 April, the Iraqi capital Baghdad had been taken by American forces. On 1 May, President George W. Bush made his famous speech claiming 'mission accomplished', though it wasn't until 13 December that the Iraqi leader Saddam Hussein was finally captured. Even when that had been achieved, allied forces would remain in the country for years to come, at the cost of many lives.

Contentious though the action was, the Queen had to be guided by her prime minister and, when President Bush visited London for a state visit that November, the Queen kept clear of controversy by using historical reference in her official address and steering away from the current situation:

Visits by American Presidents have been memorable landmarks in my reign. Unlike in the United States, the British Head of State is not limited to two terms of four years, and I have welcomed no fewer than seven of your predecessors. The first US President to stay in Buckingham Palace was Woodrow Wilson, in December 1918. America had then been fighting alongside us in the First World War and was to do so again in our hour of need during the Second World War.

Sixty years ago, Winston Churchill coined the term 'Special Relationship' to describe the close collaboration between the United Kingdom and United States forces that was instrumental in freeing Europe from tyranny. Despite occasional criticism of the term, I believe it admirably describes our friendship ...

In this twenty-first century we face together many unforeseen and formidable challenges. The leadership you showed in the aftermath of the terrible events of 11 September 2001 won the admiration of everyone in the United Kingdom. You led the response to an unprovoked terrorist attack which was on a scale never seen before ...

The end of supersonic travel by Concorde may mean that

for some it takes longer to cross the Atlantic, but in the case of the United States and the United Kingdom, the two sides of the ocean have never been closer.

Apart from the safe, if sudden, arrival of her seventh grand-child, Lady Louise Windsor, the daughter of the Earl and Countess of Wessex, the Queen seemed to have nothing but trouble to contend with during 2003. The final straw was the discovery that the *Daily Mirror* newspaper had infiltrated the palace, with one of their reporters, Ryan Parry, posing as a footman. Not only did Parry work there for two months, but he also took dozens of photographs of private areas of Buckingham Palace and Windsor Castle.

The *Mirror* chose to publish these on the first two days of President Bush's state visit, under the guise of a security scandal, and devoted fifteen pages to the story on the first day. For two days, the second of which was the Queen's fifty-sixth wedding anniversary, the royal family were humiliated by a succession of personal photographs, including pictures that Parry was able to take of the Presidential Suite, the Queen's breakfast table, the Duke of York's room and the Earl and Countess of Wessex's bedroom. The Queen was eventually able to bring a successful injunction against the paper to prevent any further publication or selling of photographs.

From the nation's point of view, the Queen came across in the newspaper article and pictures as a surprisingly ordinary woman. She obviously didn't believe in interior decoration, used an old-fashioned electric bar heater, had a transistor radio on the breakfast table – where the cereal was kept in Tupperware boxes – and liked a gin and Dubonnet at the end of the day. It was revealed that Her Majesty, like millions of her subjects, ate her supper off a tray while watching the television soap

EastEnders, and, like many husbands, Prince Philip apparently took great delight in frightening his wife's dogs.

There were no state secrets revealed, but that was clearly not the point of the story. What the newspaper did was expose the lack of security immediately around the Queen, when she was in the process of entertaining an American president who had more security than most other world leaders. Parry later claimed that no serious security checks were made on him and revealed that the palace accepted a character reference from a regular in a pub in South Wales where he had briefly worked as a bar manager.

A simple internet search would have shown Parry's name and picture next to a *Mirror* investigation he carried out into security at Wimbledon tennis. It was a prime example of how newspaper editors enjoy exposing the inefficiencies of the British system, in this instance the security at Buckingham Palace. It was not intended as a slight against the Queen or her family, but of course it sold newspapers, and to this day the thought of plastic Tupperware boxes conjures up an image of the Queen's breakfast table.

As if the year had not been troublesome enough, when the family arrived for the traditional Christmas gathering there was a fight of a different kind, which was equally if not more distressing for the Queen. When Princess Anne arrived at Sandringham on Christmas Eve with her three bull terriers in tow, there was an immediate fracas with the Queen's pack of dogs. One of the corgis, an elderly dog named Pharos, was so badly bitten by Anne's terrier Florence that he had to be put down the following day. As if confirmation were needed that she was the worst kind of doggy houseguest, a few days later Florence bit the housemaid who came in to clean the Princess's rooms. Florence was sent off to receive therapy from dog whisperer Roger Mugford, who has treated the Queen's dogs before, when her pack of corgis and the cross-breed dorgis (dachshund x corgi) had a fight in which one of them was killed.

But such domestic concerns were far from the Queen's mind when she gave her Christmas message from the Household Cavalry Barracks in Windsor, in which the theme of the armed forces was very much at the heart of it all:

> I want to draw attention to the many Servicemen and women who are stationed far from home this Christmas. I am thinking about their wives and children, and about their parents and friends. Separation at this time is especially hard to bear. It is not just a matter of separation. The men and women of the Services continue to face serious risks and dangers as they carry out their duties. They have done this brilliantly. I think we all have very good reasons for feeling proud of their achievements – both in war, and as they help to build a lasting peace, in troublespots across the globe.

In April 2004, things were more cheerful and, after the Queen celebrated her seventy-eighth birthday, she paid a three-day state visit to France to mark the centenary of the Entente Cordiale, a historic treaty by which the French and English made a defensive alliance to counter the threat then posed by Germany.

The two European neighbours had often been in conflict throughout history, from the Battle of Hastings in 1066 through to Waterloo in 1815. After the end of the Napoleonic Wars, however, the two countries had been at peace, even working together on the same side in the Crimean War. Now, although they had been allies in the twentieth century's two world wars, France was deeply opposed to American military action in Iraq, which the UK continued to support. As a non-political head of state, the Queen is supposed never to express political views, but she can articulate broad long-term concepts which politicians often find difficult. Like others who long ago deposed hereditary rulers, the French love the royalty of others and, like her father and mother before her, the Queen was an admired and popular figure in France on her fourth state visit. She also speaks perfect French and delivered all her speeches fluently.

'Of course, we will never agree on everything,' she said at the state banquet in the Élysée Palace. 'Life would be dull indeed, not least for the rest of the world, if we did not allow ourselves a little space to live up to our national caricatures – British pragmatism and French élan; French conceptualism and British humour; British rain and French sun; I think we should enjoy the complementarity of it all.'

Television might have dimmed people's appetites for lining the streets, but still the crowds came to see the Queen, accompanied by applause and shouts of '*Vive la Reine!*', which pleased the host, the impeccably mannered President Jacques Chirac, who placed great importance on the visit. The Queen met Chirac again on 6 June for the sixtieth anniversary of D-Day commemorations at the Commonwealth War Graves Cemetery in Bayeux, Normandy, then she gave an address to the dwindling group of former servicemen gathered in nearby Arromanches for the parade of the few surviving Normandy veterans, sharing her own memories of when her father addressed the nation that day in 1944, before adding:

What for you is a haunting memory of danger and sacrifice one summer long ago is for your country, and for generations of your countrymen to come, one of our proudest moments in our long national history ... I salute you and thank you on behalf of our whole nation.

On 6 July, before leaving for Scotland, the Queen opened the controversial fountain in memory of the late Diana, Princess of Wales, in London's Hyde Park. The monies raised from the Diana Memorial Fund paid for the fountain, but many thought it a misplacement of funds and that the late Princess would have preferred a hospital wing or something of more tangible benefit in her memory. The event was the opportunity for the Queen to remind everyone how much she admired her late daughter-in-law despite their well-publicised differences.

> Of course there were difficult times, but memories mellow ... To present a likeness seemed at best unnecessary for someone whose image continues to exert such a fascination the world over. To find some other way to capture her spirit has been the challenge.

Prince Charles was the only person among the royal and Spencer families present who appeared ill at ease and perhaps to wish he was somewhere else. He fiddled nervously with his cuff-links, probably wondering just how he was going to get the public to embrace the 'non-negotiable' part of his life – Camilla Parker Bowles – when their love for Diana was evidently still so powerful.

In November, the Queen went on a state visit to Germany, which symbolically echoed her earlier trip to France. Speaking in English not German, she reminded her hosts in one speech in Berlin of the importance of the European Union and the challenges we all faced in dealing with climate change. The visit was clearly a draining one: in all her seventy-seven years the Queen had always sat straight and never closed her eyes during even the dullest of speeches. During one engagement, however, she appeared to fall asleep in the middle of a talk on the use of magnets in healthcare. She must have been feeling unwell, as she slumped in her chair and closed her eyes for all of ten seconds.

The Queen and Prince Philip then returned to the UK for the funeral of 102-year-old Princess Alice, Duchess of Gloucester, at Windsor on 5 November. After the service at St George's Chapel, the Duke and Duchess of Gloucester, their family, plus the Queen and Prince Philip and the Dukes of Buccleuch and Queensberry and their families, went to the burial ground at Frogmore for a private service of interment. The Duchess, whose father was the seventh Duke of Buccleuch, was interred alongside her husband and her son, Prince William.

That year's Christmas speech had religious tolerance at the centre of it, using the parable of the Good Samaritan to make the point:

> Religion and culture are much in the news these days, usually as sources of difference and conflict, rather than for bringing people together. But the irony is that every religion has something to say about tolerance and respecting others ... Everyone is our neighbour, no matter what race, creed or colour.

The Queen also recognised the strengths brought to the country by its racial and religious diversity, recounting an anecdote:

> I particularly enjoyed a story I heard the other day about an overseas visitor to Britain who said the best part of his visit had been travelling from Heathrow into central London on the Tube. His British friends were, as you can imagine, somewhat surprised ... 'What do you mean?' they asked.
>
> 'Because,' he replied, 'I boarded the train just as the schools

were coming out. At each stop children were getting on and off – they were of every ethnic and religious background, some with scarves or turbans, some talking quietly, others playing and occasionally misbehaving together – completely at ease and trusting one another.' 'How lucky you are,' said the visitor, 'to live in a country where your children can grow up this way.'

On Boxing Day 2004, the Queen, like everyone else, woke to the horrific news that a 9.2 magnitude earthquake followed by a tsunami had devastated parts of Southeast Asia. It affected millions of people and is still remembered for its sheer destruction. Fourteen countries suffered from its effects, including India, Indonesia, Malaysia, the Maldives, Myanmar (formerly known as Burma), Somalia, Sri Lanka, Thailand, Bangladesh, South Africa, Madagascar, Kenya, Tanzania and the Seychelles. For the Queen, who knew the countries and many of the people, it was especially poignant, as five of the seven worst-affected countries were Commonwealth members. As is customary, she released an immediate message of sympathy through the foreign secretary of the time, Jack Straw.

She had also learnt a few hours later that Princess Alexandra's husband, Sir Angus Ogilvy, had died. The Ogilvys have always had close ties with the House of Windsor and Angus was a particular favourite of the Queen. His grandmother, Mabell, Countess of Airlie, was lady-in-waiting to Queen Mary for over fifty years, and his father was Lord Chamberlain to the Queen Mother. More recently, his elder brother David, the thirteenth Earl of Airlie, held the same position at Buckingham Palace, effectively running the Queen's household until his retirement. Not surprisingly, the Queen was among more than thirty members of the royal family who gathered at St George's Chapel for the funeral service, exactly two months after the one for Alice, Duchess of Gloucester.

On New Year's Day 2005, the Queen released a personal message in which she expressed her sadness for anyone affected by the tsunami and added how impressed she was that the people of Britain had given 'so generously' to the disaster relief effort. She then, as she always does, made a substantial personal donation to the disaster fund and followed it up by visiting the Central Casualty Bureau – a multi-force operations room in north London mobilised to deal with major disasters. She commented:

As the world comes to terms with the scale of the disaster, I have been impressed by the willingness of people in Britain to give generously in support of the international response, through donations, time, money or help with the relief effort on the ground. It's especially sad that these events are unfolding at the New Year, traditionally a time of celebration and hope. But it makes it all the more heartening that so many people have taken time during this holiday period to contribute in whatever way they can. To all those people, I send my heartfelt thanks.

It was a sombre end to a period that had seen the Queen lose so many family members, but the next year was to bring some happiness for her son, as well as a shocking tragedy much closer to home.

Chapter 9

TIME FOR REFLECTION

As one gets older, birthdays seem to come round quicker; they are therefore less obvious excuses for wider celebration than personal moments to count one's blessings. As Groucho Marx once said: 'Anyone can get old – all you have to do is live long enough.'

EIGHTIETH BIRTHDAY SPEECH
AT MANSION HOUSE, LONDON,
15 JUNE 2006

On 9 April 2005, the Queen made a rare personal announcement at the wedding reception of her son Prince Charles to Camilla Parker Bowles. Comparing the many obstacles they had overcome to the famous Aintree steeplechase, the Grand National, she told the assembled guests: 'They have overcome Becher's Brook and the Chair and all kinds of obstacles. They have come through and I'm very proud and wish them well. My son is home and dry with the woman he loves.'

It was a defining moment in royal history. For years the

Queen had been concerned about Camilla Parker Bowles's position in her son's life. She had witnessed Diana's tears, Charles's anger and the constant criticism of Camilla, but seldom voiced an opinion. Privately, she had said she thought the game of what she called 'cat and mouse' her son was playing with his mistress was ridiculous and had to come to an end.

'What would happen if I fell off my horse?' she asked one of her relations. 'The situation has to be resolved.'

Luckily it was. Over Christmas, Prince Charles discussed the matter with his mother and on 10 February the marriage was formally announced. The Queen happily gave the couple her blessing.

Like Charles and Camilla's relationship, the arrangements for the April wedding did not run on the usual well-oiled royal wheels. An eleventh-hour postponement due to the Prince having to attend the funeral of Pope John Paul II in Rome meant moving the date from 8 to 9 April, and a litany of errors by Prince Charles's aides overshadowed the preparations. By licensing Windsor Castle, the chosen venue for the civil ceremony, it was discovered the royal residence would have to be made available as a wedding venue for the public for the next three years. The Queen was not having that and the venue was changed to the less salubrious Windsor Guildhall.

The Queen and the Duke decided not to attend the ceremony itself, because she is the head of the Church of England, but were present at the service of prayer and dedication in St George's Chapel afterwards.

After the blessing, the celebrations continued in the State Apartments of Windsor Castle. Guests gathered beneath a spectacular floral reconstruction of the Prince of Wales feathers made from thousands of daffodils, while the immediate royal family posed for pictures in the White Drawing Room. The

Queen may not have initially endorsed her son's choice of bride, but she accepted Camilla warmly and before the speeches said she had two important announcements to make. One was that Hedgehunter had won the Grand National – the race had been put back by twenty-five minutes to avoid clashing with the television coverage of the wedding. (As an avid racing fan, owner and breeder, the Queen always considered the sporting calendar.) The other was to welcome the bride and groom into the 'winner's enclosure'.

After Camilla's 88-year-old father, Major Shand, had given a gracious thank you to the Queen for her hospitality, Prince Charles made several toasts to 'my darling wife' and thanked her for 'taking on the task of being married to me'. He also toasted his late grandmother, the third anniversary of the Queen Mother's funeral and her burial alongside George VI at St George's Chapel falling on the same day as his wedding.

'My beloved grandmother,' he said, 'I so wish she could have been here today.'

Prince Charles gave several more toasts, each greeted with cheering and stamping of feet. According to those present, the Queen appeared to be enjoying herself, despite having looked rather serious on the steps of St George's Chapel. The single-tier wedding cake was cut by the couple with the Prince's naval sword, which had originally belonged to his great-grandfather, George V. As the couple left for their honeymoon in Scotland, they drove slowly round the quadrangle, preceded by three pipers and applauded all the way by the 800 guests. Princes William and Harry and Camilla's son Tom Parker Bowles had cheekily decorated the royal Bentley with balloons, and they rushed across the grass to be the last to see the honeymooners out of the gate.

It was end of one era and the beginning of another. The

Queen was never going to relinquish her hold on the reins of the monarchy, but now that her son and heir had found the marital happiness he craved, she expected him to be able to step into her well-worn shoes on certain occasions. Not to help her – she did not need or would never accept that – but to show her subjects that the monarchy was not just for her lifetime, rather a continuing, evolving institution of which Prince Charles would eventually be the custodian.

In June, Camilla took her place on the Buckingham Palace balcony for the first time for the Trooping the Colour parade to mark the Queen's official birthday. This historic occasion marked the official status of the Duchess of Cornwall as fourth lady in the land, according to a list entitled 'Precedence of the Royal Family to be observed at court'. It was not a snub to Camilla to be positioned after Princess Anne and Princess Alexandra, the granddaughter of George V, in the royal pecking order. This was a reflection 'on the blood principles', so that neither of them would have to curtsey to Camilla when her husband was not present.

Although the etiquette may seem arcane, it is taken very seriously by the royal family, whose members bow and curtsey to the Queen in public and in private. The order of precedence affects other aspects of royal protocol, such as who arrives first at an event. For all their attempts to embrace modernity, there are still aspects of the royal family that are similar to a medieval court, if not quite in the style of *Wolf Hall*. They have their favourites and they have their fallouts. Even the Queen, the most humble of them all, has been known to go through her Christmas card list and cross off the name of anyone who has upset her. The line through the name – always in pencil – is the equivalent of being sent to the Tower in another age.

Whatever the private foibles of the royal family, the British look to them when triumph or tragedy strike. Two days after the Queen had completed an International Fleet Review at Spithead in honour of Lord Nelson's historic victory at Trafalgar, she was symbolically feted when London won the competition to stage the 2012 Olympics. Union flags fluttered in a blizzard of confetti in Trafalgar Square as the Red Arrows flew past, leaving a trail of red, white and blue smoke. As president of the British Olympic Committee, the Princess Royal was in Singapore to lend support to the bid and was beaming with pleasure at the unexpected triumph over Paris. Sadly, it was to prove a very short-lived moment of happiness for the city.

The following day, 7 July, the Union flag flew at half-mast from Buckingham Palace. Dozens of people were dead, killed by four bombs carried on to the underground and a red double-decker bus by terrorists. The theatres closed for the first time since Diana, Princess of Wales's funeral eight years before, and London ground to a standstill. In the past, the royal family had been slow to react to such disasters, not because they did not want to, but their advisors have always said that in the aftermath of an attack, their high-profile presence and the security necessary to protect them causes more problems than it alleviates. This was no longer the case, and the day after the atrocities the Queen paid a forty-five-minute visit to the Royal London Hospital in Whitechapel to meet some of the injured, and spoke directly to the television cameras.

'Yesterday's bombings in London have deeply affected us all,' she said, her voice breaking with emotion. 'But those who perpetrate these brutal acts against innocent people should know they will not change our way of life.' She expressed her 'admiration for the people of our capital city' and condemned what she called 'this outrage'.

Two days later, in an event to celebrate the sixtieth anniversary of the end of war in Europe and Japan, the Queen reflected on the attacks again when she spoke from the stage at Horse Guards Parade, having hosted a lunch for 2,000 veterans in the gardens of Buckingham Palace: 'It does not surprise me that during the present difficult days for London, people turn to the example set by that generation – of resilience, humour and sustained courage, often under conditions of great deprivation.' The Queen then returned to Buckingham Palace and watched a million poppies being dropped from the RAF's last surviving Lancaster bomber in an historic fly-past.

On Trafalgar Day, 21 October, the Queen and the Duke of Edinburgh were entertained to dinner by the First Sea Lord, Admiral Alan West, in the great cabin of Lord Nelson's flagship, HMS *Victory*, in Portsmouth. Beforehand, she had lit a beacon and started a 1,000-strong 'chain of light' around Britain to remember the great man and his last great battle exactly 200 years earlier. Standing at the mahogany table, the Queen, resplendent in diamonds and in a deep peach brocade evening suit, reinforced her strong link with the Royal Navy, and (just as important) the principles that lie at the heart of it:

The British fleet under the command of Lord Nelson faced a formidable enemy, but battles are seldom won by statistics. It was the qualities of leadership and comradeship which he gave to the Royal Navy in the years leading up to his final battle that made all the difference ... Tonight we recall his greatest battle and his death at the moment of victory, but we also remember his example of service and his humanity. Just before the battle, Nelson sat down at the desk behind me, to compose his famous prayer in terms so typical of his character:

'May the great God, whom I worship, grant to my Country, and for the benefit of Europe in general, a great and glorious victory; and may no misconduct, in anyone, tarnish it, and may humanity after victory be the predominant feature in the British Fleet.'

At Christmas, the Queen returned to the theme of adversity not victory when she spoke poignantly from Buckingham Palace of the natural disasters that had afflicted the world, including the floods in New Orleans and earthquakes in Pakistan and India, and the terrorist attacks in London. Instead of footage of the family or her son's wedding, the broadcast showed ordinary people giving practical and financial help to those who had suffered in the disasters.

I have sometimes thought that humanity seemed to have turned on itself – with wars, civil disturbances and acts of brutal terrorism ... This last year has reminded us that this world is not always an easy or a safe place to live in, but it is the only place we have.

The Queen started her eightieth birthday year opening the 2006 Commonwealth Games in Melbourne, Australia. In her annual Commonwealth Day message, she talked about the importance of health and exercise: 'As we watch our finest sportsmen and women compete, we will see clearly what exercise at the very highest level can contribute to both body and spirit. There is a traditional proverb which says, "He who has health has hope, and he who has hope has everything."'

The Queen rather enjoys dispensing these 'nanny-like' niceties. They are very much part of her generation and, although she didn't write the speech herself, she approved its content. She is a great believer in sensible exercise, even if in her case it's only walking her dogs and riding gently around her estates on horseback. None of her family has ever had a weight problem and, although he is now in his nineties and frail, Prince Philip still exercises every morning. She has seen the benefits that come from exercise, and is happy to encourage others to follow suit.

At home, the Queen attended the Sovereign's Parade at Sandhurst for the first time in fifteen years. As head of the armed forces, there is nothing the Queen doesn't know about military etiquette. She is an expert in military history and enjoys the pageant, the formality and the order of military occasions. She can spot an incorrectly worn piece of military regalia quicker than most commanding officers and has her own favourites among the heroes of history, including Lord Nelson. It was with great pleasure and grandmotherly pride that she watched 21-year-old Prince Harry, a second lieutenant in the Blues and Royals, complete his passing-out parade. As she moved through the lines chatting to some of the officers she gave her grandson a beaming smile, which he returned as his cheeks flushed red. 'Here's a face I recognise,' she said when she spotted him.

Her Majesty later addressed the newly commissioned officers: 'This is a very special occasion for me, as it is for all of you who are gaining your commissions today,' she said. 'It is also a great occasion for your family and friends. This day marks what I hope will be highly successful careers as officers in the British Army, or the armies of our friends and allies, and I am pleased to see so many cadets from the Commonwealth and other countries on parade.'

In December, it was Prince William's turn to be commissioned as an army officer in front of his grandmother and once again the Queen gave an address at the Sovereign's Parade, calling the army 'one of the most demanding but rewarding of careers'.

Both Prince William and Prince Harry have had successful army careers. Harry's might have been more exciting, as he was twice deployed to Afghanistan, once as a serving Apache helicopter pilot. They both had immensely demanding roles, achieved through their own abilities, not because of who they were. Being a Prince of the Realm and a full-time serving army officer, or seconded to the RAF as William was, is hard work, as they both discovered. After seven and a half years, Prince William left operational service and, after much soul-searching, Prince Harry chose to devote his energies to his philanthropic work and quit the army in June 2015.

If the Queen thought she was going to get away with a low-key celebration of her eightieth birthday, her wishes were ignored. The fanfare started a couple of days before her actual birthday, when she gave a personal tribute to fellow octogenarians at a lunch at Buckingham Palace. In a voice faltering with emotion, she admitted 'the last few years had not been plain sailing', but she felt thankful for her 'current health and happiness' and 'some wonderful memories'. Two days later, on 21 April, Prince Charles organised a family dinner and fireworks at the newly restored Kew Palace and paid tribute to his 'darling Mama'.

> It is hard to believe that my grandfather, King George VI, was the same age as I am now when he died and that my mother succeeded him when so young – the same age, in fact, as my sons are now. I have vivid memories of my parents being away for long overseas tours during the 1950s and of determined attempts to speak to them on the telephone in a veritable storm of crackling and static interference ...

There is no doubt that the world in which my mother grew up, in which she first became Queen, has changed beyond all recognition. But during all those years she has shown the most remarkable steadfastness and fortitude, always remaining a figure of reassuring calm and dependability – an example to so many of service, duty and devotion in a world of sometimes bewildering change and disorientation.

At her eightieth birthday lunch at the Mansion House on 15 June, the Queen thanked the Lord Mayor, Sir David Brewer, for his hospitality. For weeks, leading chefs had battled it out to create a lunch fit for a Queen as part of a BBC television contest, with fourteen cooks from seven nations and regions competing. The starter course was by Richard Corrigan from Northern Ireland, the fish course by Bryn Williams from Wales and the main course by Nick Nairn from Scotland, with the North of England winning the pudding, thanks to Marcus Wareing. Speaking in the opulent Egyptian Hall before lunch was served, the Queen was in high spirits:

I am most grateful to you for inviting Prince Philip and me to this lunch today to mark both my eightieth birthday and the eighty-fifth birthday of Prince Philip last weekend. The Corporation's generous hospitality is well known, and I have no doubt that this is now even more the case thanks to the 'Great British Menu' which I look forward to sampling shortly. Creating a good menu is a familiar dilemma for any host, but the solution of competitive cooking is a new concept to me – although I understand there are as yet no penalty shoot-outs. My Lord Mayor, as one gets older, birthdays seem to come round quicker; they are therefore less obvious excuses for wider celebration than personal moments to count one's blessings. As Groucho Marx once said: 'Anyone can get old – all you have to do is live long enough.'

The Queen also took the opportunity to highlight two charities that had been particularly close to her family's hearts: the Duke of Edinburgh Award scheme, which had been running for fifty years, and the Prince's Trust, which was then thirty years in operation. Even on an occasion that was supposedly devoted to her, she deflected the attention on to her family and the good work they had spent so long supporting.

For her birthday present to herself, the Queen decided to charter a yacht which had been converted from a passenger ferry into a luxury mini-liner, the *Hebridean Princess*. With thirty large cabins, it could take as many of her immediate family, children and grandchildren around the Western Isles of Scotland as *Britannia* used to do before it had been decommissioned in 1997.

Having the *Hebridean Princess* at her disposal meant the Queen could still reach the furthest-flung places of her realm, such as the remote isles of Colonsay and Harris in the Outer Hebrides. They are some of her favourite places and have sandy beaches which are inaccessible except by launch and perfect for royal picnics. After a year in which she had already made twenty-odd speeches and travelled to Australia and Singapore, an eight-day break sailing around the remote islands of Scotland was exactly what the Queen wanted.

On the tiny island of Gigha, with a population of just over 100 people, the local shopkeeper was surprised to see Princess Anne appear on a bicycle and enquire if there was a taxi service. She wanted a taxi to pick up the Queen from a remote beach and take her to see the island's famous fifty-four-acre Achamore Gardens. Of course, there is no taxi service on the remote isle and the shopkeeper was proud to drive Her Majesty himself. He later described the Queen, somewhat surprisingly, as 'a real chatterbox'.

After a visit to the Baltic States of Estonia, Latvia and Lithuania in October, the Queen's Christmas message was partly filmed at Southwark Cathedral. The Queen spoke again of the pressures of modern life and how she enjoyed the vitality of youth, as well as mentioning the importance of mutual respect between the generations and the wisdom that comes from long experience.

As I look back over these past twelve months, marked in particular for me by the very generous response to my eightieth birthday, I especially value the opportunities I have had to meet young people. I am impressed by their energy and vitality and by their ambition to learn and travel.

In preparation for their visit to the United States in May 2007, the Queen allowed celebrity photographer Annie Leibovitz a sitting in Buckingham Palace. The shoot was filmed by the BBC for a documentary and, in the publicity shots, the production company spliced two separate bits of film together to make it appear as if the Queen had stormed out of the photo-shoot.

What had actually happened was that Leibovitz evidently didn't know how to get the best out of the Queen, having already irritated Her Majesty's household by having eleven assistants, who took three days to prepare the session. As requested, the Queen put on her complicated, heavy Garter regalia and took her position by the window. The casually dressed Leibovitz took one look at the set-up shot and asked the Queen to remove her 'crown', as she thought it was too dressy.

The Queen was incredulous – no one tells her what to do – and, to add insult to injury, it wasn't a crown but a tiara. For one second she was speechless, then recovering her composure she said imperiously: 'Too dressy!' And, fingering her cloak: 'What do you think this is?' However much the Queen has adapted to the modern world, this was not the way she expected to be treated.

Later, Leibovitz tried to explain her misunderstanding about the situation. She said she had been inspired by the Helen Mirren film, *The Queen*, and had wanted the shoot to take place at Balmoral, so Buckingham Palace came as a second best. She had felt perturbed by the presence of the film crew, as she would never allow one on one of her shoots. When the Queen got annoyed about removing her tiara, she mistook it for a 'cranky' kind of English humour until she noticed her dresser and assistant had retreated at least twenty feet away and were watching the entire proceedings with trepidation.

The visit to America was altogether more successful than the photoshoot, although during his welcoming speech President Bush became flustered and muddled his dates.

'You visited us for our bicentennial in 1776 ...' he began, before hastily correcting himself, '... er, 1976', amid much laughter. The following evening, the Queen evened the score when, hosting a dinner at the British ambassador's residence, she began her speech, 'When I was last here in 1776 ...'

The Queen talked about her visit to Jamestown for the commemoration of the historic landing by the British in Virginia 400 years earlier and the 'future cooperation between our countries'. As the Queen said herself, 'a lot of the visits have a very strong political tone to them', and this was no different.

In October, the Queen welcomed 83-year-old King Abdullah of Saudi Arabia, Custodian of the Two Holy Mosques, to

London on a state visit. It was more politically sensitive than usual, as the King had publicly accused Great Britain of not taking terrorism seriously enough in spite of warnings. The Saudi King and some of his retinue of twenty-three all-male advisors stayed at Buckingham Palace, and on the first night enjoyed the Queen's sumptuous hospitality at the traditional state banquet. It was Gordon Brown's first state banquet as her new prime minister, after he had replaced Tony Blair. He was the eleventh prime minister of her reign.

On 20 November, the Queen became the first reigning monarch to celebrate a diamond wedding anniversary, which she marked with a service of thanksgiving at Westminster Abbey. She felt that, with the country going into its worst recession since the 1930s, a party would have been inappropriate. Five weeks later, on 22 December, she surpassed her own great-great-grandmother Queen Victoria as the oldest serving monarch. Throughout her reign, the Queen has felt reluctant to force too many birthdays and anniversaries on her subjects. She is a shy person and has never come to terms with the spotlight being shone too frequently upon her without good reason. She also remained acutely aware of when it was appropriate to mark events in lavish style.

Her Christmas address in 2007 showed film of part of her first somewhat stilted televised broadcast fifty years before at Sandringham. The broadcast also showed her assembled family gathering at Clarence House for an official photograph, with all the banter and joshing they enjoy when they get together. As she often does, the Queen talked about change, getting older and the disadvantaged:

One of the features of growing old is a heightened awareness of change. To remember what happened fifty years ago means that it is possible to appreciate what has changed in the meantime. It also makes you aware of what has remained constant. In my experience, the positive value of a happy family is one of the factors of human existence that has not changed. The immediate family of grandparents, parents and children, together with their extended family, is still the core of a thriving community.

Three months later, in March 2008, in a glittering display of pomp and ceremony, Nicolas Sarkozy, the president of France, and his glamorous wife, former model Carla Bruni, arrived at Windsor Castle for a state visit. It was an opportunity for the English to show the French a few lessons in style, as the Queen herself had explained in the 1992 documentary, *Elizabeth R*:

We are the hosts; we give the entertainment initially and have the people to stay hoping to give them a nice time to remember. And obviously we keep up as many of the traditions we can, like going in carriages.

I think in a way it's quite an old-fashioned idea to put out the red carpet for a guest. I think people don't really realise this. I do tell the guests that we put on our best clothes and everybody dresses up, and the best china and the glass and the gold plate comes out, otherwise it doesn't see the light of day, so it's very nice to be able to use it and show it. But sometimes it's worth explaining that we put it on specially, that we don't live like this all the time!

In her speech in the candlelit St George's Hall that evening, the Queen spoke of the historic links between the two countries. 'Both countries are rightly proud,' she said, 'and sometimes perhaps even a little jealous – of our respective histories ... And no one will ever win an argument over the respective merits of our rich and expressive linguistic heritage.'

In April 2008, the High Court inquest into Diana's death finally ended. After six months, some 270 witnesses and at the cost of several million pounds, the jury in the long-awaited case delivered the verdict of unlawful killing due to gross negligence of both the driver and the paparazzi. The inquest had been an unpleasant reminder of the tragedy for everyone, especially Prince William and Prince Harry, while the Queen had to hear of her husband being branded as a Nazi murderer by Mohamed Al-Fayed in one of his more volatile moments in the witness box.

A few days later, the Queen was at the Royal Naval College, Dartmouth, for the passing-out parade. It was more familiar territory for her, and in her address she talked about the significance of the Royal Navy to her family:

My grandfather, father, husband and two sons have all undergone training here, and I have had many visits over the years ... As modern technology becomes increasingly sophisticated, life in the Navy is even more demanding and challenging. The ships, aircraft, submarines, weaponry and equipment are changing as fast as at any time in our history, yet the quality required of Officers – leadership, courage, integrity, good humour, professional competence – are as important in today's Navy as they have ever been. And I am speaking to every individual one of you when I say: never forget who you are; despite all the technological advances of the last decades, nothing will ever be more important than your inner sense of humanity, decency, and regard for the dignity of others.

In May, the Queen and Prince Philip's first grandchild, Peter Phillips, married Canadian-born Autumn Kelly at St George's Chapel, Windsor. The Queen was bemused to see that the couple sold the photographs of their engagement and gave an interview to the celebrity magazine *Hello!*, and even more surprised when the magazine was also present at St George's Chapel and Frogmore House for the wedding. She gave the venue to the couple for their wedding reception and dance. The fifty pages of photographs were the first public royal wedding shots of their kind and, although the Queen likes to keep up with the way young people expect their lives to be conducted, the experiment was never repeated.

This all came at a time when the economy was heading into one of its deepest ever recessions. The problems began early in 2007 in the United States with the collapse of property values and the subsequent bankruptcy of many smaller banks that had recklessly made loans which went sour. This precipitated the worst financial crisis since the Great Depression of the 1930s. It soon spread to the UK, when the Northern Rock bank collapsed and had to be rescued by the government. There followed a domino effect, with larger banks coming under pressure, and it eventually came to a head in 2008 when the US government allowed the banking giant Lehman Brothers to go bankrupt.

The UK's largest banking group, the Royal Bank of Scotland, had to be bailed out with tens of billions of pounds, having incurred the biggest loss ever by a UK company, and to this day it is still largely owned by the UK taxpayer. Stock market values dropped everywhere and the world went into recession, with high unemployment and countries such as Ireland and Greece having to be bailed out.

Although the Queen is always kept abreast of current affairs by her weekly meetings with the prime minister, the financial crisis had little effect on her programme of state banquets, ceremonial engagements and the traditions of royal life. However, like many of her subjects, she saw the value of her investments halved, and when she was visiting the London School of Economics on 5 November 2008, she asked incredulously: 'Why did nobody notice it? If these things were so large, how come everyone missed them?'

For several years, the Queen has been a relatively proficient user of the internet, and at the end of 2007 Buckingham Palace launched a channel on YouTube for the royal family. The Royal Channel is an example of how the Queen wants to promote the vital work of the monarchy to a younger global audience. She had sent her first electronic message in 1976 during a visit to an army base, but admitted to Bill Gates in 2005 that she had not used a computer. However, when she visited the Google headquarters, she knew what was going on. She also met staff from YouTube, the video sharing site, and both she and the Duke were reduced to giggles when they were shown a clip of a baby laughing like an adult, which at the time had been viewed 63 million times. 'That's a lovely little thing, isn't it?' the Queen said after she had watched it. 'Amazing a child would laugh like that.'

Imagine the Queen's delight, therefore, when, in 2009, the newly elected President Obama and his wife Michelle presented her with an iPod containing video footage of her 2007 visit to the United States. The president admitted he was 'as excited as a schoolboy' at the prospect of meeting a woman he had only ever seen 'on stamps and documentaries'. He was not disappointed, and neither was his wife, as they spent twenty-five precious minutes with the Queen and Prince Philip ahead of the G20 cocktail party at the palace.

The Queen, who has met every US president of her reign

except Lyndon Johnson, sympathised with the young Obama, who had the hopes of millions of Americans riding with him during the country's worst economic downturn since the Depression. When the Queen put a comforting arm around Michelle Obama's back at the reception, it was not therefore perhaps so surprising. As a young woman, the Queen had had little time to be a wife and mother, and she recognised that the First Lady was in a similar position.

The two women have little in common, but they obviously share a sense of humour as they discussed their height difference and, unprecedented though it might have been, it was delightful to see that small sign of public affection from the Queen. We sometimes forget she is a *real* person and, as President Reagan once described her, 'both charming and down to earth'.

In November 2008, as he celebrated his sixtieth birthday, it was Prince Charles's turn to be praised by his mother when she visited the headquarters of his Prince's Trust charity. The Queen does not lavish praise on her children unless she feels it is genuinely well deserved. Over the years she has had a splintered relationship with her eldest son, but as he slowly matured, she appreciated how much he cared about what he was trying to do.

As we celebrate the many extraordinary achievements of the Prince's Trust today, so too I should like briefly to reflect on the role of the Prince of Wales, who has given enduring inspiration to it. In public life, highlighting the success of individuals can be a hazardous and invidious occupation. But as the Prince of Wales, our son, approaches his own sixtieth birthday, may I say that we are both enormously proud to have been reminded here today of his personal contribution to this remarkable organisation.

Countless lives have been transformed by the Prince's

Trust to which the Prince of Wales has brought vision and conviction. For Prince Philip and me, there can be no greater pleasure or comfort than to know that into his care are safely entrusted the guiding principles of public service and duty to others.

In the 2008 Christmas broadcast, Prince Charles again came in for praise for his charitable work:

Indeed, Prince Philip and I can reflect on the blessing, comfort and support we have gained from our own family in this special year for our son, the Prince of Wales. Sixty years ago, he was baptised here in the Music Room at Buckingham Palace. As parents and grandparents, we feel great pride in seeing our family make their own unique contributions to society. Through his charities, the Prince of Wales has worked to support young people and other causes for the benefit of the wider community, and now his sons are following in his footsteps.

One of the things the women of the royal family have always done is support the society that forms the Women's Institute and, during her winter visit to Sandringham, the Queen attends the New Year Sandringham WI meeting. In 1919, Queen Mary became president of the local West Newton branch of the WI and started a royal tradition. The Queen became a WI member in 1943 when she was still Princess Elizabeth, and the Queen Mother was president for sixty-five years. After her accession in 1952, the National Federation of Women's Institutes sent a loyal address to the Queen from their AGM, 'that this meeting, remembering that our young Queen has duties as a wife and mother, urges the nation as a whole not to overwork Her Majesty'.

Fifty-seven years later at the January 2009 meeting, the

Queen injected some humour into her address when she described her royal year:

> Turkey was, I am told, my eighty-sixth state visit. Even so, there are still some places that I had not been to. Two such countries were Slovakia and Slovenia, both of which I visited, for the first time, in October. These are friendly and welcoming nations – so much so that in Slovenia I was presented with a horse; a particularly impressive Lipizzaner. The captain of my aircraft was pleased to learn that the horse would be staying in Slovenia, and not flying back with the rest of the presents to London.

On 1 July 2009, the Queen broadcast to members of the armed forces around the world. With operations still ongoing in Iraq and Afghanistan, despite increasing political doubts about the continued British presence, she recognised the importance of giving her support to those carrying out such dangerous work in challenging circumstances. She said:

> As I talk to you today I am conscious that my words are being heard simultaneously across many time zones, climates and terrains. Wherever you are deployed in the world, you should be assured that I and the whole nation are deeply thankful for the part you play in helping to maintain peace around the globe ... The Armed Forces have recommended that for those servicemen and women who have given their lives during operations, a special emblem and scroll will be granted to their next of kin. I am pleased to be associated with such an initiative, which is in keeping with a tradition established during the First World War. And so I have asked that this emblem should be known as the Elizabeth Cross.

In November, the Queen travelled across the Atlantic again, this time to the Caribbean. On her way to the Commonwealth Heads of Government Meeting (CHOGM) in Trinidad, the Queen stopped off in Bermuda for the celebrations of the 400th anniversary of the settlement of the island. At the opening ceremony of the CHOGM, the Queen echoed the concerns often expressed by Prince Philip and Charles, and warned of the effects of climate change:

And on this, the eve of the UN Copenhagen Summit on Climate Change, the Commonwealth has an opportunity to lead once more. The threat to our environment is not a new concern. But it is now a global challenge which will continue to affect the security and stability of millions for years to come.

The Queen will never enter the political arena, but she is not averse to raising matters of global concern and nudging people into action, as she and Prince Philip had done years ago, when they announced they had adopted unleaded petrol, to encourage others to do the same.

Not only was the country in the continued grip of the economic downturn, but the war in Afghanistan seemed to be never-ending, with the number of servicemen and women killed on active service exceeding a hundred for the first time. In her Christmas address, the Queen decided it was a year best forgotten:

Each year that passes seems to have its own character. Some leave us with a feeling of satisfaction, others are best forgotten. 2009 was a difficult year for many, in particular those facing the continuing effects of the economic downturn. I am sure that we have all been affected by events in Afghanistan and saddened by the casualties suffered by our forces serving there. Our thoughts go out to their relations and friends who have shown immense dignity in the face of great personal loss.

Having recently returned from Trinidad, the Queen spoke again of her affection for her Commonwealth and its subjects: 'I have been closely associated with the Commonwealth through most of its existence. The personal and living bond I have enjoyed with leaders, and with people the world over, has always been more important in promoting our unity than symbolism alone.'

In the six decades since the founding of the Commonwealth, the Queen had met most of its leaders and formed personal friendships with many of them. Despite despots, such as Zimbabwe's Robert Mugabe, and their regimes of violence, the Queen still felt the Commonwealth – her Commonwealth – had come a long way in its sixty years. She was the central pivot that held it all together, the one person who was above politics and who could see it from almost every point of view. In the years to come this was to prove to be a most valuable asset.

Chapter 10

MILESTONES

Since my Accession, I have been a regular
visitor to the Palace of Westminster and, at
the last count, have had the pleasurable
duty of treating with twelve prime
ministers.

DIAMOND JUBILEE SPEECH, HOUSES
OF PARLIAMENT, 20 MARCH 2012

As the new millennium moved into its second decade and after nearly sixty years on the throne, it might have been expected the Queen would have taken things a little more easily. Most people her age would have retired long before, but, far from slowing down, the Queen increased the number of her public engagements in 2010 over the previous year.

At the age of eighty-four, the Queen carried out 444 engagements, sixty-nine more than in 2009. Her workload also featured fifty-seven overseas engagements, all of which involved the delivery of speeches. On the personal front, the Queen had the excitement of announcing the engagement of her grandson Prince William to Catherine Middleton, as well as the joy of becoming a great-grandmother for the first time with the birth of Savannah, the daughter of Peter Phillips and his wife, Autumn.

As always, both the Commonwealth and advances in technology remained high priorities for the Queen. In her annual Commonwealth Day message on 8 March 2010, she talked about the advances in telecommunications and the internet with wonder when she said:

> People can now use mobile phones to be in instant contact virtually anywhere in the world, be it with a medical centre in the Himalayan mountains in Asia, a Pacific island school, a research facility at the South Pole or even the international space station, beyond this planet altogether.

As long ago as 2001, Prince Andrew had given his mother a mobile phone with the family's numbers programmed in so she could contact them on speed dial. He has always been the technology expert of the family and used to record the racing for the Queen on a video player, which was then activated by her page. He also gave her a BlackBerry mobile phone, which gave her access to emails wherever she might be, although she dictates messages rather than write them herself.

To what extent the Queen actually uses her mobile is not certain, but when in Canada in July she made a point of visiting the headquarters of the company Research In Motion, best known for inventing the BlackBerry. After touring the facility, she was presented with the latest model and, after a close inspection, she put it firmly back in its box.

During that twenty-second visit to Canada on a nine-day, five-city tour, the Queen and Prince Philip had to endure the soaring temperatures of a North American heatwave. While the

press corps, the crowds of tens of thousands and every welcoming dignitary was soaked in sweat, the Queen remained as cool
as ever in spite of deciding to wear dresses with three-quarter-
length sleeves, big hats, brooches and long white gloves, and
always carrying her handbag over her arm. Her couturiers claim
she just doesn't feel the heat and always uses natural fabrics.
Nothing as unpleasant as viscose would line a royal garment
and even every press stud is cushioned in silk.

The tour drew record-breaking crowds in a country in which
Elizabeth II is revered as 'Queen of Canada'. When there, the
Queen always includes some passages in French in her speeches,
for the benefit of the French-speaking inhabitants of Quebec.
On leaving Canada, the Queen and Prince Philip flew by private
jet to New York to pay their respects to those who had died fol-
lowing the terrorist attacks on the Twin Towers of the World
Trade Center on 11 September 2001.

As a young Queen she had made her first visit to New York
City in 1957, arriving on board the royal yacht *Britannia*, which
steamed past the Statue of Liberty. On landing, she was given
the traditional ticker-tape welcome from cheering throngs as
she drove down Broadway in President Eisenhower's limousine.
She addressed the United Nations, at that time having been
established only twelve years earlier. She said of New York
City: 'Everyone has a mental picture of famous places they have
never seen. But I suppose the mental pictures of New York are
nearer reality than those of any other city.'

Nearly two decades later, in 1976, the 50-year-old Queen
made her second visit to New York, marking the bicentenary of
America's Declaration of Independence. She was hailed by huge
crowds and became the centrepiece of the celebrations, and
Mayor Abraham D. Beame made her an honorary New Yorker.

The visit in 2010 was of a much more sombre kind. On

arrival, she again addressed the United Nations, saying: 'I believe I was last here in 1957. Since then, I have travelled widely and met many leaders, ambassadors and statesmen from around the world. I address you today as Queen of sixteen United Nations member states and as Head of the Commonwealth of fifty-four countries.'

In the evening, the Queen visited Ground Zero, the site of the Twin Towers terrorist attacks, where she was met by an honour guard and by Mayor Michael R. Bloomberg and Governors David Paterson of New York and Christopher Christie of New Jersey. She briefly toured the sixteen-acre site where thousands died. Later, she went across Lower Manhattan to the British Garden in Hanover Square, the memorial to the sixty-seven British subjects who died in the attacks. Relatives of some of the victims met the Queen, who cut a ribbon to formally open the garden. An elongated triangle in the rough shape of the British Isles, it was set out as a landscaped version of a traditional British garden, planted with hydrangea, rhododendron, azalea, foxglove, holly and yew, and set off by a winding path of Morayshire stone with benches fashioned in Northern Ireland.

On her return to the UK, the Queen travelled to Scotland for her annual holiday at Balmoral. It is one of the very few places she can be herself and once she is in the privacy of her sitting room there, with its pine-framed windows overlooking carefully tended sloping lawns, she can be alone. The piles of papers and knick-knacks, the little gifts from her grandchildren and the collection of china dogs on the mantelpiece, all have their place and meaning.

For years and years, everyday royal life in Scotland has been organised in a similar fashion: at lunchtime, picnic baskets are spread on plaid rugs on the heather and the house party guests, without a footman in sight, lay out the feast before the guns alight from the hillside. It was King George VI who was the inspiration for it all, and there remains at Balmoral the memorial which he would have most valued, an unbroken continuation of what he himself created with so much skill, care and love.

It is unusual for the Queen to be interrupted at Balmoral except in the case of an emergency, but on 16 September the first ever state visit of a pontiff to the United Kingdom was of necessary importance. Pope Benedict XVI was greeted at Edinburgh airport by Prince Philip who, unlike the Queen, had met him before. The Queen then received the Pope at the Palace of Holyroodhouse, her official residence in Scotland. Although the Queen had made four visits to the Vatican, nearly thirty years had gone by since the previous papal visit to the United Kingdom, by Pope John Paul II in 1982. The Queen gave her welcoming speech from the podium in the garden, in which she thanked the Vatican for helping to resolve the problems between Protestants and Catholics in Northern Ireland:

In this country we deeply appreciate the involvement of the Holy See in the dramatic improvement in the situation in Northern Ireland. The Holy See continues to have an important role in international issues, in support of peace and development, and in addressing common problems like poverty and climate change.

Gifts were exchanged inside the palace and the Pope was given an edition of eighty-five sketches from sixteenth-century German artist Hans Holbein the Younger – all tastefully encased in a white papal binding. In return, the Pope handed over a copy of the ancient Lorsch Gospels dating from 778 to 820. Historic though it was, the visit was brief and to the point, and within the hour the Pope was off in his Popemobile through the streets of Edinburgh before a private lunch with the head of the Catholic Church in Scotland, Cardinal O'Brien.

The Queen referred to the Pope's historic visit at the inauguration of the General Synod on 23 November 2010. The General Synod, made up of archbishops, bishops and representatives of the laity, considers and approves legislation affecting the whole of the Church of England. It was generally believed that the 2010 Synod would vote to allow female bishops. The Queen, who has always championed women's rights and the role of women in society, was disappointed that this Synod did not get the necessary two-thirds majority of votes in favour. It would be another four years before the Church's national assembly voted in favour of legislation to allow the consecration of women as bishops.

After attending a service of Holy Communion at Westminster Abbey, the Queen addressed the Synod at Church House next door. In her speech to the Synod the Queen said:

> ... as the recent visit of His Holiness the Pope reminded us, churches and the other great faith traditions retain the potential to inspire great enthusiasm, loyalty and a concern for the common good. The new Synod will have many issues to resolve to ensure that the Church of England remains equipped for the effective pursuit of its mission and ministry. Some will, no doubt, involve difficult, even painful, choices.

By coincidence, General Synod was also the name of a colt bred by the Queen which raced in her colours in 2010 and 2011. Although placed second and third when trained by Richard Hannon, the horse never managed to win a race. The Queen has always had a great affection for the outspoken

Hannon, who was champion trainer four times, and enjoyed visiting his yard and seeing her horses perform on the gallops. On one occasion, the Queen was watching her horses on the gallops from Hannon's car and he wound down the window and called out to an Indian lad cantering past on one of the Queen's horses. Hannon couldn't hear the answer and apparently turned to the Queen and said, 'You speak the lingo, don't you, Your Majesty? You should, you ran the place long enough!'

In a break from tradition, the Christmas address in 2010 was recorded in the Chapel Royal at Hampton Court Palace. Equally unusually, the Queen chose sport as her theme. She emphasised the role that sport played in life, 'bringing people together from all backgrounds, from all walks of life and from all age groups'.

She praised its role in building communities and creating harmony, and highlighted the role of volunteers: 'Apart from developing physical fitness, sport and games can also teach vital social skills,' she added. She praised the thousands of people across the country who gave up their time to participate in physical activity, highlighting the different perspective on the world offered by all sports. She added: 'None can be enjoyed without abiding by the rules, and no team can hope to succeed without cooperation between the players. This sort of positive team spirit can benefit communities, companies and enterprises of all kinds.'

In the first part of 2011, the Queen was much occupied with family matters, with the marriages of two of her grandchildren. On 29 April, the newly ennobled Duke of Cambridge married Catherine Middleton in a wedding at Westminster Abbey reminiscent of the glorious ceremonial of old. Then, on 30 July, the Queen's granddaughter Zara Phillips married her long-term boyfriend, former England rugby captain Mike Tindall, at a much smaller family service in Canongate Kirk in Edinburgh. The Queen and the Duke of Edinburgh travelled straight from Balmoral to the ceremony and allowed Zara and her guests to have the reception at Holyroodhouse.

Unlike Zara, who invited all her own friends, Prince William had been given a list of nearly 800 people he had to invite to his wedding and complained he didn't know one of them. He appealed to the Queen by asking if it was necessary and recalled, 'She said: "No! Start with your friends first and go from there." She told me to bin the list. She made the point that there are certain times when you have to strike the right balance, and it's advice like that which is really key when you know that she's seen and done it before.'

It was a great example of the Queen showing her own personal touch, but also pointing out the important lessons that needed to be passed on to future generations. The list was duly binned and another drawn up. On other matters the Queen was not quite so accommodating and insisted he should wear the ceremonial uniform of the Irish Guards, to which she had just appointed him colonel. 'You don't always get what you want,' he said, referring to his uniform. 'You just do as you are told.'

On the wedding day, the Queen looked happy and, despite having been to the christening of her first great-grandchild, Savannah Phillips, in Gloucestershire then a party the night before at the Mandarin Oriental, not in the least tired. Wearing a primrose yellow dress and coat with a matching hat designed by her trusted personal assistant Angela Kelly, she looked a decade younger than her eighty-five years as she waved to the cheering crowds.

After the ceremony, the Queen and Prince Philip travelled from the abbey to Buckingham Palace in the Scottish State

Coach, rather than an open carriage, accompanied by a Sovereign's Escort. The Prince of Wales and the Duchess of Cornwall rode in the rather dark Australian State Coach with Catherine's parents, Michael and Carole Middleton.

Although the Queen and Prince Philip hosted the lunchtime reception at Buckingham Palace for family, friends and politicians from home and abroad, she had no intention of staying on late. She felt it was a day for the young and as soon as she had departed they could let their hair down – which they did. The Royal Standard was lowered and a vast Union flag hoisted in its place as she and Prince Philip headed for the peace and quiet of Wood Farm on the Sandringham estate. There she could unwind, secure in the knowledge that the woman at her grandson Prince William's side was not a bewildered ingénue but a dignified young woman of twenty-nine with the potential to withstand the merciless adoration global celebrity brings, without losing herself.

It is a role the Queen herself played to perfection when she was Princess Elizabeth. She too had someone at her side to support and encourage her through the challenging times before and after her accession. Prince Philip made her laugh and see the funny side when she was gawped at, cheered at and almost blinded by the old-fashioned press cameras without a moment to relax. William and Kate have a similar camaraderie, which is essential for a lasting royal partnership in an age of such relentless social media attention.

As is her custom, the Queen made only the briefest of references to her family in her Christmas address: 'The importance of family has, of course, come home to Prince Philip and me personally this year with the marriages of two of our grandchildren, each in their own way a celebration of the God-given love that binds a family together.'

Other family matters were not so happy. The Queen's second son, Prince Andrew, was forced to give up his role as Britain's special representative for international trade and investment because of his friendship with Jeffrey Epstein, a convicted sex offender, and his association with several unsavoury characters including Colonel Gaddafi's son Saif. Prince Andrew's former wife Sarah Ferguson yet again caused embarrassment to the royal family, this time by offering to sell introductions to Prince Andrew for hundreds of thousands of pounds.

The Queen took the opportunity to return to a subject dear to her heart in her Commonwealth Day message on 14 March 2011, when she talked about the important role of women in society:

> This year, the Commonwealth celebrates the important role that women already play in every walk of life and in every Commonwealth country ... and faith, recognising that women are 'agents of change' in so many ways: as mothers and sisters, teachers and doctors, artists and craftspeople, smallholders and entrepreneurs, and as leaders of our societies, unleashing the potential of those around them. And also this year, the Commonwealth reflects on what more could be achieved if women were able to play an even larger role.

Later that year, on 28 October, the Queen addressed the Commonwealth Heads of Government in Perth, Australia, with women again at the top of the agenda:

> The theme of this year is, 'Women as Agents of Change'. It reminds us of the potential in our societies that is yet to be fully unlocked, and it encourages us to find ways to allow girls and women to play their full part. We must continue to

strive in our own countries and across the Commonwealth together to promote that theme in a lasting way beyond this year.

A hugely significant political event took place as a result of the efforts of another woman – the President of the Republic of Ireland, Mary McAleese. The Queen and the president of Ireland had met on six previous occasions going back to 1998, and it was Mary McAleese who issued the invitation to the Queen to visit her country. It would be the first visit by a British monarch to the Republic of Ireland since the 1911 tour by King George V, when the entire island of Ireland was still part of the United Kingdom. In the fight for Irish independence in the streets of Dublin, British Army soldiers were renowned for their ruthless treatment of the Irish rebels. After the suppression of the Easter Rising in 1916, when the rebels occupied Dublin's General Post Office, sixteen ringleaders were taken prisoner and executed by a British firing squad. As a result, those killed became martyrs and much bitterness towards the British ensued for many years. The Queen's visit in 2011, and the respect she showed for those who died in the struggle for independence, helped put an end to much of that bitterness at last.

On 17 May, the day of their arrival, the Queen and Prince Philip, accompanied by Mary McAleese and her husband, paid a visit to the Garden of Remembrance in the heart of Dublin for the first official engagement of their four-day state visit. Opened in 1966 on the fiftieth anniversary of the Easter Rising, it is dedicated to 'the memory of all those who gave their lives in the cause of Irish freedom'. The presence of the British and Irish heads of state side by side in a place regarded by many as a shrine to republicanism was deeply significant. Having laid her laurel wreath, the Queen stepped back and bowed her head in a hugely symbolic act of reconciliation between the two countries.

The next day, the Queen took a tour of the world-famous Guinness brewery at St James's Gate in Dublin and was given a lesson in how to pour a perfect pint, although neither she nor Prince Philip, who is partial to beer, was prepared to taste the stout. The high point of the state visit was to come that evening at the state banquet in Dublin Castle, where the Queen and Prince Philip were joined by the Conservative prime minister David Cameron, who had been elected the previous year to head a coalition government.

The content of the speech, which was written by the Queen and her deputy private secretary, drew widespread praise from the Irish media and from politicians. The Queen began her speech by speaking in Irish: '*A Uachtaráin agus a chairde*,' she said, 'President and friends.' President McAleese turned to others at the table and said 'Wow!' three times. The Queen went on: 'Together we have much to celebrate: the ties between our people, the shared values, and the economic, business and cultural links that make us so much more than just neighbours, that make us firm friends and equal partners.'

While she did not apologise for the atrocities carried out under British rule, she did refer to the past when she said:

It is a sad and regrettable reality that through history our islands have experienced more than their fair share of heartache, turbulence and loss. These events have touched us all, many of us personally, and are a painful legacy. We can never forget those who have died or been injured, and their families. To all those who have suffered as a consequence of our troubled past I extend my sincere thoughts and deep sympathy.

For most of the events of the state visit, the Queen was dressed appropriately in green. For the state banquet, she wore one of her emblem gowns specially made for the occasion, which had hand-sewn shamrocks on the bodice, while on the left shoulder was an Irish harp made from Swarovski crystal. She wore the Girls of Great Britain and Ireland tiara, a wedding gift from her grandmother Queen Mary, who wore it on one of her trips to Ireland.

The next day the Queen indulged her passion for horse racing with visits to the National Stud of Ireland and to some of Ireland's most famous breeding establishments. The state visit ended in Cork with a walkabout where the Queen, ignoring formality and the heavy security that surrounded her in Dublin, was able to mingle with the crowds. She was seen on television chatting with stallholders in the English Market in Cork.

'Ireland was fantastic,' Prince William recalled in an interview later. 'We all wanted it to go smoothly because it was such a big deal. I know a lot of Irish people and so many of them were so excited about the visit that I knew it would go well.' The visit to Ireland was reciprocated three years later when the Queen entertained the Irish president at Windsor Castle.

No sooner had the Queen returned home than she welcomed President and Mrs Obama to London on a state visit on 24 May. In her speech at the state banquet at Buckingham Palace, the Queen, as well as stressing the usual subject of the 'special relationship', spoke humorously about 'our common language'. On the subject of entertainment she said:

Over the years, we have enjoyed some of America's most spectacular musical productions and any number of what we call films – and you might prefer to call movies. In return, British films and theatrical productions have achieved considerable success in your country. This exchange of people and projects has enlarged and invigorated our common language – although I think you will agree we do not always use it in quite the same way!

The Queen is not afraid to play up to national stereotypes when the time is right to do so, and it often reflects how comfortable she feels in a particular situation.

On 15 July 2011, the Queen paid a visit to Bletchley Park near Milton Keynes to pay tribute to the codebreakers who worked there in the Second World War and who cracked the German Enigma codes. The fact that they did so made an incalculable contribution to the Battle of the Atlantic, allowing the movement of U-boats to be discovered. The existence of Bletchley was one of the most closely guarded secrets of the war. Its contribution to the Allied victory in that conflict was such that one historian has said that, without it, the war would have lasted for at least two more years. Although the work of the genius Alan Turing and other wartime codebreakers is now well known thanks to the several films that have been made about them, their work in cracking the Enigma and other German and Japanese codes during the war remained a secret for thirty years after the end of the war.

The Queen spoke about the secrecy and the important work done by women in Bletchley when she unveiled a memorial designed and sculpted by the artist Charles Gurrey to remember those codebreakers who had died:

It is impossible to overstate the deep sense of admiration, gratitude, and national debt that we owe to all those men and, especially, women. They were called to this place in the greatest of secrecy – so much so that some of their families will never know the full extent of their contribution … Necessity is indeed the mother of invention, and … battles can be won, and many lives saved, by using brainpower as well as firepower; deliberation as well as force.

Turing and his team at Bletchley went on to build what is considered to be the father of all computers – the Colossus. The Queen and Prince Philip viewed a restoration of a Colossus machine and a rebuild of a Turing Bombe machine, which was used to crack the codes.

In 1945, Turing was awarded the OBE by King George VI for his wartime services, but his work remained secret for years. Two years before he died of cyanide poisoning in 1954, Turing was convicted of a homosexual offence and stripped of his security clearance. In 2009, following an internet campaign, Gordon Brown made an official public apology on behalf of the British government for 'the appalling way he was treated'. The Queen subsequently granted him a posthumous pardon in 2013. The Queen's action is only the fourth royal pardon granted since the conclusion of the Second World War and it remains the only pardon granted where the party involved was guilty of the offence of which he was convicted. However, the Queen felt it was important to reflect the changing times by giving him this pardon.

Before the year was out, the Queen made her sixteenth and possibly final visit to Australia. The short trips 'down under', combined with the time change, were now too exhausting, and both the Queen and Prince Philip felt unwell afterwards. He had celebrated his ninetieth birthday in June and, although he was still remarkably active, they were not joking when they told friends another one just might finish them off. At a reception in her honour held at Parliament House in Canberra on

21 October 2011, the prime minister, Julia Gillard, described the Queen as 'a vital constitutional part of Australian democracy'. The Queen replied by saying:

> Ever since I first came here in 1954 I have watched Australia grow and develop at an extraordinary rate. This country has made dramatic progress economically, in social, scientific and industrial endeavours, and above all in self-confidence.

The Queen added: 'The world witnessed the anguish of Australians as they lived through a summer of national disasters. We were all impressed by the courage and resolution shown by those affected in the face of crippling desolation.' She was referring to the natural disasters that struck Australia between November 2010 and February 2011, which saw more than 99 per cent of Queensland declared a disaster zone, with thirty-seven lives lost as a result of floods. During the same period, all other Australian states experienced severe weather events or bushfires.

The Queen visited Canberra, Brisbane, Melbourne and Perth during the tour. In Perth, she attended a Commonwealth Heads of Government Meeting. She ended her speech saying: 'I conclude with an Aboriginal proverb which is itself enduring: "We are all visitors to this time, this place. We are just passing through. Our purpose here is to observe, to learn, to grow, to love ... and then we return home."'

The eyes of the world turned to the UK in the summer of 2012, both for the Queen's Diamond Jubilee and for the Olympic Games, in which she played such a memorable role. Before that there were several events of note, one being the sixtieth anniversary of her accession on 6 February. Sixty years earlier, King George VI died peacefully in his sleep at

Sandringham, his favourite royal residence. As a mark of respect to her late father, the Queen likes to spend the anniversary of his death at Sandringham, keeping her only public appearances on the day to something local and appropriately low-key.

Although the six weeks she spends at Sandringham at the beginning of each year provide the opportunity for the Queen to fulfil her role as a landowner away from state duties, many of them continue. She spends a couple of hours each day working on her state papers, which are delivered to her in the red boxes. The cabinet papers and foreign and Commonwealth communications they contain have been selected and marked for her by her private secretary.

So the working life of the court continues wherever the Queen might be. The Queen has a confidential timetable published for the information of the royal household only, which is issued every Monday morning. It details every engagement and coming and going from the palace; even at Sandringham the Queen has a timetable, which lists her duties for the day. Although they may be very few, such as attending the Women's Institute meeting or visiting a local school, it gives an idea of how precise and exact the Queen's arrangements are.

The adjacent town of King's Lynn (the birthplace of Admiral Lord Nelson and home of Captain George Vancouver, who founded the Canadian city) nearly always receives a visit, and in 2012 the Queen visited the infant school at Dersingham to meet pupils and staff. The Queen likes the minimum of fuss to be made and finds it satisfying to be able to chat informally to the people of her very own local town. In contrast, during the following months, the Queen and Prince Philip would be making a great deal of regional visits, touring the country as part of the Diamond Jubilee celebrations, leaving the overseas visits to other members of the royal family, who were now sharing more of the load.

One of the Queen's first official engagements of the year, held on 14 February, Valentine's Day, was to celebrate the bicentenary of Charles Dickens's birth. As patron of the Royal Theatrical Fund, the Queen attended a short lunchtime recital of his work performed by theatrical luminaries including Derek Jacobi at London's Guildhall. In the evening, she hosted a reception at Buckingham Palace for all the many societies connected with Charles Dickens. As well as literary scholars from the UK and North America, those attending included actors from film, television and the theatre who have starred in adaptations of Dickens's novels, members of the Dickens Fellowship from around the Commonwealth and those involved in preserving the Dickensian heritage in libraries and museums.

The actor Eddie Redmayne, who was presented to the Queen, said: 'She was very interested in the bicentenary and told me about when Dickens met Queen Victoria. She seemed genuinely interested in the family and the events that have been taking place.' Julius Bryant, who looks after Dickens's manuscripts at the Victoria and Albert Museum, said: 'She seemed to know all about his working methods, which was a surprise. She knew all about how he wrote for magazines and the practicalities of that. She seemed very well informed, so she is definitely a Dickens lover. I think she must have read a lot of his work.'

Queen Victoria's meeting with Dickens is immortalised in her diary, which was on display in a glass case at the reception. That the Queen also keeps a diary, which she updates every night, was confirmed in a conversation with an American guest. When the Queen asked the American if he had seen Queen Victoria's diary, he replied in the affirmative and said he admired the penmanship. The Queen then told him that she writes her diary by hand every night. The American said he would very much like to see it. The Queen replied: 'Well you won't – not until after I am dead.'

In March, both Houses of Parliament delivered a loyal address to the Queen. In her reply, she paid respect to Prince Philip, who only a few months before had been hospitalised with chest pains and had had a stent inserted into an artery. The Queen said: 'Prince Philip is, I believe, well known for declining compliments of any kind. But throughout he has been a constant strength and guide.'

The Queen's Diamond Jubilee was marked with a spectacular central weekend, a series of regional tours throughout the United Kingdom, and Commonwealth visits undertaken by other members of the royal family in support of the Queen. On Saturday 2 June, the Queen attended the Epsom Derby and arrived with great fanfare to be serenaded with the national anthem by singer Katherine Jenkins. The big race was won by the Irish horse Camelot and, although the Queen did not have a horse running in the race, it is one of her favourite days of the year, and her presence delighted the racegoers, who cheered her wherever she went.

On Sunday, there were street parties throughout the land and in the afternoon an extraordinary, innovative tribute to the Queen. The Thames Diamond Jubilee Pageant took place on the river and consisted of up to 1,000 boats assembled from across the United Kingdom, the Commonwealth and around the world. The Queen and the Duke of Edinburgh travelled in the royal barge, *Spirit of Chartwell*, which formed the centrepiece of the flotilla.

It was one of the most magnificent royal spectacles ever, but sadly the British weather almost ruined it. It was cold and grey to start with, so the Thames looked muddy and sad, and then the rains came, accompanied by gusts of wind to ensure that even if people were under cover they got soaked. But in true British spirit everyone got on with it as if they were under a tropical sun.

The only downbeat note was Prince Philip's sudden hospitalisation afterwards. The Duke was taken to the King Edward VII Hospital on 4 June to be treated for a bladder infection. To say he must have been fuming to be forced to miss the service of thanksgiving the following day was an understatement, but he complied with his doctors and stayed in hospital long enough for the treatment to work. To keep his spirits up, he was visited by members of his family, including the Queen. Many blamed his condition on his having to stand for so many hours in the cold wind and rain during the flotilla, but the Duke, a naval man, is stoic and stubborn. Even Prime Minister David Cameron remarked, 'Our royal family are incredibly dedicated to what they do, no matter what the circumstances.'

The Queen paid particular attention to the horse puppeteers from the play *War Horse*, who appeared on the roof of the National Theatre. Towards the end of the historic and beautifully organised river pageant, twelve members of the Royal College of Music chamber choir on board the last vessel in the flotilla pulled up alongside the main royal party. As the rain lashed their upturned faces and turned their song sheets to pulp, they sang 'Land of Hope and Glory' and 'Rule Britannia'. The dozen young men and women, accompanied by the London Philharmonic, struggled to see and hear as the earpieces they wore fell out in the wet, but still they sang on.

On Tuesday 5 June, the Diamond Jubilee weekend culminated in a day of celebrations in central London, including a service at St Paul's Cathedral followed by two receptions, a lunch at Westminster Hall, a carriage procession to Buckingham Palace and finally a balcony appearance, fly-past and fireworks. President Obama released a video message: 'Your Majesty, on the historic occasion of your Jubilee, Michelle and I send you and all the British people and members of the Commonwealth the heartfelt congratulations of the American people.'

In a televised address to Britain and the Commonwealth, the Queen said she would treasure the memories of the previous week. It is one of only a handful of addresses to the nation she has made outside her traditional Christmas broadcasts, and it was a very heartfelt thanks to all those who had made the occasion so special:

> The events that I have attended to mark my Diamond Jubilee have been a humbling experience. It has touched me deeply to see so many thousands of families, neighbours and friends celebrating together in such a happy atmosphere. I hope that memories of this year's happy events will brighten our lives for many years to come. I will continue to treasure and draw inspiration from the countless kindnesses shown to me in this country and throughout the Commonwealth. Thank you all.

After her travels up and down the country and the hectic programme of the Diamond Jubilee, the Queen travelled to Balmoral for her summer court. Rarely given a moment's respite, the Queen's spell in Scotland was interrupted by the Olympic Games in London.

On 27 July, the Queen addressed the Olympic heads of government at a reception at Buckingham Palace, noting: 'This will be the third London Olympiad: my great-grandfather opened the 1908 Games at White City; my father opened the 1948 Games at Wembley Stadium, and later this evening I will take pleasure in declaring open the 2012 London Olympic Games at Stratford, in the east of London.'

None of those present could have imagined the role that the Queen was to play in the opening ceremony later that day. In the spring, amid much secrecy, the Queen and actor Daniel Craig filmed a Bond sequence at Buckingham Palace under the direction of creative director Danny Boyle for the Olympics opening ceremony. As the Queen's page, Paul Whybrew – dressed in livery with his service medals on his left lapel – announced actor Craig to the Queen, she waited a few moments with the clock ticking and then turned around from her desk to say the now immortal words: 'Good evening, Mr Bond.'

The three of them then walked through Buckingham Palace – with corgis Monty, Willow and Holly – towards the garden, where a helicopter was waiting. The world gasped as the Queen appeared to parachute from the helicopter into the stadium to open the Olympic Games. Of course, it was a stunt-double who made the jump, but the Queen displayed a sporting spirit when she appeared in the same peach lace outfit at the opening ceremony.

At the Irish state banquet at Windsor Castle two years later, the Queen joked about the famous sequence in her speech when she said teasingly: 'And it took someone of Irish descent, Danny Boyle, to get me to jump from a helicopter.'

After an extremely successful Olympic Games for Team GB, with a record tally of sixty-five medals, the Queen welcomed the Paralympians with the words: 'We look forward to celebrating the uplifting spirit which distinguishes the Paralympic Games from other events, drawing on Britain's unique sporting heritage.'

That year's Christmas message unsurprisingly devoted plenty of attention to the Diamond Jubilee and the Games, giving the Queen another opportunity to applaud the 'army of volunteers' who had made it all possible. After an incredibly busy year in 2012, the Queen understandably reduced the number of official engagements in 2013. With the spotlight on the Duchess of

Cambridge and the birth of Prince George, the Queen was less in the headlines than in her jubilee year.

The Queen is lucky enough to enjoy remarkably good health, so when she is taken ill, as she was at the beginning of March 2013, everyone made an inordinate amount of fuss. After the Queen arrived at the King Edward VII Hospital in London from Windsor Castle with symptoms of gastroenteritis, the media started to gather outside in large numbers. Like most of us, the Queen dislikes going into hospital (it was only the fifth occasion in her six-decade reign), but once there she followed the orders of her physician, Professor John Cunningham, to the letter.

In this case, it is believed she was hospitalised so that her doctors could assess her health and attach a drip to rehydrate her and speed her recovery, thus preventing the cancellation of more official engagements. The Queen loathes letting people down and takes every precaution to avoid getting sick. (Note the gloves, which are worn not only to protect her hands, but lessen the risk of infection.) If any one of the royal family has a cold, for instance, they will isolate themselves, sleep in a separate bedroom and avoid the rest of the family. As it turned out, the Queen was in hospital for only twenty-four hours and spent the remainder of the week quietly at Buckingham Palace, available for consultation but not travelling anywhere.

One of her next major engagements was a much more sombre one. When the Queen attended the state funeral of Baroness Thatcher, the longest-serving prime minister of her reign, at St Paul's Cathedral on 17 April, it helped lay to rest nearly three decades of speculation about their reportedly difficult relationship. Apart from Sir Winston Churchill, who was honoured with an official state funeral in 1965, the Queen rarely attends any such events, preferring to send a representative. In the past twenty years, she has attended only a handful of non-family funerals, including those for King Baudouin of the Belgians, Margaret MacDonald (her former nursery maid and dresser, who worked for her for over sixty-seven years) and her great friend and racing manager, The Earl of Carnarvon.

The month of June marked two milestones. On the fourth, the Queen joined 2,000 guests for a service at Westminster Abbey to mark sixty years since her coronation. More than twenty members of the royal family attended, including the Prince of Wales and Duchess of Cornwall and the Duke and Duchess of Cambridge. Several key items from the coronation were placed in Westminster Abbey for the service. Among them was the heavy, solid gold St Edward's Crown, displayed on the high altar – the first time it had left the Tower of London since 1953. Beside it was the Ampulla, the gold, eagle-shaped bottle from which the holy oil was poured for the Queen's anointing. The Coronation Chair, one of the oldest pieces of English furniture still in use, was also on show.

Two weeks later at Royal Ascot the Queen's horse, Estimate, won the Gold Cup, the first time in its 207-year history it had ever been won by the monarch. The only time the general public sees the Queen lose her regal composure is when she is watching one of her horses take part in a race. If the horse is a winner, her excitement knows no bounds. Nor does that of the crowd, and that day the spectators went wild as they roared on the filly they had made 7–2 favourite.

The Queen could not stop smiling; her bloodstock advisor, John Warren, was shouting and the entire party of royalty and guests in the box erupted with joy when Estimate narrowly won in a thrilling finish. The Queen clapped her hands with delight as the four-year-old crossed the line, while Princesses Beatrice and Eugenie jumped up and down with excitement next to her in the royal box. It is traditional for the Queen to present the trophy to the winner of one of Flat racing's most famous races, but instead her son the Duke of York had to step in to hand the cup to her. Peter Phillips, the Queen's grandson, said: 'It's been amazing. This is her passion, this is her life; every year she is here, every year she strives to have winners and to win the big one at Royal Ascot means so much to her.'

Ever since she was a small child and kept a collection of thirty-odd toy ponies on wheels on the landing of 145 Piccadilly, the Queen has loved horses. But unlike many girls whose interest in all things equine wanes when they become teenagers, her passion for these beautiful animals has never abated. From the moment she was first lifted on to a saddle and was able to move from fantasy to the real thing, horses have remained the Queen's principal recreation. Now, even as she approaches the age of ninety, the Queen is sometimes glimpsed on her favourite hack Emma – one of the fell ponies she breeds herself – with her headscarf tied firmly under chin, in the company of her stud groom, Terry Pendry.

As the Queen is not the kind of person who takes up interests lightly, only to drop them just as easily, horses have remained her constant diversion in life. During the war, a favourite pastime was to travel to the royal stud, then at Hampton Court, to see the mares and foals kept there. Armed with a Box Brownie camera, she picked out the foals she liked and proceeded to photograph them throughout the early stages of their lives.

In June 1945, dressed in her ATS uniform, she accompanied her parents to her very first race meeting to see one of the foals she had earmarked run in the Derby. The race meeting was held at Newmarket; many of the buildings had suffered bomb damage and the place was a mess. It was a memorable occasion, however, as Rising Light, the colt that the Princess had photographed since the day it was born, came fifth. Two months later, in August, two days before President Truman sanctioned the destruction of Hiroshima, the Princess joined the King and Queen at the Ascot races. This time Rising Light won by a head and the Princess was hooked.

In 2001, John Warren succeeded his late father-in-law, the Earl of Carnarvon, as the Queen's bloodstock and racing advisor. A straight-talking son of a greengrocer, Warren is the first person without a title or military rank to be the Queen's racing advisor. He describes the Queen affectionately as 'a creature of habit'. Every spring she goes to the royal stud at Sandringham in Norfolk, armed with her camera, to see her twenty or so mares with their new foals, and a few years ago Warren suggested she borrow his digital camera. 'The Queen still can't get used to looking at a digital screen,' he explained later. 'Her Majesty tried taking a picture with my camera, but it wasn't for her – she still loves her routine.'

The importance of racing to her can be judged by the fact that the first newspaper the Queen reads in the morning is the *Racing Post*, and her racing advisor and trainers can always get through to her on her private line. Sadly, her schedule means she has precious little chance to see her horses actually race. Other owner-breeders at her level would get forty or fifty days' racing a year, and they'd be on the course to watch the majority of their horses run. The Queen gets only eight or ten days, and if she's lucky sees 10 per cent of her horses race. For the most part, she has to watch them on television in the evening, the races having been carefully recorded by her page. The exception is Royal Ascot, a race meeting the Queen has never missed during her reign. Despite her love for the sport, the Queen never mentions her private passion for racing and breeding in any of her speeches, in much the same way as Prince Philip never mentions his enthusiasm for cricket.

After Ascot week, the Queen endorsed her husband's interest not in cricket, but in engineering. Prince Philip is the Senior Fellow of the Royal Academy of Engineering and has given his name to the Prince Philip Medal, awarded biennially to an engineer of any nationality who has made an exceptional contribution to engineering. In June, the Queen gave her name to a new global prize for engineering – the Queen Elizabeth Prize.

The inaugural £1 million prize was awarded to a team of five engineers who created the internet and the World Wide Web. On 25 June 2013, the winners received their award from the Queen in front of an audience at Buckingham Palace that included the three leaders of the UK's main political parties, the judges and a number of young engineers. In her speech, the Queen said: 'I have every hope that this prize will be an aspiration of the international engineering community and an inspiration to young people everywhere, by letting them know that it is an exciting time to become an engineer and that by joining this profession they, too, can make a real impact on the way we live our lives.'

In November, Prince Charles, accompanied by the Duchess of Cornwall, represented the Queen at the 2013 Commonwealth Heads of Government Meeting in Sri Lanka. He had never before attended in place of the monarch at the biannual gathering of Commonwealth leaders – it was an indication that the Queen had decided it was time for her to give up long-haul foreign travel.

'Reflection' was the theme of the 2013 Christmas message, though she also referred to the christening of Prince George, and the presence of four generations at the event. The Queen said:

I myself had cause to reflect this year, at Westminster Abbey, on my own pledge of service made in that great church on

Coronation Day sixty years earlier. The anniversary reminded me of the remarkable changes that have occurred since the Coronation, many of them for the better; and of the things that have remained constant, such as the importance of family, friendship and good neighbourliness.

In her first foreign trip since a visit to Australia in 2011, the Queen and Prince Philip flew to Rome at the beginning of April 2014. They had lunch with the Italian president, Giorgio Napolitano, and his wife Clio at the Quirinal Palace on 3 April before going on to the Vatican to meet Pope Francis. Arriving at the Vatican a little behind schedule, the Queen shook hands with the Pope and said: 'Sorry to keep you waiting, we were having lunch with the President.'

Although the visit was less formal than usual, and the Queen wore a lilac hat and coat instead of black, the monarch and the Pope still exchanged gifts inside the Vatican. Pope Francis gave the Queen a royal orb made of lapis lazuli with a silver cross on top, for her baby great-grandson Prince George. He also presented the Queen with a facsimile of a seventeenth-century papal decree upgrading the saintly status of St Edward the Confessor, the Queen's ancestor. The Queen presented the pontiff with a hamper of British produce, including goods grown in the gardens of royal palaces, honey from the beehives at Buckingham Palace and whisky. Prince Philip was happy to be photographed proffering the bottle of Scotch to the Pope.

A few days after her return from Rome, the Queen welcomed the new President of Ireland, Michael D. Higgins, and his wife, on an official state visit. It was the first visit by an Irish president. On 8 April, the Queen gave a state banquet at Windsor Castle. Among the guests at the banquet was Sinn Féin's Martin McGuinness, who once wore the black balaclava, beret and leather gloves of a commando of the IRA, an organisation that murdered members of the royal family in a bid to end the authority of the British Crown on the island of Ireland.

At the banquet, dressed in white tie and tails, McGuinness, Northern Ireland's deputy first minister, stood for the national anthem and toasted the 'health and happiness' of the Queen in a symbolically significant act for British–Irish relations. In her speech, the Queen looked back to her visit to Dublin in 2011, saying: 'In Dublin, I laid wreaths in the Garden of Remembrance for those who died in the cause of Irish freedom and at Islandbridge, where Ireland's dead from the First World War are commemorated.'

She admitted that 'Irish migrants to Britain encountered discrimination and a lack of appreciation. Happily, those days are now behind us,' and she continued by returning to a familiar theme: 'My visit to Ireland, and your visit this week, Mr President, show that we are walking together towards a brighter, more settled future. We will remember our past, but we shall no longer allow our past to ensnare our future.'

Although inside the castle, the talk was all of reconciliation and cooperation, of putting the past behind and moving on, outside the castle gates was a crowd of protesters who found putting the past behind them much more difficult. They were those who had lost relatives and friends at the hands of the IRA. Back in London the next day, Mr Higgins went to Westminster Abbey to see a memorial to Lord Louis Mountbatten, the cousin of the Queen killed in 1979 by the IRA.

In her continuing crusade for reconciliation, the Queen went back to Belfast in June. The Queen and Prince Philip were greeted as they arrived at Crumlin Road jail by members of the public waving Union flags. Inside, they were given a tour of the notorious C wing by Martin McGuinness, who had been held prisoner there in 1976. It was another symbolic gesture of reconciliation between the two sides, something that the royal family has done much to help bring about by its example. She made sure she highlighted the moment in that year's Christmas speech, as it was her visit to the *Game of Thrones* set that received more attention, but she felt this was a far more important element of her visit.

On 5 June, the Queen and Prince Philip took a Eurostar train to Paris for a state visit to France to coincide with the seventieth anniversary of D-Day. A minor diplomatic crisis was averted when it was discovered that the Citroen C5s normally used to transport state guests in France were too low for the Queen to wear a hat. Instead, she travelled in a higher-roofed and more modest Renault. The Queen was invited by President François Hollande, who had assumed office in 2012, to preside over the main international ceremony to mark the Normandy landings on Sword Beach. President Barack Obama and David Cameron were among the many heads of state and political leaders attending.

The failure to invite the Queen for the sixty-fifth anniversary of the landings five years previously was seen by many to be an insult to the memory of the British and Canadian troops who died to free France and are buried there. Nicolas Sarkozy, the then conservative French president, was criticised for regarding the commemorations as 'primarily a Franco–American occasion'. Prime Minister Gordon Brown had also been criticised for attending himself, but not ensuring that the Queen was invited, too.

After a day spent on the beaches in Normandy, the Queen and Prince Philip returned to Paris for a state banquet in their honour. In her speech to President Hollande, the Queen said:

'Today our nations are free and sovereign because allied forces liberated this continent from occupation and tyranny.' She went on to express three observations:

> The first is that the true measure of all our actions is how long the good in them lasts ... My second observation, which is that everything we do, we do for the young ... The decisions we make should always be designed to enlarge their horizons and enrich their future, from caring for our environment to preventing conflict ... My third observation is that our two nations, Britain and France, have a particular role to play in this effort. We are two of the trustees of international peace and security, and we are both ready and equipped to aid those threatened by poverty or conflict.

In July, shortly before her annual stay at Balmoral, the Queen was in Scotland, at Rosyth dockyard, to name the Royal Navy's newest and largest ship, HMS *Queen Elizabeth*. In her speech at the dockyard she said: 'Lord Mountbatten told my father on becoming King that "there is no more fitting preparation to be King than to have been trained in the Royal Navy".' She went on to refer to Prince Philip as 'The Lord High Admiral', a title the Queen had held since 1964 and which she decided to bestow on her husband as a gift to mark his ninetieth birthday in 2011 and to show her gratitude for his unstinting support during fifty-nine years as her consort.

That stay had a particular resonance for her. The Scottish referendum was only a couple of months away and since her coronation year of 1953, when she first toured Scotland as Queen, her entire being has been focused around the unity of her kingdom. At the age of eighty-eight, she had to come to terms with the unwelcome possibility that the break-up of the

Union between England and Scotland could become a reality. In her Silver Jubilee speech of 1977 the Queen made no bones about where she stood. She could readily understand the aspirations of the Scottish and Welsh peoples, she said, 'But I cannot forget that I was crowned Queen of the United Kingdom of Great Britain and Northern Ireland.'

The question of independence was especially poignant for the Queen because her family are all so essentially Scottish. All four of her children attended the Scottish boarding school Gordonstoun on the Moray Firth, as did two of her grandchildren, Zara and Peter Phillips. Prince William, educated at Eton, chose to study at St Andrews University, where he met his future wife. The Princess Royal, Chancellor of Edinburgh University, holds more Scottish patronages than any other member of the royal family. The Prince of Wales, who uses his Scottish title, Duke of Rothesay, when he is north of the border, also holds the romantic titles Lord of the Isles and Great Steward of Scotland.

The Queen has made more trips north of the border than any other sovereign since the Scottish and English crowns were united in 1603. Scotland is her home, as it was for her great-great-grandmother Queen Victoria, who was the first monarch to establish a footing in Scotland since the Jacobite rebellion. The turreted castle, with its surrounding misty hills, pine walks and immaculate gardens, became a royal home in 1852. It has been the favourite ever since. Inside the castle, it is all antique pine and gurgling pipes, with wallpaper chosen by Queen Victoria and her personal cipher, VRI, on the staircase and walls. Many things in the castle, down to the smallest item of domestic equipment, bear the imprint of things Scottish and still do to this day – a tradition laid down by Prince Albert.

No royal dinner is ever served at Balmoral without the

accompaniment of a piper. The piper marches round the table two or three times and out into the castle hall, where he is refreshed by a traditional dram of whisky. In the dining room, there are large paintings by Winterhalter of Victoria and Albert and the architect of Balmoral, and in the corridors Landseer paintings depicting stags, dogs and stalking scenes. It might look like a typically romanticised view of Scotland, but it is very real for the Queen.

Scotland is in Her Majesty's roots and she is deeply attached to the country and its people. As a baby she was taken to her mother's ancestral home, Glamis Castle, to be with her maternal grandparents, the Earl and Countess of Strathmore. As a child she spent magical summers with her paternal grandparents, King George V and Queen Mary, at Balmoral, and as a young girl she learnt to stalk and shoot deer there with her father, King George VI. As little girls, she and her sister Margaret, who was born in Glamis Castle, used to love the Highland Games at Braemar, held on the estate of the late Princess Royal, Duchess of Fife. They would attempt to escape from their nanny, Clara Knight, and run across the field, regardless of the fact they might get struck by a hammer or a caber. Once back at the castle, they would have their own contest, dancing around the lawns and tossing little sticks and whatever they could find, much to the anxiety of their mother.

The Queen has always loved the Scottish people; she was bought up by a Scottish governess, Marion Crawford, and until 1993 spent her life being looked after by her Scottish companion and dresser, Margaret MacDonald. 'Bobo' taught her mistress to be 'thrifty and frugal' and even accompanied her on her honeymoon to Birkhall, much to Prince Philip's annoyance. The Queen's personal connection with Scotland is especially emotional, as, when Prince Philip was a dashing young naval officer, he spent his leave with the King and Queen at Balmoral. The Prince developed a love for the Highlands and all the region had to offer, including the potential to marry a beautiful Princess with a substantial amount of Scottish blue blood in her veins.

When the Queen is at Balmoral, she is on holiday. 'It is the one place one looks forward to very much as the summer goes on,' she says. 'It has an atmosphere of its own and you just hibernate.' The Queen might be able to 'sleep in the same bed for six weeks', but she still has to perform some state duties. Notable among these is the annual succession of official guests who come to stay for the weekend or perhaps a few days. As we have seen, the prime minister of the day is always invited, and every prime minister who has ever visited, dating from the days of Queen Victoria, has presented a portrait of themselves to the sovereign. There is a special room on the ground floor over-looking the lawns and fountain, known as the prime minister's room, which is always set aside for his or her use.

Despite these close ties, Buckingham Palace made it clear that the Queen was entirely neutral in the matter, and that the outcome of the referendum on 19 September was a matter for the Scottish people alone. In her message following the result, she said:

For many in Scotland and elsewhere today, there will be strong feelings and contrasting emotions – among family, friends and neighbours. That, of course, is the nature of the robust democratic tradition we enjoy in this country. But I have no doubt that these emotions will be tempered by an understanding of the feelings of others.

It was a neutral response to a subject that had clearly polarised opinion, and not just in Scotland. However, a few days later, microphones caught the prime minister claiming that the Queen 'purred down the line' when he told her the news, and he added that 'I've never heard someone so happy'.

Towards the year's end, the most-visited public art installation for a generation was put in place in the moat of the Tower of London. To commemorate the centenary of the outbreak of the First World War, 888,246 ceramic red poppies were gradually planted until 11 November, the anniversary of the end of the war. Each represented one British or colonial life lost. By the end there was a sea of red; then they were all taken away and sold.

The idea for the poppies came to the artist Paul Cummins as he went through First World War archives in Chesterfield records office. By chance he found the will of an unknown soldier who died at Flanders, which contained the line: 'The blood-swept lands and seas of red, where angels fear to tread.' And it was that which inspired him. The Duke and Duchess of Cambridge and Prince Harry walked among the poppies in August, just as the display was taking shape, while the Queen and Prince Philip came to pay their respects when they visited the installation on 16 October.

In the Christmas broadcast of 2014 from Buckingham Palace, photographs of the Queen's grandparents King George V and Queen Mary were carefully placed on the table, together with an embossed brass box. These First World War boxes of chocolate, cards or tobacco were intended for 'every sailor afloat and every soldier on the front', paid for with monies dutifully raised by their daughter, Princess Mary. The theme was, of course, one of reconciliation and the Queen spoke of the sacrifices made by so many a hundred years ago:

Reconciliation is the peaceful end to conflict, and we were reminded of this in August when countries on both sides of the First World War came together to remember in peace. The ceramic poppies at the Tower of London drew millions, and the only possible reaction to seeing them and walking among them was silence. For every poppy a life; and a reminder of the grief of loved ones left behind. No one who fought in that war is still alive, but we remember their sacrifice and indeed the sacrifice of all those in the armed forces who serve and protect us today.

She went on to recall the famous Christmas truce in the trenches of 1914, which was 'a reminder to us all that even in the unlikeliest of places hope can still be found'. It was a typical message of hope and forgiveness from the Queen, who has always sought to find ways of helping to bring about peace.

In 2015, in the ninetieth year of her life, the Queen remains as busy and committed as ever. Numerous anniversaries – including her own as Britain's longest reigning monarch – have kept her busy in between the day-to-day business of her ordered life. The Commonwealth is still of utmost important to her and, in an era when it might appear to be something of an anachronism to some people, the Queen tried to inject a new spirit of youthfulness into her annual Commonwealth Day message. She began:

I think it apt that on this day we celebrate 'A Young Commonwealth' and all that it has to offer. As a concept that is unique in human history, the Commonwealth can only flourish if its ideas and ideals continue to be young and fresh and relevant to all generations. The youthfulness and vitality that motivate our collective endeavours were seen in abundance last year in Glasgow.

They will be seen again in a few months' time when Young

Leaders from islands and continents gather to make new friendships and to work on exciting initiatives that can help to build a safer world for future generations. And last November in India, talented young scientists from universities and research institutes conferred with eminent professors and pioneers of discovery at the Commonwealth Science Conference. These are stirring examples of what is meant by 'A Young Commonwealth'.

The Queen returned to another of her favourite themes, the place of women in society, at the centenary Annual General Meeting of the Women's Institute at the Royal Albert Hall when, with the help of her daughter the Princess Royal, watched by a laughing Countess of Wessex, she cut through the solid iced cake made in celebration of the anniversary.

'In the modern world, the opportunities for women to give something of value to society are greater than ever,' she said at the beginning of her address to the meeting. 'Because, through their own efforts, they now play a much greater part in all areas of public life. Over the past one hundred years, the WI has continued to grow and evolve with its members to stay relevant and forward-thinking. In 2015 it continues to demonstrate that it can make a real difference to the lives of women of all ages and cultural backgrounds, in a spirit of friendship, cooperation and support.'

On Sunday 5 July, it was the Queen's turn to celebrate once again. This time it was the Sandringham christening of her latest great-grandchild, Princess Charlotte Elizabeth Diana of Cambridge, who was born on 2 May at St Mary's Hospital. Like her brother, Prince George, Charlotte was baptised by the Archbishop of Canterbury using consecrated water from the River Jordan.

The sixteenth-century church of St Mary Magdalene on the Sandringham Estate was last used for such a royal purpose in December 1990, when Princess Eugenie was baptised during the regular Sunday service attended by villagers and estate workers. Eugenie was nine months old by then and the traditional christening gown – worn by generations of royal babies – was too small and the buttons at the back had to be left open. The church was also the place where Princess Charlotte's paternal grandmother Lady Diana Spencer was christened on 30 August 1961.

The Queen is proud of her children, grandchildren and great-grandchildren, as well she might be. Following his decision to leave the army after ten years, Prince Harry received the KCVO from his grandmother, who presented him with the insignia privately in Buckingham Palace. It was especially significant to him after his years of falling in and out of trouble and he was 'proud and pleased' to receive the honour, which is the personal gift of the sovereign.

It seems a long way off from the days of the nineties when the Queen felt she had failed with her offspring as one by one their marriages had collapsed. She turned to her mother in mock despair and asked her where it had all gone wrong. The Queen Mother looked up from her game of cards and said, 'Don't worry it will all be all right in the end.' Which it has been.

Chapter 11

CONCLUSION

When Princess Elizabeth became Queen on the death of her father, George VI, in 1952, she was twenty-five years old. Television in the United Kingdom was still in its infancy and, like most children, she had been brought up listening to the wireless with her parents. She made her first speech at the age of fourteen on a special edition of *Children's Hour* and her first Christmas Day broadcast in 1952 continued a custom started by her grandfather twenty years before. In her ninetieth year, the Queen is still giving speeches and the one she delivers at Christmas time is the only one she writes herself, albeit with the help of her husband and private secretary. The broadcast is filmed shortly before Christmas and, as soon as the television recording is complete, the Queen goes into another room and records exactly the same speech for the radio transmission only. The speech reflects her personal feelings, tells the story of her year and, in the case of this book, the story of her reign.

On 9 September 2015, the Queen becomes the oldest monarch in British history, overtaking her great-great-grandmother Queen Victoria. Victoria reigned for sixty-three years and seven months and seemed genuinely delighted by her achievement, writing in her journal from Balmoral that

23 September 1896 was 'the day, on which I have reigned longer, by a day, than any English Sovereign'. As 'the day' progressed, church bells began to ring and beacons were lit on the neighbouring Scottish hillsides and across the rest of the United Kingdom. In London, everything from printed handkerchiefs to china plates bore the legend 'the longest reign in history'. No disrespect was implied towards the Queen's grandfather, George III; it was simply because Victorians revelled in a present they considered more glorious than the past.

It will be many years before we know what the Queen puts in the diary she writes every night, but she will no doubt record the moment in her own hand, just as Queen Victoria did that day at Balmoral. Then there was huge national rejoicing, as her reign symbolised the importance of the Victorian age, with its bridges, its railways, its industry and its invention. The reign of Queen Elizabeth II will be remembered for its technological advances more than its industry, architecture or wars. The recurring theme of the Queen's reign, as revealed in her Christmas speeches, is one of tolerance, forgiveness and reconciliation.

The Queen herself has immense personal restraint in all things, which is reflected in her way of life and the manner in which she does things. She has a knack of maintaining a sense of proportion at all times. Like her late mother, she has the uncanny ability to shut off worries, putting them into one compartment and closing the door, 'so even if something pretty awful is happening, she remains resilient', as her first cousin Margaret Rhodes astutely says. She may have been accused by those close to her of compartmentalising her life, but it has proved to be expedient in a devoted sovereign. Prince Philip described his wife as having 'the quality of tolerance in abundance', which has helped her over many of the more difficult aspects of her reign – and her life.

Her judgement deserted her only once, and that was when Diana, Princess of Wales, was killed in Paris. Tucked away in the seclusion of Balmoral Castle, the Queen failed to realise that 500 miles south in London the crowds of mourners were perilously close to turning into a mob. Their growing wrath was palpable. They wanted to know why no flag was flying at half-mast over Buckingham Palace, why no royal tributes to the Princess had been forthcoming, and above all else why the royal family had decided to remain in Scotland.

The Queen had tried everything to accommodate Diana in life, bending the rules, excusing her indiscretions, making allowances for her illness, overlooking her outbursts, taking note of her grievances, ignoring the way she tried to claim centre stage and ordering her staff to treat her with respect and courtesy at all times. But what she could not and would not do was restructure the monarchy to suit her daughter-in-law. When Diana died, she did not know what to do, so she did what she has always done in times of personal tragedy and closed ranks with her family around her. It wasn't enough. It was never going to be enough for a life cut so short, sharply and painfully.

The Queen believes her role is to fulfil her duty, not define what that duty should be. On the occasion of her twenty-first birthday, while with her parents, she made an oath to the Commonwealth. Over a radio link she said: 'I declare before you all that my whole life, whether it be long or short, shall be devoted to your service and the service of our great imperial family to which we all belong.'

The British Empire is long gone and the institution she pledged her life to is no longer even the British Commonwealth, but simply the Commonwealth, a body of independent nations whose links to the mother country are ever more tenuous. But the Queen has kept her vow. She has sat through countless state banquets and listened to corrupt dictators ramble on for hours; she has met more civic dignitaries than she can remember; she has opened so many factories, schools, hospitals and welfare centres they merge into a grey blur. It is the mind-boggling boring routine of her reign, and yet she has always looked interested and involved. She never complains and the smile is still in place. It is as if the shadow of old Queen Mary is forever looming over her, ordering her not to fidget and to keep her hands out of her pockets with nothing more than a promise of a biscuit at the end of it.

By a great effort of will, the Queen has kept the course she set herself. While others fell by the moral wayside or took advantage of their royal position, she soldiered on, avoiding so much as a breath of personal scandal. But if her own life is without blemish, experience has given her an insight into the weakness of others. She sees the broader picture and counsels patience: 'Just wait and see what happens' is her frequent advice. One of her courtiers remarked that when her mother, Queen Elizabeth, died in 2002, it was as if the Queen had 'stepped into the century'. It took the death of her mother to release her personality from the strictures cast by such a luminary. Her emotions are now more apparent and, for someone who has had her life so structured, she enjoys nothing more than when things go slightly awry.

In 1995, she was taken in by a telephone hoaxer pretending to be Canada's prime minister. In the resulting conversation, conducted in both French and English, she agreed she would try to influence Quebec's referendum on the issue of whether or not to break away from Canada. Whether she would have done it or not, we will never know, but the conversation was an indication of how adept the Queen is at dealing with any situation that might arise. She has made more speeches and addresses than anyone else alive today, but is not by nature a performer. According to her son the Duke of York, the Queen often withdraws to another room when the rest of the family gather around the television set at Sandringham on Christmas Day.

'Sometimes the Queen watches it,' he said. 'And sometimes sits in another room thinking, "Has it come across in the right way."' It is very important for the Queen that her message comes across as clear and concise. She dislikes long speeches, as she does long sermons, and, as Prince Andrew explains, it is essentially a message for all fifty-three countries of the Commonwealth and has to be straightforward.

'The Christmas message reflects not just her opinions but what has happened in the year,' Prince Andrew says. 'How we can bring ourselves as a family – and we're a family of a huge number of different cultures, races and creeds – how we can bring that family together as part of the United Kingdom.'

The Queen's speech has seldom been criticised, except for being bland. She chooses not to dwell upon disasters, but to look for the positive. 'In difficult times,' she says, 'it is tempting for all of us, especially those who suffer, to look back and say "if only". But to look back in that way is to look down a blind alley. Better to look forward and say "if only".'

It could be her epitaph. In a world of sometimes bewildering change, she remains a shy and private person, less likely than most of us to be surprised by that change. She spans the generations, from those who stood quietly and solemnly around their wireless set on a Christmas afternoon when the national anthem was played to their counterparts today, who might watch her message on their mobile phone.

The continuity of the Queen's speech is so important that, in the event of a nuclear war, the script for a hypothetical broadcast was written for her by Whitehall officials. The document, which was released under the thirty-year rule, was drawn up in the spring of 1983 to prepare the country for a potential world war.

On 21 April 2016, the Queen will be ninety. At the same age, her mother was physically frailer, but mentally just as strong. As the memories of Britain's imperial past have yellowed into the history books, so has the concept of a rich, remote monarchy. Despite her distinguished age, or maybe because of it, the Queen has managed to move the monarchy into the twenty-first century. It has not always been a seamless transition, but it has been done dutifully. There will be much rejoicing and the Queen's Christmas address will no doubt carry the images of a nation in full-flooded national pride.

At the centre of it all, a tiny figure will be holding it all together as she always has done. Perhaps the Queen should have the last word, taken from her Christmas speech at the end of the old century:

> We can make sense of the future – if we understand the lessons of the past. Winston Churchill, my first prime minister, said that, 'The further backward you look, the further forward you can see'.

QUEEN'S SPEECH TIMELINE

1952	Live from Sandringham	First Christmas speech. *The Mousetrap* opens.
1953	Christmas broadcast from New Zealand	Death of Queen Mary. Everest conquered.
1954	Live from Sandringham	Roger Bannister runs mile in under four minutes.
1955	Live from Sandringham	Churchill resigns as prime minister; Anthony Eden succeeds him.
1956	Live from Sandringham	Incorporating recorded message from Prince Philip on board *Britannia*. Suez crisis.
1957	First televised broadcast from Sandringham	Harold Macmillan becomes prime minister.
1958	TV broadcast from Sandringham	Decision not to show children. Charles made Prince of Wales.

1959	No TV as pregnant. Radio address	First motorway in UK. First Mini car.
1960	Pre-recorded at Buckingham Palace	Recorded tapes sent around Commonwealth. Prince Andrew born. Princess Margaret marries.
1961	Recorded at Buckingham Palace	Viscount Linley born. Contraceptive pill becomes available.
1962	Recorded at Buckingham Palace	First communications satellite *Telstar* launched.
1963	Radio address only as pregnant	President John F. Kennedy assassinated. Profumo scandal. Alec Douglas-Home becomes prime minister.
1964	Recorded at Buckingham Palace	Prince Edward born. Beatlemania erupts around the world. Harold Wilson becomes prime minister.
1965	Recorded at Buckingham Palace	Winston Churchill dies. Vietnam war escalates.
1966	Recorded at Buckingham Palace	England win World Cup at Wembley. Aberfan disaster.
1967	Recorded at Buckingham Palace, in colour for first time	First heart transplant. Francis Chichester circumnavigates the globe single-handed.
1968	Recorded at Buckingham Palace	Martin Luther King assassinated.

1969	No broadcast. Film of *Royal Family*	Investiture of Prince of Wales. First man on the moon.
1970	Recorded at Buckingham Palace	General de Gaulle dies. Edward Heath becomes prime minister.
1971	Broadcast included film of Andrew and Edward	Decimal currency introduced.
1972	Recorded at Buckingham Palace	Silver wedding anniversary. Duke of Windsor dies.
1973	Broadcast includes film of Princess Anne's wedding	Britain joins EEC. IRA bombs in London. Thalidomide case settled.
1974	Recorded at Buckingham Palace	Attempt to kidnap Princess Anne. President Nixon resigns. Harold Wilson prime minister again.
1975	Recorded in gardens at Buckingham Palace	Global inflation and unemployment. North Sea oil starts to flow.
1976	Recorded at Buckingham Palace	Queen's fiftieth birthday. James Callaghan becomes prime minister. First Concorde commercial flight.
1977	Recorded at Buckingham Palace	Silver Jubilee. Queen's horse Dunfermline wins Oaks and St Leger. Elvis Presley dies.

1978	Broadcast included film of first grandson Peter Phillips	Also included recordings of Kings George V and VI. Princess Margaret divorces.
1979	Recorded at Buckingham Palace	Mountbatten killed by IRA. Margaret Thatcher becomes prime minister.
1980	Recorded at Buckingham Palace	Queen's speech draws record 28 million viewers. Queen Mother eighty. John Lennon shot.
1981	Recorded on terrace at Buckingham Palace	Prince Charles and Diana Spencer marry. Shooting at Trooping the Colour. Zara Phillips born.
1982	Recorded at Windsor Castle for first time	Prince William born. Falklands war. IRA bomb cavalry. Break-in at Buckingham Palace.
1983	Recorded at Buckingham Palace	£1 coin introduced. State visit to USA.
1984	Recording includes film of Prince Harry christening	Prince Harry born. IRA bomb Conservative party at Grand Hotel, Brighton.
1985	Recording includes film of investitures at Buckingham Palace	Earthquakes, flood and famine. First UK mobile phone calls. Wreck of *Titanic* found.
1986	Recorded at children's party in Royal Mews	Prince Andrew and Sarah Ferguson marry. Chernobyl nuclear reactor meltdown.

1987	Recorded at Buckingham Palace	Hurricane hits south-east England. *It's a Royal Knockout*.
1988	Recorded at Buckingham Palace	Lockerbie aircrash. First DNA conviction for murder. Princess Beatrice born.
1989	Part recorded at Royal Albert Hall children's gala	Berlin Wall comes down. Tiananmen Square protest. Hillsborough football stadium disaster.
1990	Recorded at Buckingham Palace	Gulf War begins in Kuwait. Invention of the World Wide Web. John Major becomes prime minister.
1991	Recorded at Buckingham Palace	IRA bombs in London. Collapse of Soviet Union.
1992	Recorded at Sandringham	'Annus Horribilis'. Fire at Windsor Castle. Separation of Charles and Diana.
1993	Recorded at Sandringham	IRA Bishopsgate bombing.
1994	Recorded at Buckingham Palace	Channel Tunnel opens. Nelson Mandela becomes president of South Africa.
1995	Recorded at Buckingham Palace	Bosnian war ends. Fiftieth anniversary of VE Day.

1996	Recorded at Buckingham Palace	Divorce of Charles and Diana. Dunblane massacre.
1997	Recorded at Windsor Castle	Golden wedding anniversary. Death of Diana. Tony Blair becomes prime minister.
1998	Broadcast included film of Queen Mother and Queen in France	Good Friday Agreement in Northern Ireland.
1999	Recorded at Windsor Castle including film of young achievers	Prince Edward and Sophie Rhys-Jones marry.
2000	Recorded at Buckingham Palace	Queen Mother 100. Tate Modern opens.
2001	Recorded at Buckingham Palace	9/11 Twin Towers attack in New York. Outbreak of foot and mouth disease.
2002	Recorded at Buckingham Palace	Golden Jubilee. Deaths of Princess Margaret and Queen Mother.
2003	Recorded at Cavalry Barracks, Windsor	Iraq War begins. London congestion charge introduced. Lady Louise Windsor born.
2004	Recorded at Buckingham Palace	Sixtieth anniversary of D-Day. Diana memorial fountain. Indian Ocean tsunami.

2005	Recorded at Buckingham Palace	7/7 London bombings. Charles and Camilla marry. Hurricane Katrina.
2006	Recorded in Southwark Cathedral	Eightieth birthday. Twitter is launched.
2007	Included clips from 1957 broadcast	Diamond wedding anniversary. Gordon Brown becomes prime minister.
2008	Recorded at Buckingham Palace	Financial crash. Prince Charles sixty. Diana inquest verdict. Barack Obama elected US President.
2009	Recorded at Buckingham Palace	Elizabeth Cross founded.
2010	Recorded at Chapel Royal, Hampton Court Palace	Coalition government formed with David Cameron as prime minister. Savannah Phillips born.
2011	Recorded at Buckingham Palace	Prince William and Kate Middleton marry. Zara Phillips and Mike Tindall marry.
2012	Recorded at Buckingham Palace	Diamond Jubilee, including Thames Pageant. London Olympics.
2013	Recorded at Buckingham Palace	Prince George born. Margaret Thatcher dies. Queen's horse Estimate wins Ascot Gold Cup.

| 2014 | Recorded at Buckingham Palace | Scotland votes to stay in Union. Ceramic poppies at Tower of London to commemorate start of WWI. |

LIST OF SPEECHES QUOTED

Chapter 1

1952   Christmas Broadcast
5 September 1997   Address to nation on death of Princess
                       Diana
6 February 1992   Television documentary *Elizabeth R*
20 March 2012   Diamond Jubilee address to Parliament

Chapter 2

13 October 1940   Wartime broadcast on *Children's Hour*
24 May 1946   Empire Day speech
21 October 1947   Twenty-first birthday speech
8 February 1952   Accession speech to Privy Council
4 December 1952   Speech at the Bank of England
1952   Christmas Broadcast

Chapter 3

16 April 1953   Launching of the royal yacht
                       Britannia
2 June 1953   Coronation day speech from
                       Buckingham Palace
13 June 1953   Reply to address from Provost of Eton
                       College

1953	Christmas Broadcast
16 February 1954	State opening of Parliament, Canberra, Australia
21 October 1955	Unveiling of memorial to King George VI, London
21 October 1955	Trafalgar Dinner at Royal Naval College, Greenwich
1957	Christmas Broadcast
25 July 1958	Opening of the Commonwealth Games, Cardiff
1958	Christmas Broadcast

Chapter 4

19 July 1960	Tercentenary of the Royal Society at Royal Albert Hall
1960	Christmas Broadcast
1961	Christmas Broadcast
1962	Christmas Broadcast
1964	Christmas Broadcast
14 May 1965	Inauguration of the Kennedy Memorial, Runnymede
1966	Christmas Broadcast
1967	Christmas Broadcast
1968	Christmas Broadcast
1969	Christmas Broadcast

Chapter 5

1971	Christmas Broadcast
20 November 1972	Silver wedding speech at Guildhall, London
1972	Christmas Broadcast
1973	Christmas Broadcast

1974	Christmas Broadcast
1975	Christmas Broadcast
1976	Christmas Broadcast
4 May 1977	Silver Jubilee address to Parliament
18 August 1977	To people of Northern Ireland at University of Ulster
1977	Christmas Broadcast
1979	Christmas Broadcast

Chapter 6

1980	Christmas Broadcast
1981	Christmas Broadcast
26 May 1982	Opening of Kielder Reservoir, Northumberland
1982	Christmas Broadcast
3 March 1983	State visit to USA, San Francisco
1983	Christmas Broadcast
1984	Christmas Broadcast
1985	Christmas Broadcast
1986	Christmas Broadcast
1987	Christmas Broadcast
1988	Christmas Broadcast
1989	Christmas Broadcast

Chapter 7

1990	Christmas Broadcast
1991	Christmas Broadcast
24 November 1992	Fortieth anniversary of accession at Guildhall, London
1992	Christmas Broadcast
1994	Christmas Broadcast
1996	Christmas Broadcast

5 September 1997	Speech following death of Diana, Princess of Wales
20 November 1997	Golden wedding speech, Banqueting House, London
1997	Christmas Broadcast
1998	Christmas Broadcast
1999	Christmas Broadcast

Chapter 8

20 March 2000	Speech at Sydney Opera House, Australia
2000	Christmas Broadcast
2001	Christmas Broadcast
8 April 2002	Death of Queen Elizabeth, the Queen Mother
30 April 2002	Reply to addresses from both Houses of Parliament
4 June 2002	Golden Jubilee speech at Guildhall, London
2 July 2002	Speech at Millennium Point, Birmingham
1 August 2002	Speech at National Space Centre, Leicester
2002	Christmas Broadcast
20 March 2003	Message to Armed Forces in the Gulf
19 November 2003	Address to President Bush at state banquet
2003	Christmas Broadcast
5 April 2004	State banquet in Paris
6 June 2004	Sixtieth anniversary of D-Day, Arromanches
6 July 2004	Opening of memorial to Diana, Princess of Wales

2004	Christmas Broadcast
1 January 2005	Message to the public following tsunami appeal

Chapter 9

8 July 2005	Royal London Hospital after 7 July bombings
10 July 2005	Sixtieth anniversary of VE Day, Horse Guards Parade
21 October 2005	Dinner on board HMS *Victory*, Portsmouth
2005	Christmas Broadcast
13 March 2006	Commonwealth Day message
12 April 2006	Royal Military Academy, Sandhurst
15 June 2006	Eightieth birthday lunch at Mansion House, London
2006	Christmas Broadcast
2007	Christmas Broadcast
26 March 2008	French state banquet at Windsor Castle
10 April 2008	Royal Naval College, Dartmouth
12 November 2008	Visit to Prince's Trust Headquarters
2008	Christmas Broadcast
22 January 2009	Women's Institute, Sandringham
1 July 2009	Annual broadcast to Armed Forces
25 November 2009	Visit to Bermuda
2009	Christmas Broadcast

Chapter 10

8 March 2010	Commonwealth Day message
6 July 2010	Address to United Nations Assembly, New York

16 September 2010	Holyroodhouse, visit of Pope Benedict XVI
23 November 2010	Inauguration of General Synod, Church House
2010	Christmas Broadcast
14 March 2011	Commonwealth Day message
18 May 2011	Irish state dinner, Dublin
24 May 2011	US state banquet, Buckingham Palace
15 July 2011	Visit to Bletchley Park
21 October 2011	Parliament House, Canberra, Australia
28 October 2011	CHOGM opening in Perth, Australia
20 March 2012	Diamond Jubilee address to Parliament
6 June 2012	Diamond Jubilee address to the nation
27 July 2012	Reception for Olympic Heads of Government
29 August 2012	Address to Paralympians
2012	Christmas Broadcast
25 June 2013	Queen Elizabeth Prize for Engineering
2013	Christmas Broadcast
8 April 2014	Irish state banquet, Windsor Castle
6 June 2014	French state banquet, Paris
4 July 2014	Naming of aircraft carrier *Queen Elizabeth*, Rosyth
19 September 2014	Message following Scotland's referendum
2014	Christmas Broadcast
9 March 2015	Commonwealth Day message
4 June 2015	Centenary AGM of the Women's Institute at Royal Albert Hall

BIBLIOGRAPHY

Benson, Ross, *Charles, The Untold Story* (Victor Gollancz, 1993)

Blair, Tony, *A Journey* (Hutchinson, 2010)

Bradford, Sarah, *Elizabeth* (Heinemann, 1996)

Chance, Michael, *Our Princesses and their Dogs* (John Murray, 1936)

Corbitt, F.J., *My Twenty Years in Buckingham Palace* (David McKay Company, 1956)

Crawford, Marion, *The Little Princesses* (Cassell, 1950)

Fleming, Tom, *Voices Out of the Air* (Heinemann, 1981)

Gathorne-Hardy, Jonathan, *The Rise and Fall of the British Nanny* (Hodder & Stoughton, 1972)

Hardman, Robert, *Our Queen* (Hutchinson, 2011)

Harris, Kenneth, *The Queen* (Weidenfeld & Nicolson, 1994)

Hartnell, Norman, *Silver and Gold* (Evans Brothers, 1955)

Kiggell, Marcus, and Denys Blakeway, *The Queen's Story* (Headline, 2002)

Lacey, Robert, *Royal: Her Majesty Queen Elizabeth II* (Sphere, 2002)

Noakes, Michael, and Vivien Noakes, *The Daily Life of the Queen* (Ebury, 2000)

Oliver, Charles, *Dinner at Buckingham Palace* (Prentice-Hall, 1972)

Parker, Eileen, *Step Aside for Royalty* (Bachman & Turner, 1982)

Pimlott, Ben, *The Queen: A Biography of Elizabeth II* (HarperCollins, 1996)

Seward, Ingrid, *Prince Edward: A Biography* (Century, 1995)

Seward, Ingrid, *Royal Children of the 20th Century* (HarperCollins, 1993)

Seward, Ingrid, *The Queen and Di* (HarperCollins, 2000)

Seward, Ingrid, *The Last Great Edwardian Lady* (Century, 1999)

Seward, Ingrid, *William and Harry* (Headline, 2003)

Seward, Ingrid, and *Majesty* writers, *The Queen's Diamond Jubilee* (M Press (Media) Ltd, 2011)

Shawcross, William, *Queen Elizabeth the Queen Mother* (Macmillan, 2009)

Sherbrook Walker, Eric, *Treetops Hotel* (Robert Hale, 1962)

Sheridan, Lisa, *From Cabbages to Kings* (Odhams Press, 1955)

Sheridan, Lisa, *Our Princesses at Home* (John Murray, 1940)

Sheridan, Lisa, *The Queen and her Children* (John Murray, 1953)

Turner, Graham, *Elizabeth: The Woman and the Queen* (Macmillan, 2002)

Vaughan-Thomas, Wynford, *Royal Tour 1953–4* (Hutchinson, 1954)

Warwick, Christopher, *Princess Margaret: A Life of Contrasts* (Andre Deutsch, 2000)

Winn, Godfrey, *The Young Queen* (Hutchinson, 1952)

York, Duchess of, with Jeff Coplon, *My Story* (Simon & Schuster, 1996)

Majesty magazine (Hanover magazines and Rex Publications, 1980–2015)

The Queen's speeches and broadcasts (Crown copyright, 1940–2015)

ACKNOWLEDGMENTS

Over the course of my time as editor of *Majesty* magazine I have written about almost every aspect of Her Majesty's life and reign. I have met many of her friends, family and members of her staff and household. Her Majesty keeps her private opinions to herself, but once a year she allows herself to go public with some of the issues she feels strongly about – when she makes her Christmas address. As the longest reigning British monarch in history, it seems appropriate to listen to her voice and let her tell the history of her reign through her many speeches.

In helping me with the intricate and often difficult task of putting this book together, I would like to thank my friend David Pogson, the senior communications officer at Buckingham Palace. David was an inspirational help, found me unpublished speeches and answered all my questions about when and where and how things happened, even when they happened over sixty-three years ago. I would also like to thank Sally Osman, director of royal communications and Charles Anson, who was the Queen's press secretary during the turbulent years of the nineties. Joe Little, the managing editor of *Majesty* magazine, whose brilliant memory for royal facts and details is second to none also deserves a big thank you. The back copies of *Majesty*, which was first published by Hanover magazines in 1980, were absolutely invaluable and are, without doubt, some of the only available printed records of many of the royal tours and visits. I had forgotten how many subjects we had covered over the years, including, on several occasions, the Queen's Speech, which was my inspiration for this book.

I would like to thank my agent Piers Blofeld and editors Ian Marshall and Charlotte Coulthard from Simon and Schuster. Most important of all I want to thank Nick Cowan, who is more familiar writing about rockers than royalty, but without whose help I would have been sunk in the multiple strands it took to write the book.

I have listed separately in the bibliography those books which I found most useful in my research for *The Queen's Speech*.

Ingrid Seward, London, July 2015